LAUNCHING SUCCESSFUL VENTURES

SAGE PUBLISHING: OUR STORY

We believe in creating fresh, cutting-edge content that helps you prepare your students to make an impact in today's ever-changing business world. Founded in 1965 by 24-year-old entrepreneur Sara Miller McCune, SAGE continues its legacy of equipping instructors with the tools and resources necessary to develop the next generation of business leaders.

- We invest in the right **authors** who distill the best available research into practical applications

- We offer intuitive **digital solutions** at student-friendly prices

- We remain permanently independent and fiercely committed to **quality, innovation, and learning**.

Sara Miller McCune founded SAGE Publishing in 1965 to support the dissemination of usable knowledge and educate a global community. SAGE publishes more than 1000 journals and over 800 new books each year, spanning a wide range of subject areas. Our growing selection of library products includes archives, data, case studies and video. SAGE remains majority owned by our founder and after her lifetime will become owned by a charitable trust that secures the company's continued independence.

Los Angeles | London | New Delhi | Singapore | Washington DC | Melbourne

LAUNCHING
SUCCESSFUL VENTURES

Michael W. Fountain
University of South Florida

Thomas W. Zimmerer
University of South Florida

Los Angeles | London | New Delhi
Singapore | Washington DC | Melbourne

FOR INFORMATION:

SAGE Publications, Inc.
2455 Teller Road
Thousand Oaks, California 91320
E-mail: order@sagepub.com

SAGE Publications Ltd.
1 Oliver's Yard
55 City Road
London EC1Y 1SP
United Kingdom

SAGE Publications India Pvt. Ltd.
B 1/I 1 Mohan Cooperative Industrial Area
Mathura Road, New Delhi 110 044
India

SAGE Publications Asia-Pacific Pte. Ltd.
18 Cross Street #10-10/11/12
China Square Central
Singapore 048423

Acquisitions Editor: Maggie Stanley
Content Development Editor: Alissa Nance
Marketing Manager: Sarah Panella
Production Editor: Veronica Stapleton Hooper
Copy Editor: Karen E. Taylor
Typesetter: C&M Digitals (P) Ltd.
Proofreader: Jeff Bryant
Indexer: Beth Nauman-Montana
Cover Designer: Alexa Turner

Printed in the United States of America

Library of Congress Cataloging-in-Publication Data

Names: Fountain, Michael W., author. | Zimmerer, Thomas, author.

Title: Launching successful ventures / Michael Fountain, University of South Florida, Thomas W. Zimmerer, University of South Florida.

Description: Thousand Oaks : SAGE Publications, [2019] | Includes bibliographical references and index.

Identifiers: LCCN 2018027695 | ISBN 9781506358932 (pbk. : alk. paper)

Subjects: LCSH: New business enterprises—Management. | New business enterprises—Finance.

Classification: LCC HD62.5 .F686 2019 | DDC 658.1/1—dc23
LC record available at https://lccn.loc.gov/2018027695

This book is printed on acid-free paper.

18 19 20 21 22 10 9 8 7 6 5 4 3 2 1

BRIEF CONTENTS

DETAILED CONTENTS

PREFACE

The authors firmly believe that entrepreneurship is now, and will continue to be, the driving force for global economic well-being. Entrepreneurs are the risk takers who form new business ventures, foster innovation, and create employment, economic growth, and wealth in any society. On a global basis, entrepreneurship is altering the economic opportunities for millions of people. Entrepreneurship is the vehicle that unleashes human creativity and enhances the economic well-being of people worldwide. Entrepreneurs are at the heart of the knowledge-based revolution that is reshaping the economies of nations.

New business ventures can start small yet find new and untapped markets for products and services that have a disruptive impact on markets globally. Millions of new entrepreneurial ventures are started each year, but an exceedingly large number fail due to a lack of practical entrepreneurial knowledge. This distressingly high failure rate has always been a motivating factor for our research and teaching efforts in entrepreneurship. Every new business must be prepared to face an onslaught of competition by existing businesses that simply wish to protect their market niche by taking aggressive actions to challenge any newcomers. Every new business venture must expect to face the acid test of competition. The study of entrepreneurship and the application of operational tools that have the potential to identify a new venture's strengths and potential weaknesses will go a long way to reduce the current failure rate for new businesses.

The authors believe that an increase in the success rate of new business ventures will have a dramatically positive impact on the economic growth and well-being of a nation. This book is written to assist its reader with the "tools" of analysis, tools that enhance the likelihood for success. Your success as an entrepreneur is beneficial to our society. It is our sincere wish that this book will help you achieve both your economic and professional objectives. You will be the challengers of the status quo. Your success benefits each of us.

TARGET AUDIENCE

This book has been written to serve students in an introductory course in entrepreneurship or small business management. In the writing of this book, the authors called upon both legal and financial professionals that work daily with the creation of new business ventures to insure that its content is both accurate and relevant to the process of new venture formation.

APPROACH

This book creates a synergy between the content of each chapter and the analytical tools that have been designed to evaluate objectively every step in the creation of a new business venture. Every chapter's content is followed by a series of what we have chosen to term "entrepreneurial exercises." These are simply analytical tools that allow the student to apply the information in the chapter to the proposed new business. This combination of information presentation and analytical exercise serves to enrich the student's understanding of the content of each chapter while making the learning process active and not passive. In our experience, this approach both energizes the learning process and challenges the students through their development of a serious business plan. This synergistic blending of textbook content and the student's application of the "entrepreneurial exercises" brings life to the course. The student is able to demonstrate knowledge of the chapter content while mastering the analytical tools employed by successful new venture entrepreneurs. Each analytical exercise allows the student to apply the critical content of the chapter actively to a proposed new business venture of her or his interest. This textbook is designed to encourage immediate learning through allowing the student to participate actively in the class.

The inclusion of "entrepreneurial exercises" at the conclusion of each chapter is unique in today's market. The application of the analytical tools provides every student with the opportunity to, as objectively as possible, evaluate the strategic and financial viability of the student's proposed new business venture. Feedback is therefore immediate. The instructor can actively interact with each student and therefore have a positive influence, guiding the student to recognize potential shortcomings or barriers to success, suggesting areas where additional analysis might be needed, or even pointing out possible changes that would allow the student to modify his or her business idea and avoid potential failure. The student is in control, however, completing each "entrepreneurial exercise" with the particular aim of starting a new business. The instructor and the student now become partners in the student's future success.

FEATURES

Each of the chapters of this book guides readers through the entrepreneurial process and encourages them to apply key concepts to a real-world potential business venture of their choosing. The book is therefore

1. *A logical presentation of the many factors that must be understood in order to achieve a successful business venture* (for this reason, the authors sought advice and guidance from professionals who work daily with differing aspects of the entrepreneurial process, including attorneys, accountants, venture capitalist, and the like);

2. *The source of in-depth coverage of the absolutely critical knowledge that must be mastered to create, manage, and grow a business effectively*; and, possibly most essential to the learning process,

3. *A repository of entrepreneurial exercises that encourage readers to actively apply the key concepts of each chapter to their proposed new business venture.*

TOPICAL COVERAGE

The chapters of the book are presented in a highly logical pattern that leads students to the creation of a business plan for their proposed business. From Chapter 2 forward, the student is involved in the identification and assessment of an idea for a viable new business venture. Creativity is encouraged as well as the assessment of a new product or service in terms of its ability to create value in the marketplace. The student is taught how to evaluate the market potential for her or his purposed new product or service. The chapter stresses why it is valuable to develop an accurate adopter profile and the value of building an opportunity evaluation model. The text introduces the student to the barriers to achieving market penetration. Without this analysis, the owner of a new venture is incapable of taking effective strategic actions or even of making basic and consistent day-to-day decisions.

Moving forward, Chapter 3 involves the creation of a business model for the proposed new venture through a detailed assessment of the industry in which the new product or service will compete. Industries are continually reshaped by what are termed macroenvironmental forces. Students need to understand this process to avoid becoming victims to forces beyond their control. The student develops a detailed competitive profile matrix to assess whether a market niche may exist for the planned business. In these technical areas, the "entrepreneurial exercises" allow the student to employ the needed analytical tools to greatly enhance the probably of the new venture's success. The chapters on entrepreneurial marketing, the creation of a solid financial plan, and the management of cash flow each address the absolutely essential components that must be tailored to a new business. The "entrepreneurial exercises" allow the content of each chapter to be integrated into the student's business plan. Too often, these "bread and butter" components fail to be addressed in terms of what is needed for a new start-up business. Each chapter relates the content to a new business venture and not an ongoing and well-established business. The challenges for a start-up business are unique, so the application lessons of each chapter must be focused on entrepreneurship and small business creation. These chapters do exactly that.

An area that few textbooks address is the ability of an entrepreneur to become a leader of the business she or he created. The future of the business is dependent upon the entrepreneur's ability and willingness to manage and lead his or her growing business. In Chapter 7, students are challenged to conduct a self-assessment of their personal qualities of leadership and the overall requirements for implementing an effective human resources program. Additionally, the entrepreneur must create a culture in the workplace that supports the organization's fundamental mission.

Chapter 8 allows the student to build a business plan that incorporates the work performed in the previous chapters. This is where students see the fruits of their analytical efforts, as all of the components of the business plan reinforce one another. Today's investors and lenders have exceedingly high expectations—they expect to be presented with a professional business plan in which all of the specific components of the plan are consistent and reinforcing of one another.

With the business plan completed, the book then introduces the student to the various sources of new venture funding. Both equity and debt sources are discussed in detail. When the entrepreneur has selected the optimal source of funding, the next step is the process of structuring the deal. Most textbooks do not include this process in any depth. This chapter introduces the student to actual specifics of what a financial investment deal is really like.

The final chapter discusses the various options entrepreneurs have when harvesting a business. In today's technological environment, small but successful businesses recognize that their best option is to be acquired by larger firms with the required resources to help the smaller ventures reach their full potential. Unfortunately, some firms are unable to keep up with competitors and lose market share and experience declining revenue and financial losses. For these firms, sale of the business, bankruptcy, or liquidation are their only options.

To support the students' learning process fully, the book includes a series of cases written by actual entrepreneurs about issues they have experienced in their businesses. The book also features a series of what we call "entrepreneurial spotlights"—short stories about highly successful entrepreneurs and businesses. Many of the entrepreneurs featured in the "spotlight" boxes are young and extremely successful. We hope that these and the other boxes about companies and best practices will encourage and motivate students to follow their dreams, take the risk of entrepreneurship, and become our next generation of entrepreneurs.

The authors have created a textbook that represents over 70 years of teaching entrepreneurship, creating highly successful new ventures, and consulting with fast-growing businesses. It will always be our wish that this book reaches the new generation of entrepreneurs and reshapes our economy.

DIGITAL RESOURCES

A password-protected instructor resource site at study.sagepub.com/fountain supports teaching with high-quality content to help in creating a rich learning environment for students. The companion site for this book includes the following instructor resources:

- Test banks built on AACSB standards, the book's learning objectives, and Bloom's Taxonomy provide a diverse range of test items with ExamView test generation.

- Editable, chapter-specific PowerPoint® slides offer complete flexibility for creating a multimedia presentation for the course.

- Teaching notes provide chapter outlines and answers to the end-of-chapter entrepreneurial exercises.

ACKNOWLEDGMENTS

The authors wish to express their thanks to a couple of individuals who contributed their time and energy to this project: Jennifer M. Jolly, who researched a wide variety of topics for the book and who provided initial editing of our rough drafts, and Matthew L. Daniels of the University of South Florida, who was the "leg man" responsible for almost all of the case studies and digital resources for this book.

SAGE would like to thank the following reviewers:

Aaron M. Butler, Warner Pacific College

William J. Carner, Westminster College

Violet Z. Christopher, Antelope Valley College

Peter C. Freeman, Golden Gate University

John M. Guarino, Averett University

Stephen E. Lanivich, Old Dominion University

Stan Mandel, Wake Forest University

Benjamin K. Ofili, Northeastern State University

Deborah Piscitiello, University of Jamestown

Ayisha E. Sereni, Montgomery County Community College

Jeff Smith, University of South Caroline Upstate

April J. Spivack, Coastal Caroline University

Adam Starks, Alderson-Broaddus University

Jeffrey Stone, California State University Channel Islands

W. Don Stull, Texas Tech University & MicroZap, Inc.

Kim L. Wangler, Appalachian State University

Andrzej Z. Wlodarczyk, Nyack College

ABOUT THE AUTHORS

Michael W. Fountain serves as the founding director of the university-wide Center for Entrepreneurship at the University of South Florida. He also serves as the director of the USF Student Innovation Incubator. Michael served as the national director of the National Consortium for Life Science Entrepreneurship from 1999 to 2004 and as an entrepreneur in residence at the Center for Entrepreneurial Leadership at the Ewing Marion Kauffman Foundation. Dr. Fountain currently holds many senior faculty appointments, including the John and Beverley Grant Endowed Chair in Entrepreneurship in the Muma College of Business. In addition, he holds professorships in the Department of Industrial Management and Systems Engineering, the Department of Psychiatry and Behavioral Neurosciences in the Morsani College of Medicine, the College of Pharmacy, and the Institute for Advanced Discovery and Innovation.

Dr. Fountain founded or cofounded eleven new ventures based on his research, three of which became publicly traded companies. Michael holds 30 issued United States patents and over 100 international patents. These patented technology platforms are currently utilized in over 180 products. Dr. Fountain has published over 70 peer-reviewed publications.

During his corporate career, Michael has served as the chief executive officer, chairman of the board, and chief scientific officer of a number of public and private companies.

Thomas W. Zimmerer has spent the majority of his career in academics, serving as the Entrepreneurial Scholar in Residence at the University of South Florida's Center for Entrepreneurship. Prior to that he served as the dean of the School of Business at Saint Leo University and the director of the Breech School of Business at Drury University.

Dr. Zimmerer held the Allen and Ruth Harris Chair of Excellence at East Tennessee State University. While a professor at Clemson University, he was the cofounder of the Clemson University Emerging Technology and Marketing Center.

Tom has published 10 textbooks and over 200 articles and professional papers. In 1984, he was honored by the Industrial Research Institute with the Maurice Holland award.

Tom was a consultant and executive trainer to over 100 United States and international businesses, governments, universities, and trade and professional associations.

Both of us have individuals who, throughout our lives, have given us the blessings of unconditional support and love.

For Michael:

This book is dedicated to my wife, Amanda, and our children, Miles and Leigh, for their support of my entrepreneurial life journey and for helping me to see opportunities when others did not.

For Tom:

That person has always been his wife and best friend, Linda.

1

THE ENTREPRENEURIAL VENTURE

When you reach an obstacle, turn it into an opportunity. You have the choice. You can overcome and be a winner, or you can allow it to overcome you and be a loser. The choice is yours and yours alone. Refuse to throw in the towel. Go that extra mile that failures refuse to travel. It is far better to be exhausted from success than to be rested from failure.

Mary Kay Ash, founder of Mary Kay Cosmetics

Business opportunities are like buses; there's always another one coming.

Richard Branson, founder of Virgin Enterprises

CHAPTER LEARNING OBJECTIVES

Upon completion of this chapter you will be able to

Identify the key traits of a successful entrepreneur

Explain the three entrepreneurial ventures

Compare the groups that make up today's entrepreneurs

Assess the impact of global entrepreneurship

Discuss the challenges entrepreneurs face

Define social entrepreneurship

THE ENTREPRENEUR

An entrepreneur is an individual who chooses to create a new venture based on what she or he believes is a viable business idea that can be shaped into a model, which, when operationalized, creates greater customer value than is offered by current market competitors. In some cases, the new business venture involves more than one entrepreneur. These new business ventures focus on what the entrepreneur believes is an opportunity. Entrepreneurs are willing to accept risk based on their confidence that their business model is capable of successfully overcoming the competitive forces that exist in the market. Entrepreneurship is the process of new business creation.

The eminent scholars, the late Jeffrey Timmons and Stephen Spinelli, wrote that "effective entrepreneurs are internally motivated, high energy leaders with a unique tolerance for ambiguity, a keen eye toward mitigating risk, and a passion for discovery and innovation."[1] In a 1990 article, H. H. Stevenson and J. C. Jarillo defined entrepreneurship as "the process by which individuals . . . pursue opportunities without regard to the resources they currently control."[2] These thought leaders in entrepreneurship clearly viewed entrepreneurs as somewhat unique. This does not imply that only a very limited portion of the population has the ability to become successful entrepreneurs.

In reality, most successful new business ventures may remain small in scope. Their size is often what the entrepreneur wishes it to be. Many businesses are either "salary replacement" or "life style" in nature (discussed later in this chapter). There are some scholars who discount these business ventures as not entrepreneurial; we do not. The purpose of your textbook is to provide you with "tools" to evaluate the potential success of your "dream," whether that dream is to grow a Fortune 500 corporation or establish a successful local bike shop. As you begin that evaluation, it is worth investigating this series of what might be "termed" as recognized entrepreneurial traits.

Entrepreneurial Success

Decades of research from the academic discipline of organizational behavior, human motivation, decision making, and psychology provide valuable insight into the factors that influence an individual to become an entrepreneur. Consider first the individual's fundamental belief in success itself. Entrepreneurs would have what is termed an *internal locus of control*. That is, they believe that they control their destiny and chances for success. In contrast, individuals with an external locus of control believe that success is, to a large degree, a product of external forces beyond their personal control. Other components of personality theory seem to apply to entrepreneurs: a high level of consciousness, represented by an acceptance of responsibility; dependability; and persistence. These three characteristics interact to provide the entrepreneur with the capacity to endure the frustration normally associated with new venture formation. Additionally, the personality trait of openness to experience speaks to the entrepreneur's drive to express creativity and satisfy curiosity. Entrepreneurs seek to discover new and superior solutions to problems as opposed to accepting the familiar. A third personality trait that affects entrepreneurs is termed *emotional stability*. Individuals who score high in this personality trait are capable of managing stress and tend to demonstrate more self-confidence and emotional security within themselves.

Entrepreneurial Traits

Drawing on the classic research of David McClellan, we see that entrepreneurs have a very high need for achievement. The need for achievement is defined as *the drive to excel and strive for success.*[3] As this seminal work and those mentioned above discovered, many successful entrepreneurs have some of the following recognizable characteristics:

- High levels of personal confidence in their ability to succeed

- Passion for what they do

- Preference for moderate risk

- Ability to reduce risks systematically by coping with ambiguity

- High levels of energy, focused on problem identification and solution

- Acceptance of challenge based on self-confidence in their ability to overcome obstacles

- High levels of perseverance and tenacity

When students are initially asked why entrepreneurs start new business ventures, most respond quickly with the "to make money" answer. However, while many entrepreneurs recognize that they must create financially viable businesses in order to reach their goals, they also view wealth as a result of success, not the only driving force to achieve success. The initial tendency is to focus on financial success alone, but, in reality, most truly successful entrepreneurs value achievement over the simple creation and accumulation of wealth. Money is certainly one measure of achievement; however, for individuals who are socially conscious entrepreneurs, the maximization of wealth is not always the number-one consideration. Their critical outcome is measured in terms of how all of their work directly contributes to their fundamental goals. For example, the Salvation Army and Goodwill Industries operate successful retail businesses for the purpose of using the net revenue to serve the needs of the poor, disabled, or persons attempting to get their lives back on track. We term this "social entrepreneurship."

Entrepreneurial Drive

Entrepreneurs often describe the motivation to create a business because it allows them to shape their own destiny. In many cases, it is virtually impossible to separate the entrepreneur from their business. They are motivated by the intrinsic rewards that flow from proving that their ideas were correct and that their business contributes to their community or to a specific cause. Their passion to make a difference in society through their pursuits of an opportunity drives many entrepreneurs more than the financial rewards. Success must be measured in a tangible fashion. The focus must be on the achievement of results.

Serial entrepreneur Mark Moore discusses the logical process a potential entrepreneur should follow in selecting a new business venture: "First, determine what are your best skills, abilities, and knowledge base, and what activities inspire your passion. . . . [Entrepreneurs] should always play from their strengths and be guided by their personal passions. These factors will assist . . . [them] in selecting an industry with which they will be most compatible and have an expected probability of becoming successful." Second, Moore suggests that the entrepreneur scan the business environment for energizing market segments that possess high growth potential as opposed to markets that have limited or declining growth opportunities. Last, when a market niche possessing growth potential and attractive profit margins is identified, the entrepreneur needs to make a final decision as to the creation of a business venture within the market niche that incorporates the entrepreneur's skills, abilities, knowledge, experience, and passion. The proposed business venture must also be of a size and scope that will match the entrepreneur's resources and her or his potential to attract additional financial capital and outside resources.

The process serves to guide the entrepreneur toward a business venture with the highest potential opportunity for him or her as *a specific* individual. Each person has a unique set of skills, abilities, knowledge, and passions that will influence that person's ability to create a successful business. There are always new, energizing, and exciting market niches, but not every one of them is a sufficient fit with the potential entrepreneur. The time that it takes to analyze yourself and the market opportunities objectively can help you avoid a business decision that becomes, at best, a marginal success. Focusing on the intersection between your skills, abilities, knowledge, and passions, on the one hand, and, on the other, a market niche with above average growth potential and attractive profit margins that are also compatible with your current or potential resources significantly improves the probability of creating a growing business.

Entrepreneurs are indeed very complex individuals. This diverse and expanding group will not be easily defined by any overly simplistic set of personality traits and motivational drivers. Decades of research have provided clues as to the driving forces that help us identify individuals with the potential to achieve success as entrepreneurs, yet this research does not provide a basic model that guarantees success. It is highly unlikely that a prototype entrepreneur could be created. All individuals can search within themselves for their own personal level of passion to achieve defined goals and stated dreams. Entrepreneurs struggle continually to enhance their skills and gain confidence in their abilities. Entrepreneurs succeed every day, and this reinforces the entrepreneurial spirit in us. The power to succeed, and the willingness to do what it takes to do so, shapes the lives of entrepreneurs, moves society forward, and keeps the economy evolving.

TYPES OF ENTREPRENEURIAL VENTURES

There are three major categories of entrepreneurial business ventures. Many small businesses are what can be termed **salary replacement** businesses. As this name implies, these entrepreneurs open and operate businesses to earn a living for themselves and their families. These businesses may have begun from modest initiatives, but, over time, some grow larger in size. These "mom-and-pop," family-owned businesses can be significant in size and be substantial market leaders in their local geographic region. In many ways, these family-owned and operated businesses are the backbone of many small towns, and they add flavor to many a large city, giving a "small town" experience to local customers. Many of these organizations are multigenerational family businesses that actually represent owners, managers, and employees who are actively involved in the business for decades or longer. The goal of each generation is to prosper and pass on to the next generation an increasingly competitive and financially solid business. These businesses have become the source of income for an increasing number of families. Indeed, most businesses in the United States are of this sort.

A second type of business can be termed a **lifestyle firm**. As the name implies, these business ventures are an outgrowth of a desire by the entrepreneur to pursue a specific lifestyle, such as a sport or a hobby. In this scenario, the entrepreneur already has a well-developed set of skills and knowledge. Examples can range from sailing to baking elaborate cakes, playing video games, or planning events for friends. Entrepreneurs can build thriving businesses around the activities that already inspire a lifelong passion. Individuals who love global travel may become travel agents or offer their services as travel guides. Consider the number of small bookstores operated and owned by entrepreneurs with a love of books and learning. Despite the intense competition created by the online market retailers Barnes and Noble and Amazon.com, these entrepreneurs strive to build a community around the sense that the book-buying experience should be a personalized one. Education-oriented entrepreneurs are another group who tend to be motivated by ideals greater than profits: men and women who are very often far more committed to educating children than to becoming personally wealthy have gone on to create and operate successful private schools. Lifestyle businesses are often the product of the passion to accomplish specific internal goals in the entrepreneur's life. Many are equally linked to the entrepreneurs' desire to do what they feel will contribute most to society. Social entrepreneurs use their passions to improve a segment of society.

The types of firms for which entrepreneurship is most recognized are the **new venture firms**. With this type of business, an entrepreneur will use all of the previously discussed tools, talents, resources, and opportunities in the creation of new products and services and will enter the market with new and innovative business models. These businesses stem from the creative and often highly innovative ideas of their founders. Ventures formed by these entrepreneurs face the unrelenting challenges of competitors as the new business attempts market entry. Identifying an opportunity is not enough to succeed. Having a unique product or service is also no guarantor of success. Excellent marketing tactics and business plans that remain on paper do not equate with success: **only execution matters**. Entrepreneurs must do more than recognize opportunity and then generate a new product or service to fill a perceived need; they must establish a business that is capable of creating value for their target customer while also competing effectively against all competitors. The new product or service does not operate in a vacuum but rather in a dynamic marketplace where other firms are anxious to protect their hard-earned market share and will work tirelessly to retain every customer. In reality, entrepreneurship is the most challenging career imaginable.

The entrepreneurial firms that accomplish these challenging feats are the businesses whose products and services drive the evolutionary process in our society. Joseph Schumpeter described the process that drives the economy forward as "creative destruction."[4] The process of creative destruction describes how new and superior products or services replace the existing products or services within our highly competitive market environment.

Creative Destruction and Innovation

For a brief moment, consider how our entrepreneurial process has improved the delivery of health care, communications, travel, technology, and overall quality of life. When people speak of "the good old days," seldom can anyone identify specifics as to what was better than today. Today we live longer, stay healthier, work in jobs with less physical labor, and enjoy entertainment options unheard of before. Entrepreneurs have brought each of us a better life.

Many elements of the past are still valuable. These valued elements need to be incorporated with change to achieve the combined benefits of both the "new" and the "old."

The concept of *creative destruction* will be discussed further in a later chapter where you will study environment scanning. The goal of environment scanning is simple; it is looking around to see what forces, such as technology, are creating new products or services for an evolving economy. Entrepreneurial success can be achieved by recognizing and understanding in great detail these evolutionary processes. In some cases the process of creative destruction produces changes described as *disruptive*. Market changes require serious preemptive analysis.

Every entrepreneur would benefit from a review of the following questions:

1. What do your business venture's products or services do that specifically satisfies the needs and wants of your current customers? Is your current target market evolving? If so, what will the identified projected changes mean for your venture's potential viability?

2. As the market evolves, will your products or services remain valued and needed?

3. How, specifically, will your products or services create value as the market evolves? What, if any, changes must be made? How soon?

4. Will the customers in the evolving market be able to afford your modified products or services? Will potential competitors have comparable products and services at lower prices?

5. Will the forecasted changes have a "negative impact" on your current competitive advantage?

6. How will your current business model need to change to remain competitive in the evolving marketplace? Does your venture have the resources and skills to achieve a successful new and revised business model?

7. What components of your current business model need only minor changes?

8. Will customers in the evolving competitive environment still measure the creation of customer value in the same terms as now?

9. Do your current staff members have the skills needed to produce and market products and services to meet the new customer demands?

10. Last, what will be the estimated cost to make the needed changes to compete in this evolving market, and can your business afford the investment? What is the risk level associated with the proposed investments?

Joseph Schumpeter's concept of creative destruction is linked to the role of innovation in any society. Innovation results in the introduction of new products or services, the identification of new evolving market niches, new production methodologies, and new marketing and disruption techniques.

ENTREPRENEURIAL SPOTLIGHT
KARSON HUMISTON, FOUNDER OF VANGST

Opportunities are often simply created by the environment in which business competes. The creation of Vangst might be a classic case of an entrepreneur recognizing an unmet need and quickly and aggressively carving out a niche in the market. Humiston attended a cannabis trade-show in New York and spent the day speaking with every exhibitor she could meet, asking the simple question, "What is it that you most need to be more successful?" The responses all included access to qualified employees. That evening, she returned to college and began to create her new venture, Vangst. Vangst is now, in a very short time, the leading human resources consulting firm in the cannabis industry. Vangst focuses on a single industry while offering a sole product, access to college graduates and near college graduates, at a very attractive price. Competitors were charging 20 percent of the new employee's first year salary. Vangst's fee for membership is $69 per month to post as many jobs as the client wishes.

Vangst is the nation's leading recruitment agency in the cannabis industry, having placed over 7,000 professionals in positions from entry level jobs to top executive spots. Vangst has recently created a website, Vangsters, which is designed to connect potential employee candidates digitally with her client base.

Headquarter in Denver, Colorado, Vangst has hosted major career workshops that attract hundreds of cannabis businesses and thousands of job seekers.

Karson Humiston advanced from entrepreneurial "newcomer" to a market niche leader in fewer than 5 years. Further growth may be a reality, as she predicts the cannabis industry sales will increases to $50 billion by 2026.

Sources:

Courtney Connley, "Meet the 24-Year-Old Founder Behind the Career Site for Cannabis Jobs," *CNBC Make It*, October 18, 2017, https://www.cnbc/2017/10/18meet-the-24-year-old-founder-behind-the-career-site-for-cannabis-jobs.html.

"Karson Humiston: Profile," *Forbes*, accessed June 2018, https://www.forbes.com/profile/karson-humiston/.

"Karson Humiston," *Linkedin*, accessed July 2018, https://www.linkedin.com/in/karson-humiston-64572b97/.

WHERE ARE TODAY'S ENTREPRENEURS COMING FROM?

The answer to this question is straightforward. Our entrepreneurs are coming from everywhere! As entrepreneurial education programs expand in colleges and universities across the world and more individuals master the skills of new venture formation, the ranks of potential entrepreneurs is rapidly expanding. As global economies welcome and support entrepreneurship, the addition of new entrepreneurs is likely to continue to grow in economies once philosophically opposed to capitalism. Young individuals are more willing than ever to take risks and attempt to start new businesses. The traditional view that corporate careers are the only way to provide security has proven to be false. In the United States, this is proving true across the spectrum from the baby boomers (individuals born after World War II and up to 1964) to millennials (individuals born between the early 1980s and the mid-1990s and reaching adulthood in the early 2000s). The members of these groups are forming game-changing businesses.

Boomers

The Kauffman Foundation reported in 2015 that "boomers" were more than twice as likely to start a new business than millennials. Some boomers (aged 55–64) were starting businesses at a rate nearly twice what this generation did in the mid-1990s. These boomers have been described as the wealthiest generation due to their inherited wealth and savings from their careers. Eighty percent of the boomer entrepreneurs start businesses for lifestyle reasons.[5]

At the other end of the age continuum are the millennial entrepreneurs (born from 1981–1997, according to the Kauffman Foundation's categories). Researchers see great promise that these millennials have the potential to become the greatest entrepreneurial generation. This generation is better educated: 18 percent had a master's degree or higher in 2014. Millennials have been exposed to many more opportunities for entrepreneurial education than has any previous generation. A factor that could potentially support or hinder entrepreneurship for this generation is its level of student debt. A data point provided by the U.S. Department of Education in 2014 puts average student debt per borrower at $27,689 in 2014, up from $18,233 in 2007.[6] If the millennials view that working in the traditional corporate environment will never provide them with salaries sufficient to pay off these loans, they may be motivated to become entrepreneurs because the opportunity for financial success, freedom, and a sense of self-determined progress is perceived to be much higher on this career path. Hollywood films, TV shows, and the success of many celebrities in the entrepreneurial world due to social media could be contributing factors in the rise in these perceptions. For many of the boomers, new business ventures are attractive because they wish to remain active and contribute to society. Additionally, they often have savings and investments to draw upon for capital needs to support the creation of their businesses.

"Young Guns"

The driving force for young entrepreneurs may vary, but one component is surely the visibility of highly successful individuals achieving breakthroughs in science and technology, which have resulted in globally recognized businesses. Social media was created by individuals of these generations. Computer software, and all associated technologies, has proven lucrative for forward-thinking entrepreneurs. Today's professional investors and venture capitalist have learned to welcome, for review, the business plans of highly creative and innovative persons regardless of age, gender, or national origin. The 2010 drama *The Social Network* featured the story of the founding of Facebook and the subsequent lawsuits. According to the Internet Movie Database (IMDB), the film had grossed over $220 million worldwide as of February 2011. The film took considerable creative license with the true story of Facebook, but it solidified in the mind of a generation that young college students with a brilliant idea can become billionaires. Popular media has started to embrace the image of the rogue entrepreneur—in this case, Mark Zuckerberg—striking out to find success through a battlefield of personal and business obstacles. The popularity and familiarity of the story of his success will undoubtedly inspire future entrepreneurs. Facebook, as a company, gave rise to another important icon of technology who also sparked a significant series of conversations, this time about women in technology and as entrepreneurs: Sheryl Sandberg, Facebook's CEO, bestselling author, and activist.

Women

Over the past forty years, women have been increasingly important contributors to the growth of new business start-ups as well as assuming entrepreneurial roles within existing companies. Well educated and with solid business experience, many women believe that their personal success can be achieved faster and with fewer barriers, as entrepreneurs. Although still lagging behind men in the creation of new businesses, women are making a significant impact on the United States economy.

Although individual psychology plays the largest role in determining a person's potential for success as an entrepreneur, the ability to work within a group to create a consensus and then to execute the agreed-upon measures is key when forming successful new ventures. The interdisciplinary nature of most businesses will require entrepreneurs to work with teams to achieve the best results from multiple, divergent viewpoints. Women are not just starting businesses in the traditionally noted industries such as retail, childcare, food service, or beauty products. Women are now founding many entrepreneurial businesses requiring technical education and expertise. As reported by the National Center for Education Statistics in 2011, the percentage of master's and doctoral degrees earned by females increased over the decade between academic year 1998–99 and 2008–09 from 57 to 60 percent and from 44 to 51 percent, respectively.[7] In 2015–16 (the most recent year for which statistics are available), women earned just over 59 percent of all master's degrees conferred in the United

States and just under 53 percent of all doctoral degrees.[8] Women are now on an equal footing with men in terms of the number of privately owned businesses in the United States, in fields as varied as construction, transportation, agribusiness, communication, and the sciences.

Corporate Castoffs, Immigrants, and Minorities

When the economy experiences a significant decline, some firms attempt to maintain their profit level through aggressively cutting employees. Ever increasing numbers of these "corporate castoffs" decide to become entrepreneurs. In a number of cases, these men and women are well educated and may have well-established industry contacts. They also often have new product ideas that have never been accepted by their former employers. These new products or product modifications have the potential advantage of being highly focused on the industry or industries served by the former employer and well known to the new entrepreneur. Former contacts serve to improve the entrepreneur's opportunity to get a new product or product improvement before decision makers in the industry. In these cases, the original employer freed the individual to become a new competitor. Other "corporate castoffs" reject their past and choose to become entrepreneurs in a business that they always wanted to try. Many of these individuals choose to open what was described earlier as a "lifestyle" business. These "corporate castoffs" have significant experience and many also have graduate degrees relevant to their field. They possess skills and knowledge to open a new business, and they are very likely to succeed.

Entrepreneurship is also the vehicle of choice for minorities and immigrants. Minorities have not historically participated in business ownership, but new data are showing a positive turn, which impacts the US economy. Although a 2008 publication of the MIT Press reported that only 5.1 percent of African Americans and 7.5 percent of Latinos owned businesses in the United States, the *2012 Survey of Business Owners* shows an increase to 9.35 and 11.96 percent, respectively.[9] In 2011, immigrants created 28 percent of new businesses and were more than twice as likely to start a business as native-born Americans. Indeed, over the period from 1996 to 2011, the rate of new business formation by immigrants grew by 50 percent.[10] The Fiscal Policy Institute reported that the immigrants' share of business ownership had risen to 18 percent from 12 percent between 1990 and 2010.[11]

Both women and minorities have recognized that business ownership allows them the best avenue to becoming financially independent and achieving their personal goals. Free-market economies, such as that of the United States, welcome all contributors to the achievement of economic prosperity. There has been significant discussion regarding the creation of an "express lane" to US citizenship for international students being educated in the United States. Students who have demonstrated exceptional potential can be immediate contributors to our society and can become successful entrepreneurs. The logic is simple: be successful here and not back home. The opportunity to open a business and possibly become successful is the most powerful magnet in the attraction of skilled immigrants to our economy. New business formation is an important measure of the economic health of any economy. Business success inevitably leads to increased employment and a rising standard of living for a nation.

YOUR CHALLENGE

The twenty-first century is proving to offer entrepreneurs of the global community unprecedented opportunities to enhance their economic well-being. Opportunities will require entrepreneurs to accept the challenges before them and continuously strive to solve the problems facing them through the creation of businesses driven by creativity, innovation, risk taking, and personal courage. Entrepreneurs are problem solvers who willingly accept these challenges. Our global heroes are now the entrepreneurs whose actions are changing economies across the globe. Business history has taught us that established businesses are not necessarily the sources of our best new creative ideas. Established businesses seem to lose their once acute risk-taking attributes as success typically results in increasingly bureaucratic behaviors. Although founded by aggressive entrepreneurs, these businesses evolve over time into ridged structures populated by risk-averse leaders whose overall leadership focus changes from that of a problem solver to a defender of the profitable status quo. Despite an abundance of financial, human, and material resources, the established firms in some industries display insensitivity to emerging opportunities. Problems are often opportunities in disguise. When established firms choose to respond to market reality in what appears to be an apathetic fashion, new competitors can emerge with solutions never predicted by their forebears. Consequently, entrepreneurial opportunities abound under these conditions.

Revolutionary products and services successfully brought to market replace existing products and services. Many of today's pioneering new products are the result of the efforts of risk-taking, innovative entrepreneurs. New business models replace existing ones, and the beneficiary of this process of creative destruction is the consumer. Economies prosper as new products and services generate ever-increasing employment and wealth. Business history abounds with stories of drastic declines of once powerful industries and well-established business firms. The replacements are new entrepreneurial firms that customers decide better serve their needs and wants.

Entrepreneurs will always flourish in an economic system where the true power rests in the hands of consumers with freedom of choice. The entrepreneurial process is evolutionary in nature. Survival of any business is dependent on its leadership to continue to act as an entrepreneur. Professor Schumpeter did not condemn all businesses to decline but only those that fail to remain alert and sensitive to the market and to evolving consumer needs and wants. The economics of a free market system places the power of business survival in the hands of the consumer. Every business must recognize and respect the dynamic and often volatile nature of a competitive marketplace. Entrepreneurs must face and conquer the competitive pressures to meet or exceed the ever-changing expectations of target customers in both domestic and global markets.

External forces serve to accelerate and shape change as well. The continued evolving forces of science and technology, economic conditions, social norms and demographics, government policies, and regulation serve to generate a dynamic, competitive environment in which all businesses must struggle to survive. External realities, trends, and events continually interact to reshape and redefine the landscape in which firms must compete. In reality, all firms operate in a business environment whose nature is shaped by the demands of customers, the behaviors of competitors, and the often-volatile forces of numerous external factors. For entrepreneurs to be successful, they must master the complexity provided by a truly dynamic marketplace.

GLOBAL ENTREPRENEURSHIP AND THE ACCELERATION OF COMPETITION

Competition has rapidly become global in scope. Access to the Internet has leveled the playing field and serves to provide a vehicle that supports and facilitates global commerce. This increasingly expanding global market facilitated by modern technology is an example of an external force that continues to impact entrepreneurship. Entrepreneurs will quickly discover that this explosive technology is truly a competitive "double-edged sword." A US entrepreneur can market and deliver products worldwide, but so can global competitors. The clear beneficiary will continue to be the global consumer. And American consumers have demonstrated that they are virtually immune from prejudice against the products manufactured in countries other than the United States. The question of choice is rooted in the product that best meets the consumer's needs, at a price that the consumer is willing to pay. Customer loyalty is simply not what it used to be. Global competitors are confident that if their product meets, or exceeds, expectations they will win customers. Customers practice what is termed "enlightened self-interest."

Entrepreneurs the world over are discovering that financial resources are themselves global. New and innovative products and services are increasingly able to attract capital. Money, in the form of new venture investors, flows to entrepreneurs whose products and services are viewed as having potentially high profitability. The national origin of the business has become much less important than it once was. The entrepreneur with the potential to serve global economic needs, therefore, has the potential to contribute to his or her nation's well-being.

Changing Realities

Some of the realities of the changes in our global environment include, but are certainly not limited to, the following:

1. Increasing competitive opportunities that stem from international trade agreements that open markets for goods and services are benefitting entrepreneurs through increased access to global markets.

2. Global communication via the Internet has had the effect of making consumers aware of products and services far beyond their traditional purchasing boundaries. The Internet allows entrepreneurs to target potential customers without the expense of a physical location. In effect, the Internet has served to reduce the competitive barriers to entry through providing a more level competitive environment.

3. Global economic change is accelerating. New technologies are spreading across the globe rapidly, aided by the Internet and sophisticated information collection

methods. The speed at which new knowledge becomes available to all members of the competitive environment has served to enhance global competition. Beyond technology, changes in national economic systems offer economic freedom and present new market opportunities. Economic transparency and openness serve to inform the world of potential market opportunities. Consider the rapid growth of the demand for luxury items in China: this shift created tremendous growth in the middle class in that nation and has led to true wealth among the upper class. Global entrepreneurs driven by consumers with the wealth and desire to possess what might be termed a "higher personal lifestyle" responded to meet these previously unmet needs. The growth in global economics can be linked to the expansion of entrepreneurship and increasing economic well-being in both the developed and developing nations.

4. A global explosion of new knowledge and innovation led to the realities discussed above. Research is being conducted by more scholars worldwide than ever before. Nations have identified that investment in research and development produces new knowledge that is understood to be the raw material needed for innovation. Innovation is clearly an initial and critical component in the entrepreneurial process.

5. There exists a higher level of transparency of actions and information. Fewer innovations remain secret. As stated previously, the Internet supports the transfer of information and seems to encourage its sharing. In some ways, there seems to be a declining respect for intellectual property rights. In a global market, many nations do not recognize intellectual property rights to the same extent as developed nations. Entrepreneurs in nations who do not recognize intellectual property rights often exploit patented subject matter. Products based on these patents then appear in the global marketplace at prices that reflect the lack of consideration for the expense incurred in the original technological development.

6. The pace of economic change has also accelerated. Thus competitive pressures have produced a continuing effort to make individual organizations more efficient. Developed countries have witnessed organizational downsizing to reduce expense, while also outsourcing organizational functions to achieve lower cost to attempt to retain lower product pricing. Established firms have recognized that the "bloated," top-heavy organizational structures of the past are no longer competitive and are attempting to behave in a more entrepreneurial fashion.

Jeff May recently published an article that details the best countries in which to start a business. The United States ranks third behind Denmark and Canada. Some of the most compelling statistics focus on how supportive a country is to the establishment of a new business. As an example, a reduction in "red tape" barriers serves as a major benefit in lowering start-up costs and encouraging new venture formation. In this category, the United States ranks fourth overall behind Singapore, New Zealand, and Hong Kong. On a global basis, the countries that erect the highest barriers to new venture formation include a large number of African and South American nations.[12] These barriers include the imposition of high government "fees" and numerous never-ending bureaucratic procedures.

Entrepreneurs in lesser-developed countries may often find a lack of a supportive climate for new venture formation. These countries will need to support internal sources of new venture financing. Developed countries have more sophisticated sources of financial capital in the form of professional venture capitalist and "Angel Investors." In some cases, entrepreneurs have no previous experience in starting and operating a business, and, consequently, external investors may be reluctant to support that "first" venture. In developing countries, the rising middle class may have technical expertise and experience but lack sound entrepreneurial skills. Investors may view these individuals as having great potential but remain concerned regarding their unproven entrepreneurial skills.

Enhancing Economic and Social Well-Being

Economic systems and nations must recognize the importance of assisting individuals to think like entrepreneurs. There is a need to create an entrepreneurial mind-set in people. An entrepreneurial mind-set in a nation is enhanced both by educational opportunities and through a conscious effort to display entrepreneurs as the individuals changing a society for the better. Entrepreneurs bring the population new technologies that can enrich our lives, make us healthier, reduce poverty, and enhance economic well-being. Entrepreneurs frequently raise society's quality of life and therefore are the type of men and women society would wish to recognize publicly for their contributions and encourage others to emulate. Gradually, societies across the globe are replacing corporate executives, government leaders, and military leaders with a new sort of role model: the entrepreneur. Societies have begun recognizing the economic power and wealth created by entrepreneurs.

New business ventures bring to market innovative products and services and are a source of new employment in the economy. Government economic policy would benefit from directing its efforts towards the creation of an economic environment that supports and rewards the entrepreneurial process. This redirection is proving to be difficult. Policy makers need to become aware that governmental actions taken to support new business ventures result in dramatically higher returns on society's investment than those made to support large businesses that have, in too many cases, stagnated.

Governmental policies that assist in providing support for the financing of large firms may not be available to new entrepreneurs who, by traditional leading standards, often do not qualify for bank loans. Should the tax policies serve to encourage investors in entrepreneurship? Such a national policy is a serious question that needs to become a national debate. We all fundamentally recognize that increased access to capital from the private sector would be an accelerator of growth. Would all new business ventures succeed? Not likely. However, when we reflect on why so many new businesses fail, we discover that many had limited or no access to an early, objective pre-investment assessment of the potential of the business.

As an example, most university faculty members in science and engineering are rewarded more on the discovery and publication of new knowledge than on the development and commercialization of that knowledge in the form of new products. The gap between the creation or discovery of knowledge and its commercialization represents a hidden loss unrecognized or even addressed by our society. It is possible that an investment in technology maturation (efforts taking a discovery from patent to commercialization) would result in a dramatic growth in the introduction of new products. If we are confident that new products are a driving force in our economic system, it seems logical to support their creation.

Our economy will benefit greatly through new and creative methods of enhancing the process of moving from patents to product commercialization. A national policy that encourages and supports the entrepreneurial process through tax incentives for technology maturation would be a positive first step. Free markets operate best for all of society when entrepreneurship is encouraged and supported. Recognition of the critical linkage between the entrepreneur and the economic well-being of a nation needs to be firmly established in order to support the creation of economic policies that encourage the entrepreneurial process. Policy change begins with the recognition of the value of these important elements of entrepreneurship: the entrepreneurial mind-set, patent protection, technology maturation, and (if a discovery is proven viable) product commercialization.

Ultimately, ideas have the power to result in products that alter markets. Ideas, which lead to new technologies, represent both enhanced economic power for the researcher and the potential of enhancing the well-being of society. The patent process must be open and free of bureaucratic roadblocks. However, once patented, the new technology must be protected. Failure to protect patents extremely and aggressively sends an open invitation to those who would steal our long-term economic future and negatively impact our economic growth. Society benefits if new and good ideas in the form of patents are assisted in the maturation process and become, if warranted, new products. Society needs to recognize the value of a freely functioning entrepreneurial pipeline. Entrepreneurship, under these circumstances, will demonstrate its contribution to an increasingly sound economy.

The twenty-first century is witnessing exponential growth in research and development. The world leader in economic development will be the society that is most

Airbnb

Little did Brian Chesky, an industrial designer and strategist, and Joe Gebbia, passionate about landscape and architecture, realize in 2007 that the company Airbnb would execute a vision to transform the way travelers secure and utilize housing accommodations while away from home. From a personal experience of not being unable to secure and utilize housing accommodations for a month at an affordable rate to founding and growing Airbnb from Airbed and Breakfast, the pair has created a disruptive force in the travel space by establishing a company that has over 3 million listings in 65,000 cities in more than 191 countries with a 2017 market valuation of $31 billion. From identifying an unmet customer need to creating a dominant corporate innovation, Brian and Joe have turned the travel industry on its ears and provided a strong, internationally recognized, and valued travel service.

Sources:

"Airbnb," *CNBC Disruptor/50*, May 16, 2017, https://www.cnbc.com/2017/05/15/airbnb-2017-disruptor-50.html.

"About Us," *Airbnb*, accessed June 11, 2018, https://press.atairbnb.com/about-us/.

competent at facilitating the movement of new knowledge through the maturation pipeline into market-focused commercialized products. The economic models and policies of the past must be replaced with policies and actions that center on entrepreneurial principles. The time has come to take positive action across all institutions of a society to support the entrepreneurial process. The evidence is clear that entrepreneurship creates enhanced economic well-being through products and services that generate employment, earnings, and wealth.

CUSTOMER-FOCUSED BUSINESS MODELS

Decades ago, because of the geographic limit of markets, customers often had to accept whatever products or services were available. Customers bought what was available where they lived or worked. The US economy had regulations that offered only one telephone provider, AT&T, and normally a sole provider of utilities such as electricity, gas, and water. Deregulation in the 1970s encouraged competition. Economic systems operate best when consumers have choice. Customers are the driving force determining the economic viability of supplies of good and services. Business competition in an open and free market allows for new business ventures to succeed when they provide customers with the goods and services that they desire, at a price that they can afford. The result is not one single winner but potentially a variety of winners, each chosen by a distinct group of customers. Competitive markets allow producers to tailor their products and services to attract, and hopefully retain, a sufficient number of customers to remain profitable. In reality, the competitive battle for success never ceases.

Customers exercise the ultimate control over the economy through the power of choice. Customers with choice always rule the market. The results have been products and services that meet increasingly higher levels of quality, reliability, and durability at ever-lower prices. The message to entrepreneurs is simple and direct: continue to innovate and offer customers increasingly superior products or services and lower prices if you plan to survive. The market will never stabilize at a point of equilibrium as the pressure of the competitive dynamics continues to grow. Customer loyalty is a concept in decline as consumers encounter new products and services that bombard them with features designed to appeal to unrealized wants and needs. Customers regularly shun the products and services of the past as they eagerly anticipate new, superior product replacements. These consumer behaviors are a result of what our economic system has produced. Entrepreneurs continually strive to gain a foothold in the market through developing and marketing increasingly attractive new products and services. The customer's behavior in an economic system based in free choice continues to spin the market cycle ever faster.

Entrepreneurs must continually search for market niches capable of producing profit at a level high enough to sustain their businesses. If initially successful, many firms opt to expand to even larger market segments. Creating a lasting competitive advantage in the market place will require a business both to operate highly efficiently (at the lowest cost) in the present and to continue to be highly innovative in order to bring future products and services to market. This balance of efficiency and innovation is difficult to achieve. Some firms damage their future capability to compete as they concentrate exclusively on cutting their costs and expenses to the bare bones to remain competitive in the current market. Such excessively lean strategies can result in reducing the firm's strength and its ability to remain highly innovative. Investments in research and development and in creative thinking are often drastically reduced as management attempts to ignore actions that it thinks do not directly contribute to the firm's bottom line.

In many highly competitive markets characterized by the expectation of a continuous stream of new product introductions, a firm risks losing market share because customers choose newer and more innovative products. Equally dangerous to long-term survival is what business history has shown us to be the fate of bloated, bureaucratic organizations that prove to be too slow to respond to the dynamic environmental forces that serve to restructure the marketplace. Like the firms whose strategies "cut to the bone" their capabilities to meet future customer needs and wants, overly bureaucratic firms have diminished capabilities to respond to change in a timely manner. Such firms are equally vulnerable to new entrepreneurial business ventures. In a market comprised of established competitors who display either of these bipolar strategic or organizational orientations, the entrepreneurial firm will have a serious competitive advantage. Entrepreneurs never keep the "status quo." The goal is to remain highly competitive in the current and future markets.

DEVELOPING AN ENTREPRENEURIAL CULTURE

The more unstable or dynamic the marketplace, the more it becomes essential for the entrepreneur to ensure that the firm's entrepreneurial culture and its organizational structure remain flexible, both strategically and operationally, in order to respond quickly to market forces. Organizations that are sensitive and attuned to their dynamic, competitive environment are better equipped to respond quickly to clues from the external environment, as well as to the unmet needs and wants of the customer base. An entrepreneurial organization that creates a culture committed to remaining flexible in response to the sources and magnitude of change has a higher probability of long-term survival. In order to accomplish this level of responsiveness, an entrepreneurial organization needs to attract and retain employees who bring specific and relevant knowledge to the firm. This operational knowledge needs to be in all supportive areas. An excellent product built on superior technology needs to be supported fully by individuals with knowledge about marketing, quality, finance, and customer service.

The entrepreneurial organization needs a balance between its knowledge of how to meet the initial market demands sufficiently and its ability to continue to evolve to meet future customer demands. From its initial inception, an entrepreneurial venture is shaped by whether it is tangibly focused on its targeted customer. The value proposition for your product or service must be specific and never vague. Your value proposition must be directly linked to the customers' needs and wants. A business must have a solution and identify a market that needs it. Success happens when the entrepreneur clearly understands specific unmet needs of the target market and the firm's products or services are able to meet or exceed the customers' expectations.

Addressing the specific ways in which your product or service is superior to those of your competitors needs to be the essential component of your business model. A definitive understanding of a firm's target market must be determined based on market research. There needs to be significantly greater depth than an entrepreneur's assumption that he or she knows what these customers want and need. Knowledge of the target market allows for the creation of a business venture that has a higher probability of success because it can provide specific answers to the ten questions posed earlier in the chapter.

THE NEED FOR CONTINUOUS CHANGE

What we know from a historical study of business in America is that powerful businesses seldom retain their market leadership. For example, only 60 companies that were on the list of Fortune 500 firms in 1955 were still on that list in 2016.[13] Although once founded by aggressive entrepreneurs, these firms too often grow into bureaucratic organizations populated by risk adverse managers who prove to be insensitive to changes in the makeup of the market. Change is organic and natural. The powerful and uncontrollable external environment in which business operates has no respect for a firm's historic importance. As an example, in our lifetime, changes in technology and science have drastically reshaped competitive realties. Professor Schumpeter, as stated earlier in the chapter, hypothesized the concept of "creative destruction." This theory has accurately forecasted the rapidly evolving rise and fall of business models. Firms lost customers due to their unwillingness to act entrepreneurially. These firms often declined and were overtaken by entrepreneurs who incorporated the outcomes of these powerful external forces into more relevant products or services.

Business history spells out, in graphic detail, these "battles" between the established, financially powerful firms and the new "upstart" entrepreneurs. The process of change is normal in nature.

Environmental forces such as technology, economics, social change, demographics, regulation, and governmental actions continue to alter the competitive landscape. Today's globally integrated business landscape provides us with increasing market potential but also results in competitive environments never faced before. Consumers are, and have always been, the beneficiaries of competition that provides them with expanded product selection and lower prices. Many marketers believe that "there is little customer loyalty that cannot be overcome by a lower price." What becomes even more concerning for a business, however, is a situation in which consumers' decisions taken against that business's products or services are not based solely on price but rather on consumers' perceptions that an alternative purchase provides better quality or style and a superior "fit" with their needs and wants. Entrepreneurs must be sensitive to their customers and respond to their needs in an aggressive entrepreneurial way. Consumer loyalty can be as short as customers' memories. What customers want today may have little to do with what you provided yesterday. The result is that the entrepreneurial process never stops.

In the twenty-first century, the pace of introducing new products and services has never been faster. The entrepreneur has absolutely no opportunity to rest on mere accomplishments. Today's market-leading firm may be tomorrow's bypassed competitor. The dynamic process is at the heart of what is studied in an entrepreneurship course. Barriers to success are falling as industries are reshaped through global competition. Key to preventing stagnation is establishing and reinforcing an organizational culture that supports and rewards innovation and creative thinking. The existing entrepreneurial venture organization must create a laser focus on the always-evolving external forces that may alter the desires, needs, and wants of its customers. New competitive products and product improvements continue to flow from the imagination of its employees. Consequently, investment in entrepreneurial thinking and culture can result in continuing reinvention of the firm's core products as well as the creation of new products.

SOCIAL ENTREPRENEURSHIP IN OUR ECONOMY

A rapidly growing segment of entrepreneurship has been termed *social entrepreneurship*. There are a large number of evolving definitions of what social entrepreneurship is, but Arthur Brooks gives the following as common elements of these definitions:

1. Social entrepreneurship addresses social problems or needs that are unmet by private markets or governments.

2. Social entrepreneurship is motivated primarily by social benefit.

3. Social entrepreneurship generally works with, not against, market forces.

Brooks goes on to state that the primary difference between commercial entrepreneurship and social entrepreneurship "is not the nature of the entrepreneurial process itself but rather the denomination of the rewards sought."[14] Social entrepreneurs choose to act as potential "change agents" whose mission is to achieve a direct positive impact on society.

An excellent example of social entrepreneurship is seen in Dana Freyer, board chair and cofounder of Global Partnership for Afghanistan (GPFA):

Global Partnership for Afghanistan is a nonprofit organization that seeks to give Afghani farmers the tools and knowledge they need to rebuild orchards, vineyards, and woodlots. Although at one time Afghanistan was a major agricultural exporter, producing 30 percent of the world's raisins, decades of war have devastated the country leaving it with only 2 percent of its land in forest. The idea for GPFA began to take shape in the weeks following the 9/11 terrorists' attacks close to Freyer's workplace. She was then a senior partner at the law firm of Skadden, Arps, Slate, Meagher & Flom. As she sat in her Times Square office, watching the smoke rise from ground zero, she recalls thinking: "How can we turn an incubator of terror to a responsible economy?" As the idea grew and took shape, Freyer and her core team raised $150,000 from family, friends, and colleagues to start their venture in 2003. According to Freyer, "Since 2003, GPFA has helped 12,000 Afghan farmers—including 1,500 women— plant and care for more than 8 million trees in some 450 villages."[15]

In fiscal year 2010, GPFA's budget was $3.5 million, and it was supported by donors that included the U.S. Government, the European Commission, and the Afghanistan Ministry of Agriculture, Irrigation, and Livestock, as well as by private foundations and individuals.[16] The organization operated with a mostly Afghan staff of 180 (including 40 women) and an American executive director. As of spring 2011, the organization was responsible for the planting 11 million trees. Also, the Tree House Training Center in Guldara, Afghanistan, was responsible for instructing hundreds of farmers in forestry, horticulture, and entrepreneurship and for aiding in the construc- tion of storage facilities, so farmers can market their produce past the harvest, when prices are higher.[17]

The focus of social entrepreneurship is on producing a positive value creation outcome that impacts a specific social need. In some cases, the entrepreneur has the dual purpose of being both profitable and supportive of social outcomes. In these situations, the entrepreneur produces a product that directly benefits society, such as a new medical treatment or device. As social entrepreneurship becomes a deeply entrenched concept among entrepreneurs, it is not unexpected to discover that an increasing percentage of new entrepreneurs are including social values as a com- ponent of their mission statements. More traditional profit-driven entrepreneurial organizations are being founded by individuals who expect that their business will be capable of achieving a position of reasonable profitability and contributing to the betterment of society.

CONCLUSION

The study of entrepreneurship is not a theoretical study but a highly practical series of analytical exercises that assist in the determination of the financial and strategic viability of the proposed new venture. Way too many businesses fail because the entrepreneur never took the time to conduct these exercises objectively. This analytical process helps the entrepreneur develop "facts," which will serve to replace perhaps overly optimistic "assumptions" about the proposed new business venture. The causes of a new venture's failure are often found in these unrealistic and inaccurate assumptions.

The analytical exercises at the conclusion of each chapter, therefore, will assist in pro- viding you with the "facts" that will serve as a guide for determining the viability of your business venture. We advise you to complete, in detail, every entrepreneurial exercise and then analyze your answers to the exercises to evaluate if your proposed new business venture will be successful. *No theory*: only hard work!

When we measure the societal impact of many of the innovations of the past few decades, it is easy to understand how entrepreneurs have successfully achieved both sets of outcomes. New drugs have mitigated serious illnesses and suffering. Technology has produced a higher standard of living for our society. It might be safe to say that entrepreneurship has always produced societal improvement. Even the once maligned entrepreneurs of the early twentieth century—Andrew Carnegie, Cornelius Vanderbilt, and Leland Stanford—used their fortunes to endow what are now "world-class" universities. Graduates from these prestigious universities have gone on to further shape the well-being of our society. At the most basic level in our economy, it is the entrepreneur who takes the risk of new venture formation, which, in turn, creates employment opportunities and contributes to the well-being of society.

The remaining chapters in this textbook will serve as a guide to the successful creation of a new business venture. Each chapter will present material that will allow you to evaluate the components of a new venture. Each chapter will include a series of "Entrepreneurial Exercises" designed to teach the analytical steps you need to take to ensure that the business has the potential to become financially viable. New venture creation and the entrepreneurial process are at the very heart of our economic system. Each of you can play a vital role in new business creation or in shaping an existing business's entrepreneurial efforts. It is your entrepreneurial journey. Enjoy the ride.

ENTREPRENEURIAL EXERCISES

Entrepreneurial Exercise 1: Part A

Based on Joseph Schumpeter's concept of "creative destruction," what industries, markets, or products are most likely to experience dramatic changes in the next five years? What are the principal forces that are going to create these changes, and how will our economy and society need to respond?

Entrepreneurial Exercise 1: Part B

Based on the changes that you foresaw when completing Exercise 1: Part A, what specific opportunities do you forecast being created? (Please be specific and as detailed as possible.)

Entrepreneurial Exercise 2

Five years from now, how would you describe the economic structure of the global economy and the role that entrepreneurship is playing in this global economy?

Entrepreneurial Exercise 3

As the global economic environment becomes increasingly capitalistic, which countries have the potential to benefit most? Why and how?

Entrepreneurial Exercise 4

Based on the discussion of the characteristics and motivational components of entrepreneurs in Chapter 1, please score yourself on the following brief exercise.

(Very high = 5; Very low = 1)

Need for achievement		5	4	3	2	1
Confidence in my abilities		5	4	3	2	1
Passion for what I do		5	4	3	2	1
Preference for moderate risk		5	4	3	2	1
High level of energy		5	4	3	2	1
High level of perseverance and tenancy		5	4	3	2	1
Ability to cope with ambiguity		5	4	3	2	1
High internal locus of control		5	4	3	2	1
Emotional stability		5	4	3	2	1

Drive to be successful		5 4 3 2 1
	Total Score:	Maximum Score = 50 Minimum Score = 10

1. What does your self-assessment tell you about yourself? Remember, only thoughtful and honest assessment will help you; no one is likely to have a perfect score.

2. What are your greatest strengths?

3. How might your personal entrepreneurial profile impact your choice of a potential new business venture?

CREATIVITY AND MARKET VIABILITY

Creativity is a function of leadership. It requires navigating uncharted territory and having the courage to face adversity to bring your vision into fruition.

Linda Naiman, founder of Creativity at Work

Today, innovation and creativity are not only highly prized; they are regarded by financial markets as one of the most important drivers of value in an organization.

Michael H. Zack, author of *Knowledge and Strategy*

CHAPTER LEARNING OBJECTIVES

Upon completion of this chapter you will be able to

Explain the connection between entrepreneurship and creativity

Summarize the screening and evaluation process

Identify the steps of market evaluation

Create a potential adopter profile

Construct an opportunity evaluation model and explain your findings

Paraphrase the assessment model

IN SEARCH OF THE VALUABLE IDEA

An original idea is the beginning point of a new business venture. But that original idea is usually the result of problem solving. When entrepreneurs observe problems or unmet needs, they see them as opportunities and begin to contemplate solutions. In other words, the recognition of problems or opportunities stimulates creativity in the entrepreneur, allowing for a different perspective, and the result of that unique view may become a tangible reality—a product or service. The initial idea is a mental image or concept of how to better solve the problem or meet the need. Thus, unmet needs and unsolved problems are the sources of potential opportunities. The majority of entrepreneurs create new business ventures based on products or services that create value through solving problems. Problems create opportunities, and entrepreneurs take advantage of opportunities.

An entrepreneur is typically the type of individual who is fascinated by how objects and systems operate. As children, entrepreneurs may have been the ones who took electronic and mechanical objects apart in order to determine the how and why behind the way these things worked. New ideas are the products of a creative mind—the people who learned to repair whatever was broken or who enjoyed solving puzzles in their youth have a great start in forming successful ideas that solve problems in a new way.

Ideas, as creative as they might be, are not necessarily viable as a source for the establishment of businesses. Creativity involves thinking new thoughts, whereas innovation is the ability to apply creative thinking to problems and opportunities. From this process of innovation comes the birth of new business ventures. The study of entrepreneurship helps us to evaluate analytically the market feasibility of our ideas. Because entrepreneurs often have many potential solutions, even in response to the same problem, there is usually a competition of ideas. This battle of ideas is a powerful driver in the entrepreneurial process. The majority of these competing ideas, however, fail when tested in the marketplace. Other solutions are found to be superior, which points to the benefit of good market assessment.

In so many cases, creative and innovative ideas do not translate into market-viable products or services. They simply do not solve the problems as effectively and efficiently as another entrepreneur's products or services, or the businesses are not executed in a timely or efficient fashion. In most situations, the new product or services simply fails to generate an adequate market demand.

THE POWER OF HUMAN CREATIVITY

Creativity is a product of a mind-set that is unwilling to simply accept what others view as a **creativity fixed reality**. Some people would describe this perceived reality as a paradigm, which means a preconceived idea, or set of ideas, about some aspect of the world in which we operate. Creative individuals are not bound by these traditional assumptions and preconceived limits. Creative individuals challenge the thinking of others in search of original, new concepts and possibly new and increasingly accurate realities.

Entrepreneurs are what might be termed *creative thinkers*. Scientists have identified that the left side of the brain serves to aid us in what is termed linear vertical thinking. This is the logical side of our brains. In contrast, the right side of the brain processes emotional thought, intuitive thinking, and spatial functions. The right brain thinks in a lateral fashion and tends to be less structured, less systematic, and less conventional. Right-brain thinking allows the entrepreneur to challenge existing paradigms through questions that challenge conventional views of the world.

Why are certain assumptions accepted? Is there possibly a better way? What is the root cause of this problem? All these questions help creative entrepreneurs master the ability to integrate thinking from both halves of the brain. Most individuals have a dominant brain function and may believe that they are logical (left-brain) or emotional (right-brain) thinkers. Creative thinkers learn to use both sides of the brain and to integrate the contributions of both linear and lateral thinking in problem identification and resolution. The coordination of the complementary functions of each brain hemisphere produces what might be termed "using your fully functioning creative brain."

You can take a variety of steps to enhance your creative skills. One critical step is to improve your knowledge of a subject through factual investigation and gaining specific, relevant knowledge. A person with minimal knowledge about a problem or the underlying situation is severely limited in his or her ability to discover a creative solution. Entrepreneurs need to have "done their homework" in preparation for solving any complex problem. Relevant knowledge stems from a combination of hands-on experience and a detailed study of the situation. Some entrepreneurs fail because their solutions to problems demonstrate little actual knowledge of the issues at hand. In essence, failure can stem from developing a solution first and then looking for a problem related to that solution. It is not wise to assume that customers will be automatically lining up to make you the next business superstar simply because you bothered to create something new. Products and services must address a real and crucial need experienced by existing customers.

Convergent and Divergent Thinking

When the entrepreneur has completed the needed research and preparation, the next step is to apply the "full brain" approach, which uses both convergent and divergent thinking. Convergent thinking is the ability to recognize similarities and the connections among various seemingly unrelated data and events. Divergent thinking is the ability to recognize differences among seeming related data and events. The reason for viewing a problem using both types of thinking is to discover previously unrecognized realities of the situation. A clearer picture of the situation emerges and new solutions can appear. The final creative solution may require additional steps to achieve its final form. Many researchers suggest that the initial solution needs to mature, giving its originator time for mental reflection. The brain needs to digest new information.

Granted, neuroscientists have a long way to go before fully unraveling the mystery of how the human brain processes information and comes to conclusions. However, there is growing evidence to support that remembering events accurately or providing correct answers can depend on first forgetting and then retrieving the information from memory—a paradox that means that the most potent learning environments arise from retrieving information at the most relevant time. Thus, contrary to traditional educational models, which suggest that the study of static information is the way to create new knowledge, the best way of learning may actually be testing information as it interacts with real-world phenomena, according to neuroscience. In this process, the brain will normally add increasing specificity, resulting in significant improvements and, often, in wider applications. The last steps will involve the testing and verification of the creative solution and its implementation in the form of a new product or service.

Building a More Creative Brain

It is often necessary to remind people that they possess the power to be creative. Creativity is not limited to only a few special persons. All people can enhance their creativity through exercising their minds to employ both hemispheres of the brain. As an example, if you tend to be "left brained" consider a series of exercises that force you to think in an unconventional manner. Take steps in an attempt to understand individuals whom you believe to be quite different. Speak with these people in a nonjudgmental fashion. Attempt to be objective and to understand and accept their thought processes.

Ask them what it was that triggered their thinking on a critical issue. Read what they say they read in an attempt to expand your connectivity to their thought processes. Then, attempt to integrate their thinking with yours to gain from their perspectives and expand your understanding. In most cases, this process involves a great deal more listening than speaking. It is not a debate but a learning process. Individuals lacking in creativity have often ceased learning and become trapped in what they think they know. Creativity prospers in an open mind that is always in search of additional knowledge and the insights of others.

Become a person who can honestly say, "I have never met a person from whom I have not learned something." Creativity dies when the mind closes to new ideas and concepts.

Challenging Established Paradigms

Successful entrepreneurs are never ashamed to ask questions in search of new insights and knowledge. In fact, they are extremely inquisitive and integrate what they learn with what they know. Often, the outcome of this process is new knowledge or an innovative solution to an existing problem. Successful entrepreneurs are not afraid of challenging the established paradigms of thinking—or of possibly looking irrational as they search for new insights. Successful entrepreneurs accept that they might be wrong in their thinking and actively attempt to learn from every experience. It takes a relatively high level of personal courage to behave like a creative thinker attempting to become a successful entrepreneur.

ENTREPRENEURIAL SPOTLIGHT
HENRY BURNER—BUTTONSMITH

Buttonsmith began as the fourth-grade class project of Henry Burner in 2013. By 2018, at age 15, Burner headed a firm with 12 employees. He took this company from his initial pin-back button selling to classmates to marketing his pins at a local farmer's market and then to online sales. In September of 2017, Fast Company described how Burner's business has blended new state-of-the-art technology with old equipment to produce a globally competitive manufacturing facility, capable of responding quickly to changing market demands and new opportunities.

Revenue growth is impressive. In 2014, revenues were $250,000, but by 2017, they had risen to $2 million. The company's growing relationship with Amazon has added to its success. Buttonsmith is part of the third-party Amazon Prime option, which places very high performance criteria on sellers, including meeting Amazon's two-day shipping requirement. Buttonsmith is a family business. Henry Burner's father, Mike, a former software developer, created the complex software that serves to interconnect the firm's equipment. The product might be simple, but demand is high. Buttonsmith produces buttons, magnets, lanyards, and fixed-to-badge reels. Henry Burner has even received a patent for his invention of the Tinker Reel®—a retractable badge reel with swappable tops. The products on offer grow to meet customer demands. The streamlining has become so smooth that the business was able to respond to an Amazon customization ordering system in eight minutes.

Sources:

"About Us," Buttonsmith website, accessed June 14, 2018, www.buttonsmith.com.

Glenn Fleishman, "This 10-Year-Old's $2 Million Amazon Business Is Leaving Competitors in the Dust," *Fast Company*, September 12, 2017, https://www.fastcompany.com/40453740/meet-the-10-year-old-who-built-a-2-million-button-business-on-amazon.

SCREENING AND EVALUATING IDEAS

One recognizable sign of potential failure is blind faith. The person who believes, without careful thought and analysis, that every idea will become a successful business venture is often heading for failure. There is a long analytical road between a seemingly good idea, a new product or service, and a successful business venture. Successful entrepreneurs aggressively employ all of the analytical tools at their disposal to attempt to screen out effectively those ideas with low potential while concentrating their efforts on those with exceptional potential. Successful entrepreneurs use these analytical tools to separate financially viable and feasible products or services from the seemingly chaotic seas of ideas.

An idea must have the capacity to create value for your business. Experience has shown that if a business is based on a solution without a problem, the business will soon have a problem with no solution. The goal is to set forth a process that will serve to differentiate a viable opportunity from just another idea. For the idea to be an opportunity, it must have the capacity to create value for its intended users. The first principle is fundamental: the opportunity in the form of a product or service must create value for the buyer or user. Creating tangible and measurable value is often a function of meeting an unmet or previously unrecognized need that is at the foundation of a problem or an opportunity.

Products or services are capable of creating value if they produce both tangible and positive results, such as

1. Increases in productivity,

2. Increases in quality, and

3. Reductions in cost.

Some products or services enhance personal satisfaction, increase prestige, or help redefine the user. The value may well be more psychological than purely tangible. Value, like beauty, is in the eyes of the beholder. What is quickly evident is that the value created must be greater than the cost of the product or service. A potential buyer or user may appreciate that a product or service increases productivity but is not interested when the cost of that innovation exceeds the value created. All business ventures operate in a competitive environment where multiple variables interact to determine winners and losers. Value creation is essential but not a guarantee of market success.

The screening and evaluation process is normally a series of questions designed to place a potential value on the new product or service. The answers to some questions may result in the idea being discarded or, at the minimum, redeveloped.

Understanding the Targeted Market

An attribute or benefit derived from the customer's perception of the product or service is critical in market assessment. Market research needs to be conducted in every market segment the entrepreneur plans to serve to determine whether both potential customer and the entrepreneur hold mutual perceptions of the product or service. If the potential customer does not view the product or service in the same way as the entrepreneur, steps must be taken to correct this misconception prior to the product or service's introduction. Changing the market's view of a product or service *after* it is introduced will almost always cost more than modifying the product or service as a result of front-end market research. A product or service cannot succeed in the appropriate target market unless there is accurate consumer awareness of the product or service.

Understanding Buyers' Behavior Patterns

The "best" potential markets, as determined through the entrepreneur's research, must be introduced to the product or service in a way that supports or reinforces the buyers' behavior patterns. After determining the critical attributes of a product or service required by buyers, the entrepreneur must present the product or service to the buyers by clearly delineating its superior and critical attributes over existing products or services. The key is to make it as simple as possible for the buyer to recognize the superiority of the product or service.

Target Customer Satisfaction

Many products or services fail because entrepreneurs mistakenly assume the marketplace will automatically recognize the superiority of their efforts. But changing buyer behavior is not easy or automatic. In most cases, the new product or service must replace an existing one. Also, since buyers may not be dissatisfied with the product or service they presently purchase, entrepreneurs must analyze the targeted market to determine how the new venture's product or service can achieve an acceptable depth of market penetration. The degree of market satisfaction or dissatisfaction with the existing product or service needs to be determined by some tangible measures. **Table 2.1** lists standard questions designed to determine the degree of satisfaction of potential customers with the products or services they presently purchase. Involving the targeted customers at this early stage is very valuable in the measurement of their current satisfaction.

The answers to these simple questions will provide the entrepreneur with an initial assessment of the customer's current level of satisfaction with the competitor's product or service on key criteria, including technical satisfaction with the product or service; to

TABLE 2.1 ■ Assessing Present Market Satisfaction

Instructions: Please circle the number that best represents the degree of your satisfaction or dissatisfaction with the product or service you currently purchase.

1. To what degree does the product or service you presently purchase satisfy your technical needs?

1	2	3	4	5	6	7
Extremely Satisfied						Extremely Dissatisfied

2. To what degree does the product or service you presently purchase create tangible value?

1	2	3	4	5	6	7
Creates Exceptional Value						Creates No Value

3. To what degree is the price of the product or service justified by its quality or performance?

1	2	3	4	5	6	7
Very Fairly Priced						Excessively Expensive

4. To what extent would you be willing to purchase a product or service that is, by your criteria, slightly superior to that which you are presently purchasing?

1	2	3	4	5	6	7
Very Willing						Not Willing

5. To what extent would you be willing to purchase a product or service comparable to the product or service you presently purchase, but at a lower price?

1	2	3	4	5	6	7
Very Willing						Not Willing

Additional Key Questions

The entrepreneur's research should also capture specific information regarding the purchasing processes of customers or clients. Here are some additional questions that can be very valuable:

- For an industrial or commercial product or service, who makes the final buying decision? Is it, for example, a purchasing agent, the technical staff, or possibly upper management?

- Are purchases of a consumer product or service made annually, monthly, or weekly?

- How willing is the decision maker to evaluate comparable products?

- To what degree has the business selling the existing product or service created significant customer loyalty?

- How essential is the current product or service to the success of the buyer?

- Does the purchase of this product or service represent a significant financial expenditure on the part of the buyer?

what extent it creates tangible value; price compared to quality or performance and to product or service superiority; and, last, price sensitivity.

Answers to questions such as these help the entrepreneur assess the feasibility of the product or service in each market segment or niche. A market, or market niche, is

SpaceX

SpaceX was launched in 2002 by serial entrepreneur Elon Musk, a South African–born Canadian/American business leader, to seize upon the opportunity to privatize the aerospace launch industry and develop a nongovernmental platform for the exploration of space with an ultimate goal of colonizing Mars. SpaceX has capitalized on the United States government's desire to privatize the launch of satellites and support materials for the International Space Station by creating and manufacturing reusable launch rockets. These enable the company both to reduce significantly the costs of placing materials in space and to design and develop new generations of launch vehicles for the exploration of the Moon, Mars, and beyond. Elon Musk, the cofounder of Tesla, Inc., and of Neuralink, has leveraged his technical background and entrepreneurial business leadership experience to create a disruptive vision for the future of space exploration. With the current market valuation of SpaceX at over $25 billion, the sky is defiantly not the limit.

Sources:

"About SpaceX," SpaceX website, accessed June 14, 2018, http://www.spacex.com/about.

Michael Sheetz, "Latest SpaceX Valuation Shows 'an Unlimited Amount of Funding' Available in Private Markets, Equidate Says," *CNBC: The Edge*, April 13, 2018, https://www.cnbc.com/2018/04/13/equidate-spacex-27-billion-valuation-shows-unlimited-private-funding-available.html.

comprised of individuals or businesses that have the ability and willingness to purchase because the product or service satisfies a need they have. The need itself may be tangible, clearly defined, and even quantifiable, or it may be intangible and not easily defined or measured.

Market assessment is not a one-time snapshot but a continuous motion picture. Successful businesses have mastered the timing of new product or service introduction to correspond with the market's acceptance, or even demand, for a valued product or service. A potentially "revolutionary" new and even technologically superior product often fails to gain market acceptance due to the entrepreneur's ineffective market assessment. In some cases new and superior products and services will not immediately be accepted. Market timing is an essential component in the successful introduction of new products or services.

Identifying Unmet or Under-Met Needs

After analyzing the satisfaction or dissatisfaction of the relevant market segment with existing products or services, the entrepreneur must identify any specific unmet or under-met needs of each of the defined market niches. Then the entrepreneur can evaluate the attractiveness of the new product or service in light of these needs (**Table 2.2**).

The new product or service must be able to address the unmet or under-met needs of the market niche effectively. The stronger the ability of a new product or service to meet these needs, the higher the probability that the product or service will be successfully adopted. However, even if a new venture has positive value-creating features, success is not a sure thing. There can be a wide gap between the technology on which a product or service is based and the nature and characteristics of the targeted market niche.

TABLE 2.2 ■ Evaluating Value Creation and Market Niches	
Matching unmet or under-met needs of the market niche with the specific superior features or attributes of the new product or service	
Specific Market Niche: _____	
Brief description of the unmet or under-met needs of this market niche	Specific "value-creating" features of the new product or service relevant to the unmet or under-met need
1.	1.
2.	2.
3.	3.
4.	4.

FIGURE 2.1 ■ Market Niches and Product or Service Technology		
Nature and characteristics of Technology	**Targeted Market Niche** *Presently* ⟷ *Well-established* *Non-existing* *Market Niche*	
New and Highly Innovative ↕ *Established*	New and very innovative product or service targeted at a presently non-existing market niche	New and very innovative product or service targeted at a well-established market niche.
	Product or service based upon established technology being introduced into a nonexistent market niche (need to demonstrate superior value creation capabilities)	Product or service based upon established technology being introduced into an established market niche (need to demonstrate how the new product or service is superior to the existing product or service)

Figure 2.1 illustrates a simple example of four extreme matches between a product or service's level of technology and the existence or state of development of a market niche, and it highlights the level of difficulty various new technologies might have in achieving successful market acceptance. Products based on new and innovative technologies often find high levels of initial resistance, even in established market niches, because the product is unknown and its results are unproven. A two-fold problem exists when a new and innovative product or service is targeted at a nonexistent market segment. Can a new market segment be created based on the unmet or under-met needs of a specific target group, and will this new market segment accept an untested or unproven product based on new and innovative technology? The second situation is normally the most difficult in which to gain acceptance.

When a product or service is based on established technology the worst-case scenario deals with the reality of head-to-head competition against existing products or services in a well-established market niche. The key question to answer is why a potential customer would be willing to switch to the new product or service. How much will it cost, in both time and money, to gain a needed level of market penetration? When the new venture develops its marketing plan, great weight must be given to the whole issue of gaining market share against established competitors. A good rule is never to underestimate the level of retaliation that a new venture can expect from competitors defending their market positions.

The critical questions that serve to help in assessing the feasibility of a new product or service include the following:

1. Is there a problem or potential opportunity that the new product or service has the potential to improve or solve?

2. Do the current buyers or users recognize the nature and scope of the problem?

Responses to these questions can serve to categorize the problem as being either universally recognized and in need of resolution or already recognized but not of significant concern to the buyer or user. Clearly, the more that the new product or service is addressing a problem that is identified by most of the potential consumers, the greater its potential for successful adoption. On the contrary, if the market does not have significant concerns about a recognized problem, the initial sales of a new venture addressing this problem may not be sufficient for that venture to survive. If your product or service is focused on a problem that the market currently does not recognize, the "window of opportunity" may not yet be open. This situation exists when a product or service is ahead of its time and the market is not yet ready to accept it. It is a tough sell when the market has yet to discover the value of your product or service. Entrepreneurs can become frustrated under these conditions.

The perfect scenario for failure would include blind faith and unrealistic optimism by entrepreneurs based on the untested technical superiority of a product or service, coupled with an assumption that the market will automatically accept the new product or service and that customers therefore cannot wait to purchase it. Unfortunately, all too many entrepreneurs and their supporters buy into unbelievably simple and unrealistic assumptions that are untested and unchallenged. Entrepreneurs are too often prone to make errors in judgment when they lack any measure of objectivity regarding their product or service or regarding the behavior of the market. Obviously, it is highly important to believe in the product or service on a number of levels, but when the entrepreneur's involvement is based solely on emotional and personal psychological desires for success and financial gain, the results can range from failed launches to spectacular company flameouts.

MARKET EVALUATION STEPS

Bad assumptions or failure to revise initial positive assessments based on new information can lead the entrepreneur into a false sense of potential success. The result is denial of the need for reality-based analysis. Business history has taught us that product superiority alone does not always win adoptions. Only a small segment of the market is even ready to consider the adoption of a new and often untested product. Entrepreneurs who may be inexperienced in the process of new product introduction, with its numerous barriers, pitfalls, and landmines, need to create for themselves a "map" that will help guide them in their analysis of the hostile marketplace in which they plan to embark. The box entitled "Analytical Steps in Market Evaluation" provides an overview of the steps involved in market evaluation.

Identifying Potential Adaptors

It is always difficult to pick a starting point for the market analysis. But why not begin by identifying the realistic number of potential adopters of a new product in what is a very time-sensitive window of opportunity? This limited **window of opportunity** is created by the internal **burn rate** of the new venture's financial capital in contrast with the profit the firm derives from sales to adopters of the new product. Most firms, and especially entrepreneurial start-ups, have limited and finite financial capital.

Analytical Steps in Market Evaluation

1. What is the actual market for the product measured in terms of sales revenue? Are these sales revenues adequate to generate a profit and maintain the viability of the new venture?

2. What is the projected "burn rate" of cash in the new venture, and will the sales revenue projections you created in response to the previous question arrive in adequate time to meet your financial needs?

3. Does the product have the demonstrable ability to produce a tangible and measurable impact on the potential adopter's profitability? If so, aggressively demonstrate the relevant features.

4. Whenever possible, describe the high level of compatibility between the product and the potential adopter's current system; also describe the low cost of reversing the decision to adopt if the product were to fail.

5. If the potential adopter is known to have an existing problem that the new product can solve, focus the marketing efforts on demonstrating the product's ability to correct the problem

6. Focus all marketing efforts on potential adopters who have the technical staff to implement the new product or service and the management confidence to risk the adoption.

The entrepreneur must recognize how the total available investment that the firm began with has been reduced by the money spent on the design, development, and manufacturing of the product or service. What funds remain is all that is available for the marketing efforts. The need for marketing is too often underestimated. Consequently, underfunded marketing efforts are often the norm. In many cases, the entrepreneur fails to consider the market retaliation of competitors, which often results in the need to spend additional, and normally limited, financial resources on marketing the new product or service. Potential adopters cannot buy products or services of which they are not aware. Therefore, it is crucial to target the firm's limited and finite marketing resources at potential customers or clients with the highest adoption potential. Efficient information acquisition and new product performance data have been demonstrated to result in greater financial performance because, with this research, valuable marketing resources are used judiciously and in a precisely targeted fashion.

Innovators and Early Adopters

As **Figure 2.2** indicates, the realistic potential adopters for a new product have traditionally been termed as innovators or early adopters. The firms that belong in these two categories have demonstrated through their consistent behavior that they will consider and often adopt new products. On the other side of this coin are most of the firms in any market; they tend not to purchase new, innovative products. These firms are found in the categories marketing authorities label early majority, late majority, and laggards.

FIGURE 2.2 ■ Diffusion of Innovations

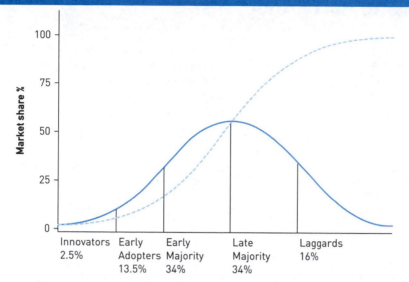

Source: Based on Everett Rogers's *Diffusion of Innovations* (New York: Free Press, 1962). Retrieved from https://commons.wikimedia.org/wiki/File:Diffusion_of_ideas.svg.

It is dangerous to generalize, but these categories typically represent 75 to 85 percent of the market. Thus, the market segments relevant to a firm attempting to sell its new products or services are those labeled "innovators" and "early adopters."

The next step in the analytical process would be to evaluate the realistic purchasing potential of innovators and early adopters (based on historical and projected data). Discovering the annual capital expenditures made by these firms is a starting point. Here is another critical question: Of the typical capital expenditures of these firms, how much is spent on products such as yours? This macro-level analysis is far from precise, but it will provide a "rough" estimate of the sales potential for the new product. Basically, you should ask whether there is adequate evidence of potential adopters reaching a sufficient purchasing volume (in both units and dollars) to support the business venture. If the product is one with a long life expectancy once sold, there is the reality that it might be years, even decades, before a follow-up sale can be expected. Revenue estimates should be based on most likely, optimistic, *and* pessimistic sales scenarios. The entrepreneur should further estimate the period between sales to early adopters and to the next wave of adopters. Furthermore, entrepreneurs must accurately project sales magnitude estimates for the next wave of adopters as well as the cost that will be incurred to meet these sales targets. Will the firm need to make significant investments in capacity to meet the projected market demands? Early adopters must sustain the firm until the larger group of later adopters enters the market.

It is beneficial to conduct this analysis early in the development of a new product, and, if the results of the analysis suggest that there is a strong likelihood of market rejection, the project can be terminated and financial resources preserved. Consequently, before a

Innovators and Early Adopters

1. The potential adopters for the market are only 15 to 25 percent of the firms that comprise the total market. If the window of opportunity is short, the percentage is even smaller.

2. It becomes essential to know the firms that are considered innovators or early adopters because they represent the target market for any firm attempting to sell a new product into the market.

Note: Although presented as static, the process of categorizing firms in this way may be further complicated by the fluidity with which they move through stages of innovation acceptance. How open to innovation a firm is can be affected by how well established it is, what strategies it is implementing, whether it has new leadership, and many other factors. Also, firms are created and fail regularly.

firm's financial resources are spent in the production and extensive marketing of a new product, it is essential to determine the extent to which firms in the defined target market will be financially capable of and likely willing to purchase at a level that makes the continuation of the venture viable. Conducting this purchasing power assessment as early as possible helps you avoid spending the project budget on manufacturing only to discover that the remainder of the funds are inadequate to support the sustained introduction of the product. The new venture is justified by a demonstrated level of demand, measured in terms of sales dollars and profitability. Time is the enemy of new product introduction, as success must be achieved before capital runs out and opportunities disappear, so any assessment must consider both **burn rate** and the **window of opportunity**.

Only cash from sales revenues can stop the hemorrhaging of financial capital. If sales are insufficient to produce the requisite cash, a new entrepreneurial venture simply runs out of capital, or the firm reaches a level of losses beyond which its owners choose not to continue. In the simplest terms, positive and timely cash flow is critical for a firm's viability.

Consequently, these initial analytical steps in the evaluation process for the introduction of a new product determine the adequacy of market demand and the critical time for earning adoptions and revenues, considering the financial realities and corresponding constraints of the situation.

Because it is essential that a new venture invest its marketing resources initially by targeting only serious potential adopters, a first step in this evaluation is a detailed study of the firms that comprise the industry to which the new product or service will be offered. The focus here is to eliminate the firms that have never displayed the initiative to adopt early-stage products. The second step would be to assess the financial capability of the targeted firms to adopt the product or service; obviously, there is no need to waste marketing resources on unlikely adopters. The third step would be to exclude all remaining firms whose ethical record indicates that they are likely to avoid payment or default on their promises to pay. The detailed study of the industry will uncover the past and present names of these unethical firms. The fourth step is to search for firms that are currently experiencing operational or performance problems that your firm's product or service can resolve. If you are successful in resolving the problems of these firms, additional doors will open.

CREATING A POTENTIAL ADOPTER PROFILE

The questions in **Table 2.3** address the behavioral history of the targeted firm as an early stage adopter. The research must discover whether each firm is consistently an early adopter of new products and whether being an early adopter and implementer of technology is extremely important and has proven to be valuable to the management of the firm. Based on these results, you can verify whether each potential adopter qualifies as a logical recipient of an intensive investment of marketing resources. In almost every case, this newly defined target market is very likely significantly smaller than the original group.

The second question in **Table 2.3** asked whether your firm's product could produce a tangible and measureable positive impact on the potential adopter's profitability. Few factors excite potential adopters more than the ability of the new product to have a positive and significant impact on their profitability. If the product has the demonstrated ability to produce either, or both, an increase in productivity or a reduction in operating expenses, this reality should be the lead factor in promoting its adoption. Demonstrable capabilities along these lines usually open the doors with potential buyers.

The third question assesses the degree of compatibility between the new product and the potential adopter's current operational system. A new product that is not compatible at all is very likely to be rejected out of hand because of the perceived need for the potential adopter to incur significant cost to revamp its operating system. If only a few inexpensive modifications are needed to ready the potential adopter's operating system, and the new product has demonstrated its ability to increase productivity or reduce expenses, the barriers may be breached. Clearly, if there is complete compatibility with the potential adopter's operating system, no barrier exists, and the potential adopters should be informed by the marketers of this fact.

The fourth question often possesses what can be a frightening pitfall: the reversibility of the adoption decision. Executives are fundamentally uncomfortable with making a decision that places them in a complete win-lose situation. If the new product performs up to expectations, the decision was a winner. If, however, the product fails to meet expectations and has to be completely replaced, the adoption decision may have been extremely costly and *has* exposed the decision maker's failure.

Potential adopters will often shy away from irreversible product decisions. In these situations, executives will often refrain from adopting and installing the new product until "others" have proven its value. The pitfall of irreversibility is as much psychological as economic.

Some of the questions, like the fifth, can identify potentially positive situations: for example, the targeted adopters could recognize that they have an existing problem that might be remediated by the new product. When the targeted potential adopters recognize a problem, it serves to open the door for the sales representatives to demonstrate the new product. Firms with recognized operational problems should be at the top of the sales call list. Entrepreneurs will need to be prepared to demonstrate the new product's superiority in resolving a potential adopter's problems.

A real, practical concern, often overlooked yet critical, is the ability of potential adopters to pay for the new product (Question 6). It is critical to ensure that the buyer can and will pay in a timely fashion, especially if a start-up firm with limited financial resources offers the new product. Accounts receivable may be assets but not the type that are available to pay current expenses. Some firms have a very poor track record for meeting their financial obligations, and once a new product is sold (and often installed), getting your product returned when payment is not forthcoming can be difficult. The more expensive the product the bigger the potential "hit" to a firm's cash flow.

On a potentially positive side, if the cost of implementing the new product is low, this may serve to reduce one of the barriers to adoption (Question 7). A new product that can be made operational quickly and at a low cost is much more appealing to adopters than ones whose implementation is time consuming, costly, and, the worst case, requires operational downtime.

Another barrier to adoption is the lack of competence of the potential adopter's current staff to implement the new product or operate it once installed (Question 8). This obstacle is often present when a new venture is marketing highly sophisticated technology-based products to potential adopters whose employees may be unfamiliar with the technologies of the product and would require additional training to become competent in the new product's operation. The barrier to adoption is the additional training cost as well as the uncertainty as to whether the current employees have the ability to learn the skills or knowledge associated with the effective operation of the new product. Most firms will resist adopting products that they believe are beyond the skill level of current employees. When a new product's technology is truly new and different, it is not unusual to discover that this barrier to adoption exists. Every effort must be made to demonstrate to potential adopters that their staff can master and apply the new product.

A serious pitfall to adoption occurs when a firm's management does not support spending on new technologies (Question 9). Often, the firm may be experiencing an ongoing organizational conflict between the operations or technology staff and the managers. The new product will face a serious uphill battle unless nontechnical management types can understand the value of the new product. Do not sell only the technology; sell the ability of your product to increase productivity or lower cost. Nontechnical managers may not understand the technology underlying the product, but they do understand increased profitability. Focus at least half of your marketing efforts on reducing the adoption barriers by selling to the nontechnical decision makers. Consummating the sale may require contacting multiple decision makers within the firm (e.g., technical or operational implementers, nontechnical users, and supervisors), and each may require a different approach.

A serious psychological barrier to adoption exists in firms that have recently failed to implement a new product successfully (Question 10). Resistance to accepting another new product is reasonable and should be factored into the marketing effort when you are attempting to sell to a firm in this situation. Although it is seldom possible to guarantee that your product will solve their problems, it is imperative to focus on every aspect of the new product that you are confident *does* meet the adopter's needs.

TABLE 2.3 ■ Potential Adopter Screening for New Products: In Search of Market Viability

	Scale Always					Almost Never	Value Very Important				Very Unimportant	Factor Score (Scale x Value)
1. A history of being an innovator or early adopter of new technology-based products	10	8	6	4	2	0	1.0				0	
2. New product can produce a tangible and measurable impact on the potential adopter's profitability	10	8	6	4	2	0	1.0				0	
3. Degree of compatibility between your new product and the potential adopter's operational system	10	8	6	4	2	0	1.0				0	
4. The reversibility of the adoption decision	10	8	6	4	2	0	1.0				0	
5. Potential adopter's need of a superior product to solve an existing problem	10	8	6	4	2	0	1.0				0	
6. Potential adopter's financial ability to buy your new product	10	8	6	4	2	0	1.0				0	
7. Low cost of implementing your new product	10	8	6	4	2	0	1.0				0	
8. The competence of the staff of the potential adopter to implement your new product successfully.	10	8	6	4	2	0	1.0				0	
9. Internal support for your new product by the management of the potential adopter	10	8	6	4	2	0	1.0				0	
10. Previously successful management of technology risk	10	8	6	4	2	0	1.0				0	
11. Your firm's reputation with the potential adopter	10	8	6	4	2	0	1.0				0	
											Potential Adopter Factor Score:	

On the other side of the same coin, the firms whose management is successful at managing the risk of new product adoption should be specifically targeted. These decision makers have earned a level of confidence in their abilities. They will be more willing to accept the risk associated with the adoption and implementation of a new technologically based product because of their previous successes.

The final question posed in **Table 2.3** uncovers a major possible landmine for newly formed firms because it is not likely that they have any reputation with the potential adopters. This is the liability of newness. Some potential adopters have unwritten policies that result in ignoring initial marketing efforts from new businesses, so new firms have difficulty gaining an audience with the critical decision makers. Even if this policy is not in place, when a firm lacks stable relationships with buyers, the risk of failure is great. The best hope for new businesses with a product that can be clearly demonstrated to be superior to what is currently being used, or one that has significant improvements in performance, are national or regional trade shows attended by the firms that have been identified as potential early adopters. Communicate with them prior to the trade show about the number and location of your booth. If your budget allows, invite these selected potential adopters to a special social event or product demonstration. They must meet both you and the product in order to gain confidence in their decision to buy. In most cases, you must be very aggressive in making a connection with the firms upon which the success of your business depends. Methods may vary, but the potential adopters need to see the product, understand how the product will create value for them, and meet the key people behind the product and the firm. References can be utilized to generate future sales. Knowing others have purchased can positively influence other potential adopters.

BUILDING AN OPPORTUNITY EVALUATION MODEL

It is essential that the entrepreneur know the critical time horizon of their business, as discussed earlier in the chapter. New businesses will normally have a finite amount of financial capital. The tangible process of designing, developing, testing, manufacturing, and marketing a new product requires expenditures of capital. **Only cash from sales can replenish the supply of financial capital**. Although this is an extremely fundamental concept, in too many instances, the entrepreneur fails to calculate the time horizon in terms of the point at which the new firm will have expended its total financial resources. Most new products descend into what has been described as the "valley of death" when financial resources are expended with few, if any, sales. Sales, and only cash sales, can replace the money expended during the entire process from initial design through marketing, final sale, and collection. The concept of "burn rate" became a harsh reality for the hundreds of firms that crashed during economically challenging times. Many firms expended millions of dollars of invested capital without emerging from the "valley of death."

Figure 2.3 provides a diagram or model that the entrepreneur can follow in the analytical assessment of the opportunity for a new product or service. This analysis requires

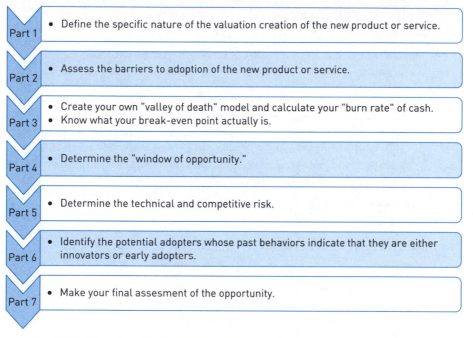

FIGURE 2.3 ■ Opportunity Evaluation Model

Part 1
- Define the specific nature of the valuation creation of the new product or service.

Part 2
- Assess the barriers to adoption of the new product or service.

Part 3
- Create your own "valley of death" model and calculate your "burn rate" of cash.
- Know what your break-even point actually is.

Part 4
- Determine the "window of opportunity."

Part 5
- Determine the technical and competitive risk.

Part 6
- Identify the potential adopters whose past behaviors indicate that they are either innovators or early adopters.

Part 7
- Make your final assesment of the opportunity.

the entrepreneur to describe in detail his or her product, how specifically it creates value for the targeted market niche, the potential barriers to its adoption, and whether these barriers be overcome. It allows the entrepreneur to evaluate the firm's "window of opportunity" for its product or service. The model next requires the entrepreneur to address the ever-present issues of technical, financial, and competitive risk, which are possibly unique and specific to the market niche the firm intends to penetrate. Last, the model allows for the identification of potential adopters whom research has identified as either innovators or early adopters. The model enables entrepreneurs, based on their analysis, to determine if a window of opportunity for the product exists and the potential time frame availability.

THE SEVEN-PART ASSESSMENT MODEL

This model is easily operationalized through the entrepreneur answering a series of fundamental questions designed to determine the extent of the business opportunity. These questions will serve to guide the entrepreneur in the objective evaluation of both the business and its probability of success.

Part 1: Value Creation

- Write a detailed description of the new business venture's product or service.

- Discuss the specifics of the product or service that create value for the customer.

  - For example, does the product or service serve to enhance the performance of the customer's products or services or of its operations? If so, how and to what extent? Are these enhancements easily recognized by the buyer? On a scale of 1–5, with 5 being extremely valuable and 1 being minimally valuable, how important will your product or service be in enhancing the performance of the customer's product or operations?

- Does the product or service serve to reduce the cost of the customer's operations?

- How does the product or service accomplish these cost reductions?

- Can the customer easily recognize the impact of your product or service on the cost of that customer's operations? On a scale of 1–5, with 5 being extremely significant and 1 being little or no significance, how would you rate the significance of the impact of your product or service on the potential adopter?

- Are there other tangible or intangible measures of value that are derived through the product or service?

- Based on the combined tangible and intangible value-creating components of the product or service, how confident do you feel that the potential adopter will find this innovation of significant enough value to consider seriously its adoption?

Always remember that value, like love, is in the eyes of the beholder. The more obviously the product or service can generate enhanced value for the potential adopter, the greater is the likelihood of an opportunity to make a sale. The key is often *both* a product or service that produces tangible value *and* the ability of the potential adopter to recognize that value. Consequently, never assume that the product speaks for itself. The job of marketing and personal selling is to help potential adopters see clearly the value, to them, of the product or service.

Part 2: Barriers to Adoption

Assessing the Barriers to the Adoption of the Product or Service

- New products and services invariably must gain market share in the targeted market niche against competitors who are not likely to be welcoming. The entrepreneur needs to be aware of the existing competitors' tactics that are designed to keep new entries out. These aggressive, and often unethical, competitive tactics are normally discovered by new businesses only as they attempt to introduce their new products or services. It is essential, therefore, that the entrepreneur has studied the past behavior patterns of the current competitors in the market niche in order to predict what tactics they might use to try to keep their market share. One under-recognized entry barrier is the possible radical, new, or revolutionary nature of the product or service. The innovation may very well be significantly superior, but the barrier is the reluctance of potential adopters to "be the first to try" it. In many cases, the entrepreneur has an exceptional grasp of the new technology and how the application of this new technology will have a significant positive impact on the potential adopters in the targeted market niche. However, the potential adopters may not possess the same level of knowledge about the technology and how its products could impact their businesses. Consequently, the entrepreneur normally needs to educate potential adopters through an understandable series of presentations that clearly demonstrate the potential for the new product or service to have a positive impact on each adopter's business. Whenever possible, an opportunity to demonstrate the new product/service to the potential adopter in a face-to-face situation is extremely valuable. A successful demonstration normally provides the best opportunity for the entrepreneur to make a sale. It is important to understand that, when bringing a new, radically different product or service to market, you will need additional time to overcome this natural barrier of skepticism erected against the new technology. Additional marketing and selling expenses will also need to be budgeted. One often-overlooked component is the time factor. When it takes additional time to introduce the radically new product or service to the potential adopters in the targeted market niche, the new firm's cash "burn rate" is running and eating up the firm's financial capital.

- Is the new product difficult to use or learn how to operate? The most serious problem would be that the product required a redesign to make it easier to use. In most cases, the entrepreneur will need to offer "hands-on" training for an adopter's employees in order to gain the adoption. The entrepreneur needs to determine if, in any way, the introduction of the product increases the adopter cost of operations. This reality would be a barrier to adoption that is tangible and must be addressed by the firm.

- As discussed previously, the failure to have a new product introduction strategy that results in achieving needed sales and cash endangers the firm's ability to meet its financial obligations. If the " burn rate" results in a deeper than anticipated decline in the firm's cash flow, the always present "valley of death" claims another new business venture. A great number of what might have been successful businesses fail because entrepreneurs do not conduct the needed analysis to determine accurately how much time they have to reach the financial breakeven point. Without a financial contingency plan, the business virtually runs out of cash to pay its bills and is forced to close.

- Normally, the most difficult barrier to adoption is the situation in which the new product decision produces an irreversible condition. Potential adopters fear this irreversible situation. If the product fails to work, the adopter needs to completely remove the product and replace it with the previous, "known" product. The huge cost to the adopter is the down time during which their business is not able to operate and therefore fails to produce any profits. To overcome this barrier, the entrepreneur will probably need to provide the potential adopter with some form of financial guaranty or product warranty that protects the adopter.

Part 3: "Valley of Death"

Create Your Own "Valley of Death"
Model Unique to Your Business Situation

- Based on the model that you constructed, which represents your unique business situation, calculate your "burn rate" and the time that the firm has until it becomes financially unable to continue. Attempt to discover ways in which the firm can act to reduce its "burn rate" while still being aggressive in the targeted market niche.

- The entrepreneur needs to have a fairly accurate estimate of these numbers because they directly affect the firm's possibility of success.

Part 4: Window of Opportunity

- Each new market entry has what is termed a "window of opportunity," which is normally a limited time during which it can earn product or service adoptions before competitors begin to focus their attention on aggressively eliminating this new intruder into their market niche.

- The entrepreneur will need to survey the competitive landscape to determine if any of the current competitors have themselves new products or services that are about to enter the market. This situation would be serious because the current competitors already have established business relationships with the firms that the entrepreneur will be courting.

- The entrepreneur must be prepared to invest the firm's limited financial resources in ways that expand its window of opportunity. Focusing the firm's marketing on the most attractive potential adopters is a necessity. The entrepreneur can expect that competition will be intense as current competitors are seldom passive in defending what they believe is their turf.

Part 5: Risk

A. Technical risk normally exist at two stages:

  1. Premarket technological risk includes the development of an initial product model, an engineering prototype, and the final production

prototype. If the entrepreneur fails at any of these stages, the final product does not get created.

2. The second technical risk is that, once built, the product does not solve the adopter's problem effectively or efficiently. In this situation, the entrepreneur will need to make all efforts to determine the reason for the failure and attempt to make the needed modifications to ensure client satisfaction. In the event that the entrepreneur is successful in making the needed modifications to the product, it must be recognized that the potential adopters in the market niche will be aware of the initial product failure and may be reluctant to be the first to try the redesigned product. In simple terms, initial technical failure tends to erect an even higher barrier to entry.

B. Competitive risk, which we have often alluded to, includes the following situations:

1. The very dangerous, ruthless, and aggressive competitors who are fully committed to retaining their place in the market niche you have targeted. Competitors have no requirement to act in a rational manner. The question that must be answered before engaging in combat with competitors is this: Can the battle be won? The entrepreneur may need to develop a unique entry strategy that gives the new business venture time to get established.

2. There is normally at least one competitor who has established a strong customer base due to its fully integrated business system, which might include an established distribution system, an experienced national or international sales force, extensive knowledge of the economics of the market, knowledge of the key decision makers within each firm, and a long-term positive business relationship with these decision makers.

3. Loyalty to a specific supplier may have been earned through years of mutually beneficial dealing. These are very difficult bounds to break. The risk is that it takes years to match this type of relationship.

Part 6: Potential Adopters

An essential component of an opportunity evaluation must be the identification of the most likely potential adopters of the business's products or services. To be accurate in the identification of potential adopters requires both an intimate knowledge of the market niche and a great deal of research to verify the facts. Research into the firms that might become adopters is primarily for the purpose of verifying both their status as innovators or early adopters and their financial capability to pay in a prompt professional fashion.

A. In order to attain an accurate evaluation of the market niche, market players, and their revenue potential, it is useful to divide the firms being evaluated into two groups: those whom your research indicated were innovators and early adopters and those less likely to take risks. Focus on the first group. It is valuable to note any unique behaviors regarding their adoption practices.

B. The size of their possible purchases is next to be estimated along with what you believe they would be willing to pay per unit based on their needs and the value of your product or service to their business performance. What this section of the opportunity analysis is designed to achieve is the determination of the revenue potential for the targeted market niche. If the revenue numbers are not sufficient to achieve profitability, it will be necessary to explore additional market niches that might benefit from your product or service.

Part 7: Cost

An often-overlooked component of an assessment of market viability is a relatively accurate estimate of the actual cost of creating the final new business venture. **Table 2.5** (page 50) provides a model that can be modified to fit the specifics of your proposed business. Without these cost numbers, you will have difficulty calculating your breakeven point and the shape of the "valley of death" model.

ASSESSING THE ACTUAL MARKET POTENTIAL: THE UGLY REALITIES

Every entrepreneurial adventure should include as detailed a forecast of expenses as possible. **Table 2.4** provides a template that can be easily modified to fit most new ventures. In reality, outside financial support is highly unlikely if the entrepreneur is unable to provide an investor with a moderately complete and accurate estimate of all costs and expenses. Generally, the initial cost estimate should outline the business venture's cost through development, start-up, manufacturing, marketing, and distribution.

Cost must then be allocated according to when they will be expended and whether they are fixed or variable. The entrepreneur must be able to ascertain the total financial requirements on a month-to-month basis for the new venture. When evaluating the feasibility of new products, you must recognize that some of these expenses will occur even if no product is ever sold. These expenses are normally referred to as "sunk cost."

The entrepreneur has a price in mind for the product or service, and that initial price estimate is the basis of all revenue calculations. The price for a product or service is almost always the result of a variety of calculations, including the firm's total cost to design, produce, market, and distribute the product plus all related start-up and overhead costs, as well as the prices being charged for similar products by existing competitors currently in the market niche. The product's price needs to take into consideration the economic reality of economies of scale. That is, as a firm produces higher volume, it will learn and implement superior production methods that result in a lower unit cost. Second, established competitors who currently produce in much higher volume often have lower operating costs due to the quantities at which they purchase raw materials, parts, supplies, and even services. A new firm seldom enjoys any of these traditional economies of scale (i.e., proportionate savings gained by increased levels of production).

Sales revenue projections should reflect the entrepreneur's most realistic estimation of sales but also include a sales projection that is both optimistic and pessimistic. Anticipated gross profit is the residual of sales revenue less the cost of goods sold. **Table 2.5**

TABLE 2.4 ■ Initial Cost Estimate for a New Venture	
Activity	**Estimated Cost**
Production Development	
Proof of concept and development of a prototype	$
Final product design	$
Equipment for manufacturing	$
Materials for manufacturing	$
Labor cost	$
Overhead expenses	$
Living expenses for the entrepreneur	$
A: Total Production Development	$
Marketing and Distribution	
Market research	$
Advertising and promotion of the product	$
Holding necessary inventory to supply the market	$
Expenses associated with a sales staff or distribution network	$
Sales support expenses	$
Serving the product or installation expenses	$
B: Total Marketing and Distribution	$
General Business Operations	
All unique (one-time) start-up costs	$
Administrative expenses (office labor, equipment, etc.)	$
Building expenses (rent)	$
Insurance expenses	$
General office overhead	$
C: Total Business Operations	$
TOTAL ESTIMATED EXPENSES	
A: Total Production Development	$
B: Total Marketing and Distribution	$
C: Total Business Operations	$
GRAND TOTAL	$

TABLE 2.5 ■ A: Anticipated Financial Performance

Firms in the Market Niche	Adopter Factor Score	Unit Cost Per Product	Anticipated Selling Price	Anticipated Number of Units Purchased	Anticipated Sales Revenue	Anticipated Gross Profit
AAA	82	$20,000	$30,000	500	$15,000,000	$ 5,000,000
BBB	76	$20,000	$30,000	300	$9,000,000	$ 3,000,000
CCC	74	$20,000	$30,000	250	$7,500,000	$ 2,500,000
DDD	72	$20,000	$30,000	150	$4,500,000	$ 1,500,000
EEE	70	$20,000	$30,000	100	$3,000,000	$ 1,000,000
				1,300 Units	$39,000,000	$13,000,000

B: Actual Financial Performance

Firms in the Market Niche	Adopter Factor Score	Unit Cost Per Product	Actual Selling Price	Actual Number of Units Purchased	Actual Sales Revenue	Actual Gross Profit
AAA	80	$20,000	$22,500	400	$9,000,000	$1,000,000
BBB	76	$20,000	$24,000	300	$7,200,000	$1,200,000
CCC	74	$20,000	$23,500	200	$4,700,000	$700,000
DDD	72	$20,000	$23,000	150	$3,450,000	$450,000
EEE	70	$20,000	$25,000	50	$1,250,000	$250,000
			AVG = $23,600	1,100 Units	$25,600,000	$3,600,000

Note: This example simplifies analysis by not accounting for the offering of quality discounts or changes in fixed cost according to volume sold. Real-world applications must adjust total cost based on allocating overhead by volume.

represents a depiction of what an entrepreneur believes his or her firm's anticipated gross profit will be, based on the assumption that there are five potential adopters and a selling price of $30,000 per unit. With product cost of $20,000 to bring each unit to market, the entrepreneur would anticipate a $10,000 per unit gross profit. Based on the entrepreneur's adoption factor score of each of the five targeted firms, gross sales would be 1,300 units generating $39,000,000 in sales revenues and $13,000,00 in gross profits. On the surface this seems to be a new venture with excellent profit potential. However, the ugly realities of customer behavior can change these outcomes.

Conservative estimates should be produced by evaluating the potential factors that might cause an adopter to delay its decision and, as a result, reshape the time frame in which the sale might occur. How will such extensions impact the viability of the new product venture? Many unfortunate entrepreneurs have business plans that were created based on what, in reality, proved to be overly optimistic projections of sales, with the result that organizational operations "burned through" the initial capital before an adequate level of revenue was achieved. The result: business failures that, on the surface, seem linked to inadequate funding but that, in reality, were brought about by the failure of entrepreneurs to analyze, in appropriate depth, the possible behavior of the market and who thus overestimated sales targets and related profitability.

In addition to customer delays in responding rapidly to the initial introduction of the new product, other issues can affect revenue estimates. For example, it is naïve to assume that customers will be willing to pay the asking price for the product. The normal behavioral characteristics of firms in the market indicate that they will "bargain tough" with the new potential supplier, knowing the risks associated with new products or services. The result is often a negotiated selling price below that anticipated by the entrepreneur. Because the clock is ticking and the entrepreneur needs to make those initial sales to prove the worth of the new product or service, the entrepreneur is inclined to accept a unit price below initial estimates. In the case presented in **Table 2.5**, the market does not purchase in the anticipated quantities either. Part B of this table illustrates how the realities of the market lower the firm's profit projection.

The behaviors of the firm's in the market could have been anticipated. When the potential buyers conducted their "due diligence" of the entrepreneur's firm, they quickly concluded that, in price negotiations they (the buyers) have the upper hand. The buyers concluded that the new firm had to make sales in order to survive, so it was in the buyers' short-term interest to bargain tough. Firm AAA was purchasing the largest number of units, and negotiated the price down from $30,000/unit to $22,500/unit. Firm EEE was purchasing the fewest number of units, but it successfully negotiated a purchase price of $25,000/unit.

Experience suggests that an entrepreneur should project a "worst-case" or pessimistic scenario that incorporates the reality that the initial profit projections are subject to error if the targeted firms either order fewer units or negotiate a lower selling price. The entrepreneur must recognize that firms will have different negotiation strategies and leverage when purchasing. Many potential adopters may be very strident negotiators, so even when they do purchase, the sale price may be significantly less than anticipated. Understand that price for initial sales may be lower than that for subsequent sales. Both of these situations are illustrated in Part B of **Table 2.5**: total anticipated units sold only declined by 200 units or 15 percent (1,300 − 1,100 / 1,300), but each of the five firms in the market niche negotiated a purchase price below the anticipated selling price of $30,000. The actual negotiated prices ranged from $25,000 per unit to $22,000 per unit (with an average selling price of $23,600). The anticipated gross profit was 13 million dollars. In this example, the actual gross margin dropped by 72 percent ($13,000,000 − $3,600,000/$13,000,000).

CONCLUSION

Very often, business failure can be avoided through a detailed, thorough, and objective evaluation of the business idea. On the other side, a positive assessment of your business idea serves as a motivator to continue your research. The entrepreneurial assessment process is driven by research and guided by the critical questioning of every assumption upon which your proposed business is based. There is never a shortcut in conducting your analysis.

The journey from the creation of the original idea through market assessment allows the entrepreneur the opportunity to evaluate the possible viability of a business based on that idea. In the next chapter, entrepreneurial readers will continue their analysis through a detailed assessment of the industry in which their businesses will compete, the specific market niches they will target, and their competitors. Last, an entrepreneurial business model will be detailed.

ENTREPRENEURIAL EXERCISES

Entrepreneurial Exercise 2.1

Part I

Creativity and innovation are the hallmarks of successful entrepreneurs. In the past few years, what have been your most creative and innovative ideas?

1.

2.

3.

4.

5.

Part 2

Of these listed ideas, which one "best" focuses on a well-defined opportunity?

IDEA	Opportunity

Entrepreneurial Exercise 2.2

Using **Table 2.1**, please build on your ideas identified in Part 2 of of Entrepreneurial Exercise 2.1, and discuss the level of satisfaction in your targeted market niche. How positive is this analysis? Is there an opportunity for your proposed new product or service to be successful? **What does your analysis tell you about your target market niche?**

Entrepreneurial Exercise 2.3

Using **Table 2.2**, determine the match between your proposed product or service and the unmet or under-met needs in your selected market niche. Clarify specifically how your product or service "creates value" for the customers in your selected market niche.

Entrepreneurial Exercise 2.4

Using the box entitled "Analytical Steps in Market Evaluation," address each of the seven (7) issues raised. **What additional market knowledge have you learned?**

Entrepreneurial Exercise 2.5

Part 1

Please research the market niche in which you plan to introduce your product or service and identify or at least be able to describe the potential adopters.

Part 2

Using **Table 2.3**, complete the profiles of your potential adopters and discuss your findings.

Entrepreneurial Exercise 2.6

Please use all seven parts (7) of the opportunity evaluation model presented in **Figure 2.3** to assess the market potential for your product or service. Please discuss your findings.

3

INDUSTRY AND COMPETITIVE ANALYSIS

The future ain't what it used to be.

Often credited to Yogi Berra

*An organization's ability to learn, and translate that learning
into action rapidly, is the ultimate competitive advantage.*

Jack Welch, CEO of General Electric (1981–2001)

CHAPTER LEARNING OBJECTIVES

Upon completion of this chapter, you will be able to

Defend the importance of macroenvironmental analysis

Summarize the components of the macroenvironment and their impact on
business ventures

Compare the different stages of industry development

Apply the five forces model of competition to your new business venture

Describe different types of competitive analyses

Explain the process of creating a new business model

ASSESSING THE INDUSTRY

In Chapter 2, you evaluated your idea for a new or modified product, service, or
business, as well as assessing the idea at the root of this innovation, the idea in search

of one or more potential opportunities. You analyzed the essential steps that need to be taken in evaluating the potential market niche. Potential adopters were next identified as those categorized as either innovators or early adopters. Issues such as the "burn rate" of your financial capital and the length of time needed to obtain sustaining sales revenues were determined. Your potential adopter screening was employed to evaluate the market viability of your proposed new business venture. Your research allowed you to define clearly how your product, service, and business create value for your potential adopters. Business to adoption was analyzed in depth to avoid attempting to create a new business that is likely to fail. Both technical and competitive risk were analyzed. Your research was not theoretical, but it was seriously analytical.

In this chapter, your analytical research continues as you master the application of macroenvironmental analysis, cross impact analysis, and environmental screening, all for the purpose of being better at recognizing the reality that most forces of change come from without. The more analytical expertise you gain, the more skilled an entrepreneur you become at the early recognition of new market opportunities, as well as serious potential threats. You will learn how to evaluate the level and nature of competitive behavior by applying Michael Porter's "five forces model." Competitive assessment will be determined through your asking and answering a series of questions designed to provide you with insight into the behaviors of the anticipated competitors. This analytical assessment of the behaviors of each competitor will lead to answers regarding the entrepreneur's business model form and function.

THE MACROENVIRONMENTAL ANALYSIS PROCESS

A humbling reality is the power of the external macroenvironment to change or reshape the competitive environment of any industry. Radical and disruptive technologies have become an accepted force in many markets and within many industries. Some macroenvironmental forces, trends, and events happen gradually while others take the market by surprise. An entrepreneurial firm attuned to potential changes can benefit dramatically through developing new products or services based on where the market is trending rather than where the current market focus resides. By correctly forecasting trends, an entrepreneur can achieve rapid market penetration and high levels of profitability through having new products or services available when the market changes. Sometimes, these changes create new market niches.

"First to market" business strategies can produce outstanding profits and help establish a new business venture in the evolving market.

Critical Forces, Trends, and Events

Unfortunately, many entrepreneurs do not focus on what they choose to describe as "futuristic events." Assessing the potential forces, trends, and events that are the foundation of the macroenvironment may be perceived to be less relevant to business leaders than understanding the short-term competitive forces that are influencing their immediate decisions. Entrepreneurs need to recognize the value off mastering the skills that allow them to be capable of "looking both ways." Being skilled at recognizing and tracking the forces, trends, and events that comprise the drivers of change allows the entrepreneur the time to gather and redirect a firm's limited resources in order to develop and deliver new products and services to gain a competitive position in the emerging new market niche. In today's competitive environment, the ability to reposition a business through superior flexibility can be a major factor in achieving and retaining market growth.

Figure 3.1 represents the interactions that exist among the major macroenvironmental forces in the competitive environment and demonstrates the dynamics of those interactions.

Observe that a change in one of the macroenvironmental factors produces changes to all the other factors. A classic example of this interaction was the development of a safe and affordable female contraceptive pill. More than just a new piece of technology, "the pill" allowed women to feel more empowered because they had greater control over their lives and reproductive health. These lifestyle changes resulted in women having an increased opportunity for higher education, increased participation in the workforce, and increased active participation in changing federal and state laws. This new piece of technology ushered in unprecedented reproductive rights, which led to changes in the legal structure of our own society, changes in the timing of family creation and to traditional familial roles, on the individual level, and changes in the redistribution of earnings among the genders, on the national level. So the invention and marketing of the pill led to changes in both the US society and economy. Globally, laws that promote equal pay for equal work in an attempt to level the economic playing field and address gender discrimination have been written and enacted in response to these changes, though there is still work to be done on this front. Clearly, the list of impacts on society could go on for pages. The key point to understand is that all components of the macroenvironment are interconnected, and these dynamic forces can result in the modification of society while creating a wide array of new business opportunities.

Cross Impact Analysis and Environmental Scanning

The exciting and dynamic insights provided by a macroenvironmental model lie in what is termed **cross impact analysis**. The occurrence of any single event changes the probability of the occurrence of all other events. What **cross impact analysis** does for the entrepreneur is generate an increasing awareness of the need to scan the environment actively. Environmental scanning is the process through which changes in the environmental sectors are tracked and evaluated. The goal is to identify the impact of those factors with the highest probability of influencing the future of the market niche in which you plan to compete. Scanning, evaluating, and assessing these factors is essential to determining potential impacts on the business. The value of environmental scanning is the identification of new opportunities and potential threats in time to take advantage of the first and avoid or defend against the second. Shifts in a major environmental factor, such as demographics, occur very slowly yet have a profound impact on our society. As an example, due to improvements in medicine and changes in lifestyle, Americans in the baby boom generation are living longer and staying healthy longer. Also, many are quite wealthy, as the passing of their parents' generation produced the greatest transfer of wealth in recorded history. Consequently, new market opportunities have been created to serve the needs and wants of this older, healthier, and wealthier population. For instance, a new market niche that might be termed "wealth preservation" has been created; businesses in this niche provide financial services designed to ensure that this aging population will not outlive resources.

As discussed, cross impact analysis is an analytical tool that further enriches the entrepreneur's understanding of the dynamic interactions of the macroenvironment. The occurrence of an event in the macroenvironment has the effect of potentially altering the occurrence of other events. The analysis of the "cause and effect" provides the entrepreneur with a deeper and richer understanding of the forces that continually impact to alter the macroenvironment. Scanning the macroenvironment for these *cross impact* occurrences allows the entrepreneur to recognize new opportunities early enough to possibly profit from their creation. Environmental scanning and cross impact analysis are analytical tools that, when mastered, enhance the entrepreneur's ability to achieve first mover advantage in new or evolving markets.

Your macroenvironmental analysis will need to focus on the four most critical major components: the economic environment, the technological environment, the sociopolitical environment, and the demographic and lifestyle environment. Understanding the virtually continuous interactions of these components within the overall macroenvironment will provide greater insight into current and future changes.

FIGURE 3.1 ■ Macroenvironmental Interactions

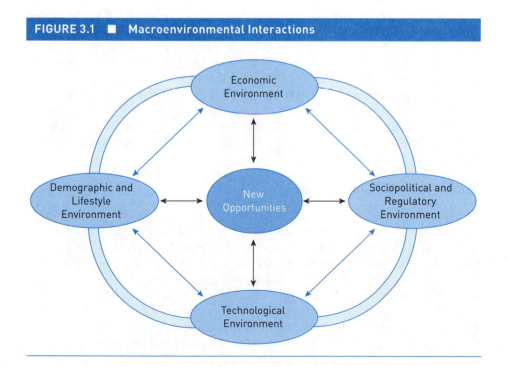

COMPONENTS OF THE MACROENVIRONMENT

Economic Environment

In a global economic environment, the entrepreneur is required to remain vigilant about any and all economic changes that have the potential to impact her or his business. As an example, the supply and demand for essential raw materials and commodities are truly global in scope. The price that an entrepreneur will be required to pay for a commodity such as oil, corn, wheat, copper, or other natural materials is determined by global supply and demand. A failure to track trends and make needed adjustments can be devastating to profit margins in a period of rapidly rising costs if an entrepreneur is unable to raise prices due to competitive pressures. Entrepreneurs who are dependent on critical commodities need to scan the futures market continually looking for trends related to needed commodities and take action to hedge their long-term cost.

On a national level, the entrepreneur is bombarded by economic factors that could be either an opportunity or a serious threat. For example, if interest rates are a critical factor in the firm's operations, it is necessary to follow closely the actions and pronouncements of the United States Federal Reserve and those of similar entities in other politically and economically dominant nations. Anticipating higher interest rates in the near future, for example, an entrepreneur might arrange for long-term borrowing to be done quickly to avoid the rising cost that higher interest rates will create. What if you discover indications of a growth in family income? How might your business be affected by this growth? Do increases in housing starts in your community impact your sales? Entrepreneurs need to develop models that reflect accurately the economic variables with positive and negative effects on their specific businesses. The next step is to identify an accurate and reliable source of economic data and forecasting that will inform their economic models of what actions need to be taken.

In reality, the number of economic variables that interact to shape the environment in which a business operates can become overwhelming. The entrepreneur does not want to experience "paralysis from analysis" in making timely decisions, but the most significant economic variables that impact critical decisions must be noted, analyzed, and integrated into the decision-making process.

Technological Environment

The past few decades has witnessed a series of one major technological breakthrough after another. By all indications, this pattern of explosive and often disruptive technological change has become the norm for our society. Technological advances are now global in scope and are a worldwide phenomenon. Facilitated by the Internet, new technologies are quickly distributed to an eagerly awaiting audience. As a global society, we have an increasing expectation that technology will solve problems and provide for a better life. Technology has, for many industries and markets, become a disruptive and volatile force driving the other components of the macroenvironmental model. Explosive technological changes have reshaped industries and created new, untapped market niches. In many of these cases, the biggest beneficiaries have been the entrepreneurs who were prepared to enter, and even dominate, these emerging markets.

Sociopolitical Environment

Social and political forces, trends, and events are analyzed to determine the long-term societal forces that will likely affect the behavior of society. Political trends analysis attempts to forecast future laws and regulations that either support or impede a business's ability to operate efficiently and achieve its targeted growth. In America, industries and companies continually lobby lawmakers to enact legislation that will provide a positive economic environment, one that is to their competitive advantage. An entrepreneur needs to track carefully the progression of federal, state, and even local legislation to become alert to potentially damaging legislation that could negatively impact markets and products.

Changes in the makeup of society will often generate new potential market. On a very simple and basic level, the immigrants to the United States bring with them their cultural preferences for particular foods and lifestyles. Thus, new market niches in the restaurant industry are continually reflecting changing tastes and a demand for ethnically rich cuisine. When we consider a variety of societal changes in process, our analysis must provide an understanding of deep-seated trends. Professional couples with two above-average incomes and one or two children, who were motivated to ensure that the children would attend the better universities, were responsible for creating a market niche of high-end prekindergarten schools, as well as academically intensive afterschool programs designed to prepare their children for exceptional scholastic achievement. For many parents, their children's academic achievement is a positive or negative reflection of their performance as parents. Another niche market exists to serve those whose incomes allow for the search for physical perfection; body modification businesses now offer plastic surgery, nutritionists, and personal trainers to assist in shaping the body.

Society is divided into an almost unlimited number of segments based on any combination of demographic: gender, age, ethnicity, sexual orientation, income, marital status, religious orientation, and the list goes on. Entrepreneurs can often identify market niches among the nearly limitless combination of people in our society and create a business that meets their needs and wants.

Demographic and Lifestyle Environment

Sociopolitical changes are closely aligned with demographic and lifestyle trends on a variety of levels. As discussed earlier, the demographics of the population change relatively slowly. Trends such as birth rates provide a steady and accurate assessment of potential market needs. For example, manufacturers and retailers of children's clothing know, with accuracy, how many children will be of a certain age next year as well as the gender of those children. Parental disposable income can be projected based on economic data. Housing trends would provide insight into where the parents and children live. In fact, the U.S. Census data can provide extremely precise and detailed demographic, societal, and economic information to guide the entrepreneur's decision making.

Lifestyle trends evolve at a faster pace. Some lifestyle trends begin in specific parts of the country and are adapted by other regions or specific communities later. Some lifestyle trends show signs of becoming permanent for a section of the population. An example would be exercise and fitness. Insightful entrepreneurs recognized that some women were reluctant to exercise around men due to cultural taboos, being offered unwanted male attention or advice, or just plain awkward self-consciousness. Consequently, "women only" fitness centers are thriving, driven in part by the same lifestyle trend for health that fuels the vitamin and supplement industry. As of 2018, the fitness industry, which was practically nonexistent 40 years ago, now accounts for a market worth of more than $25 billion. Membership in a gym or health club in the United States has grown 33.6 percent since 2008, not to mention the growth in health-related apps and wearable activity trackers.[1]

Demographic and lifestyle trends can be compared to a train. An entrepreneur must find out early where the "trend train" is going and decide whether or not to get on board. It is normally too late to get on board when the train has picked up speed and is roaring down the track. However, by conducting proper research, entrepreneurs can get on board early and position themselves to be at the train controls. Entrepreneurs who recognize and analyze demographic and lifestyle trends early can position themselves to gain an ever-increasing share of a growing market.

Creating Opportunities

The process of determining the interactions among the components of the macroenvironment that will produce potential opportunities for a new business venture is not complete until the entrepreneur assesses the probability of the occurrence of these

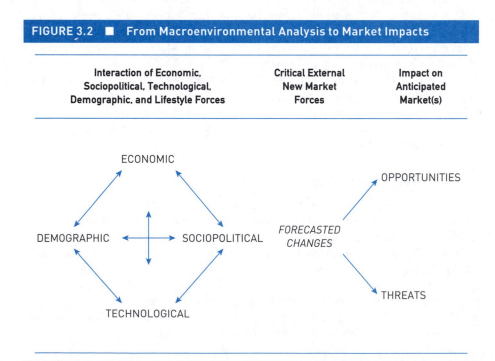

FIGURE 3.2 ■ From Macroenvironmental Analysis to Market Impacts

Interaction of Economic, Sociopolitical, Technological, Demographic, and Lifestyle Forces	Critical External New Market Forces	Impact on Anticipated Market(s)

forces and the strength of the impact supporting the feasibility of the new venture. It is essential to remember one thing at least. Just because the interactions of the macroenvironmental forces create significant potential opportunities does not guarantee that those opportunities fit the core competencies and resources of the entrepreneur's business. The entrepreneur benefits from making a detailed and painstaking evaluation of all the relevant information regarding the nature and scope of the anticipated opportunity. Only then can it be determined to be an accurate "fit" with the firm. If the anticipated opportunity has merit for the business, a plan of action needs to be created and necessary resources allocated to move in an appropriate and timely manner. The goal is to place the firm at the "front end" of the new emerging market. The creation of a new business model in line with an emerging trend can have a sweeping impact on the market, sometimes creating entirely new niches. **Figure 3.2** illustrates how forces, trends, and events from the interactions of macroenvironmental components can produce changes in the forces that drive markets and impact how business operates. These forces can drive the creation of new opportunities or possibly create threats to existing businesses.

STAGES OF INDUSTRY DEVELOPMENT

After gaining an understanding of the role macroenvironmental forces play in changing and reshaping markets through threatening some business models while creating opportunities for others, our next step is a detailed analysis and assessment of the competitive behaviors of the industry offering a new opportunity. The first step in an industry assessment is determining the basic nature of the industry in which the entrepreneur's business will need to compete. The size, scope, and maturity of the industry all generate characteristics that need to be understood in depth.

Mature Industries

Mature industries are composed of established firms that have survived past battles. As the name of these industries implies, they compete in already-developed markets, so demand for their products and services may be slow, but it is steady, and often there is little need for innovation if they are content with the status quo. New ventures can only penetrate a mature market effectively through innovative products and services, those that challenge that status quo. Entrepreneurs can expect aggressive competitive pressure from existing firms with market positions that they need to defend. A second drawback of competing against this type of industry is the possible difficulty of gaining initial adoptions from customers who have established relationships with the current suppliers. Entrepreneurial firms must ensure that they have the resources to survive a lengthy battle in gaining a foothold in the market. The entrepreneur must have confidence in the new product, must know that it is technologically sound and that its superiority and value creation capability can be demonstrated

Mature industries are often comprised of customers who are reluctant to change from established suppliers. Consumer products are equally well established in the minds of buyers, and you may discover that market penetration can become a lengthy and costly process. For some customers, there are deeply rooted psychological barriers that must be overcome before switching to a different seller, good, or service. When asked why they don't change, they will often say, "I always buy that product."

Declining Industries

Declining industries are experiencing decreasing demand for their products or services. Although the demand for these industries' products or services may be in decline, there may be a few market niches experiencing growth. The entrepreneur will need to investigate very carefully to establish if this growth trend is short lived or has the potential to continue to grow. In a few cases, new competitors might have innovative products or services that can gain market share through providing the market niche with a lower-cost alternative.

Declining industries may have market components with the potential for rapid growth, or they may offer opportunities that the existing competitors are not capable of servicing or even willing to make the effort to serve. In this scenario, an innovative entrepreneur with a fresh idea would experience limited competitor resistance. Competitors might chose to leave the market due to their assessment that it is in steep decline, thinking they would benefit by reallocating their efforts elsewhere. In other cases, an entrepreneur might find a market niche large enough to be viable, even in a declining market, if he or she is able to focus a product or service on the specific needs and wants of that unserved or underserved niche. However, you should be aware of how the most aggressive firms in the industry are working to avoid the overall decline. These firms are striving to avoid obsolescence by reinventing themselves with new products or services. Your goal is to become their new supplier with products or services that meet their new needs.

Fragmented Industries

Fragmented industries are normally easy to enter because the industry is comprised of firms of relatively equal size. There are no dominant competitors to oppose the entry of the entrepreneur's business, but there are equally no barriers to entry by other new competitors. The potential opportunity may be in the introduction of a business model that is so attractive that the firm can rapidly achieve a leadership position in the market and erect barriers to potential "copycat" competitors. As an example, an entrepreneur may create growth and market share through franchising. Outback Steakhouse, Olive Garden, Hooters, and the Tilted Kilt have built national chains in the highly fragmented restaurant industry.

The fragmented industry has what might be considered behavioral or operational norm. The businesses in such an industry all operate with similar performance expectations. A new business venture that can significantly exceed the standard norms of behavior and operation can "stand out" from competitors. These businesses are able to establish and maintain practices viewed by the market as superior to those of the other competitors. The customers determine what the most important criteria are in any market niche, but often it will be operational behaviors—such as superior quality, honesty in all dealings, or friendly and courteous service—that enable your customers to recognize your superiority. Delivery of the criteria important to customers will give you the opportunity to grow your business rapidly. (This subject is investigated in depth in the chapter on marketing.)

Emerging Industries

Emerging industries are normally viewed as providing the best opportunities for new ventures. When an entrepreneur has products or services that serve a previously unrecognized or unmet customer need, these will face fewer established existing competitors. In an ideal situation, the new venture achieves what is termed "first mover advantage" and becomes recognized by the market niche as the firm best suited to meet these new needs. The analytical question to be studied is the demand stability of the market niche. Will the niche continue to grow? Is the niche still evolving, and if so, to where and at what pace? The greatest source for identifying emerging industries is almost always macroenvironmental analysis, as discussed previously. New market niches can be traced directly to the emergence of the trends produced by the interaction of the external environment.

Global Industries

Global industries are market niches that have common characteristics in multiple nations. In most cases, some modifications of the firm's products or services need to be made to tailor these to the unique requirements of each potential market. At times, product or service modifications may be superficial in nature. Opportunities for growth in sales can occur rapidly through mastering strategies supportive of global market growth. One of these, termed a *multi-domestic strategy*, emphasizes responsiveness to the local requirements of multiple domestic markets, adapting products and services to fit these

Uber

Launched in 2010 by Internet entrepreneur Travis Kalanick, Uber has grown into a company with one of the highest market valuations in the world, with a valuation greater than Tesla, Ford, or General Motors. In spite of internal challenges, the company continues a trajectory of growth; 2016 gross bookings by users of the service exceeded $20 billion. Although reported 2016 net revenues exceeded $6.5 billion, the company's net losses were $2.8 billion. Dara Khosrowshahi has now become the CEO of Uber although its founder, Travis Kalanick, remains as a member of the company's board of directors. Khosrowshahi's vision for continued disruption in the transportation space has now begun to take shape through the development and deployment of autonomous driving vehicles. Because of the company's execution of its mission to decrease the costs for dispatched taxis from central service providers, Uber had attained a market valuation of $62 billion by the first quarter of 2018.

Sources:

Eric Newcomer, "Uber, Lifting Financial Veil, Says Sales Growth Outpaces Losses," *Bloomberg*, April 14, 2017, https://www.cnbc.com/2018/05/23/uber-q1-financial-data-increased-sales-valuation-with-new-tender-offer.html.

Jillian D'Onfro and Josh Lipton, "Uber Posts Big Sales Jump in First Quarter and Boosts Valuation to $62 Billion," *CNBC: TECH*, May 23, 2018, https://www.cnbc.com/2018/05/23/uber-q1-financial-data-increased-sales-valuation-with-new-tender-offer.html.

"Leadership," Uber website, https://www.uber.com/.

markets. At the opposite end of the spectrum is a truly global strategy that sacrifices responsiveness to local requirements in favor of efficiency and does not make too many modifications of the firm's products or services. Serving global industries can become potentially complicated, whatever strategy a company follows. The entrepreneur must factor in issues such as government laws and regulations, cultural differences, and economic factors, for example, the customers' ability to pay and the company's ability to force payment in a foreign country.

ANALYZING INDUSTRY BEHAVIOR

Porter's Five Forces Model

Michael Porter of Harvard University developed the *five forces model of competition*. This model is a powerful tool for assessing the anticipated level of competition that will exist in an industry. Figure 3.3 illustrates this analytical method.[2] Using the "five forces," an entrepreneur can evaluate the likelihood of a proposed venture surviving and prospering

FIGURE 3.3 ■ Five Forces Model

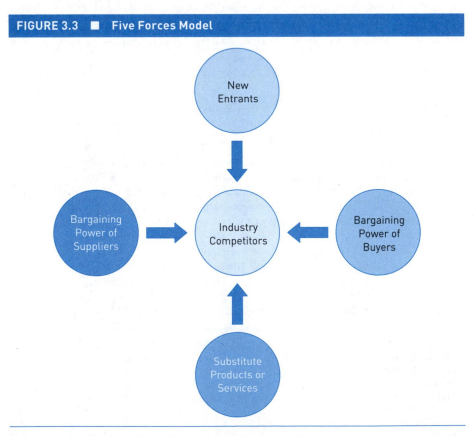

Source: Based on Michael E. Porter. "The Five competitive Forces That Shape Strategy," *Harvard Business Review*, January, 2008, pp.86–104.

under a variety of difficult competitive situations. Each element of the model provides the entrepreneur with a series of potential strategic challenges, which have the power to shape the intensity of the rivalry that exists in the industry.

The threats experienced by new market entries are determined by economic factors that include economies of scale and brand identity. Competitors who possess absolute cost advantage, high capital requirements that restrict entry, and high switching costs, as well as those with proprietary technologies and intellectual property, further inhibit the market entry of new firms. Each of these components is tangible and measurable. The economics of the industry and the existence of established competitors who can exercise power to restrict entry into the industry need to be understood.

This analysis is far from theoretical. As an entrepreneur, you can evaluate any industry that you are considering entering to determine objectively the nature of the competitive forces you are likely to encounter. The conclusions you are able to reach based on your assessment will serve to assist you in determining the potential of strategic success and strategies for attaining it. Porter's five forces model is a highly valued analytical tool for the assessment of new venture success.

Impact of Suppliers

Suppliers have power to influence the competitive environment of a business when they are highly concentrated and control potential access to needed components. In many cases, their economic power allows them to set prices. Suppliers have no motivation to negotiate due to their ability to control product prices; therefore new ventures need to be concerned about the stability of supply under conditions in which suppliers can artificially limit or withhold vital components. The new venture might not be able to purchase needed critical components if it does not pay a supplier's "asking price." Suppliers will normally demonstrate a preference for their larger and long-term customers. This preference is a very serious issue that could be harmful to revenue and success.

Impact of Buyers

Buyers possess the power to negotiate lower prices when a new business venture needs their orders to survive. Typically, buyers who make larger than normal purchases have the capability to exercise strength in negotiating lower prices in the form of volume discounts. Entrepreneurs quickly discover that their assumptions regarding their "proposed product price" and associated profitability are proving to be unrealistic.

The negotiating power of larger buyers normally exists due to the economic reality that it is less expensive to sell in high volume. New ventures will always be at a disadvantage until they are on a more equal footing with the buyers. The new venture will have a negotiating advantage when their products or services are uniquely superior to those of competitors. A new venture can gain additional economic power when products possess intellectual property protection, such as patents, copyrights, and trademarks.

Impact of Substitute Products or Services

Another component of the five forces model that impacts the intensity of competition is the threat of **substitute products or services**. Competition is enhanced when the industry players feel pressure from a potential competitor who is capable of offering products or services comparable to their own. The closer these substitutes are in price and quality to those of the entrepreneur wanting to enter the industry, the greater the competitive pressure.

Competitive pressure is one of the factors determining the profitability of an industry. There is no logical reason to invest in a business venture that will operate in an industry where competitive pressures produce unacceptable profits. The entrepreneur needs to search for market niches that have less competitive pressures and the potential to achieve higher profit margins. Thus, entrepreneurs must evaluate the operational components of their business models and the dynamics of the industries in which they are considering competing to determine if proposed ventures have the potential to meet their profitability expectations.

COMPETITIVE ANALYSES AND COMPETITIVE PROFILE MATRICES

If the entrepreneur finds the characteristics of the industry to be favorable, the second step is the evaluation of the competitors currently or potentially in the market niche the business intends to enter. A detailed competitor analysis requires the collection of what is described as *competitive intelligence*. Competitive intelligence focuses on gathering and evaluating all of the information that can be learned about each competitor's capabilities and behaviors. For publicly traded companies, there is an abundance of information through such sources as these:

- Required SEC filings

- Competitors' websites

- Third-person analyses of other firms

- Discussions with suppliers and vendors who serve the market niche

- Publications of the trade associations in which the companies are members

- Current customers of the competitors

- Industry conferences and trade shows, which are normally sponsored by the relevant trade associations

- Speeches and reports by the executives of competitive firms

Much of this research is available through the assistance of a qualified research librarian. There are many completely ethical sources of competitive intelligence. Entrepreneurs have no reason to enter a market without conducting a modestly sophisticated analysis of the competitors in the market.

Competitive Critical Factors

Competitive intelligence is not complex or even overly sophisticated. Competitive intelligence involves the collection of critical information about the businesses with whom

Lyft

Serial entrepreneurs Logan Green and John Zimmer cofounded and launched Lyft in 2012 as a logical outgrowth of their earlier ride-sharing venture, Zimride, which was begun in 2007. Created in the disruptive space of on-demand personal transportation replacing traditional taxi and limousine services, Lyft has grown to provide over 1 million rides daily and expanded its business operations to include all 50 states in the United States. In 2017, the company began its expansion into Canada with the launch of services in Toronto. The company's cofounders, having grown a substantial, profitable business, have now turned their attention to another disruptive business offering. Working in partnerships with General Motors, Ford, Waymo, and NuTonomy, Lyft has begun the development of autonomous driving vehicles. Through the insightful and directed leadership of its cofounders Green and Zimmer, Lyft reached a market valuation of $7.5 billion in April 2017.

Sources:

Biz Carson, "Lyft Doubled Rides in 2017 as its Rival Stumbled," *Forbes*, January 16, 2018, https://www.forbes.com/sites/bizcarson/2018/01/16/lyft-doubled-rides-in-2017/.

See also the Lyft website and blog: https://www.lyft.com/ and https://blog.lyft.com.

Andrew J. Hawkins, "Ford and Lyft Will Work Together to Deploy Autonomous Cars," *The Verge*, September 27, 2017, https://www.theverge.com/2017/9/27/16373574/ford-lyft-self-driving-car-partnership-gm.

Eric Newcomer, "KKR Among Lyft Investors at $7.5 Billion Valuation for Startup," Bloomberg, April 11, 2017, https://www.bloomberg.com/news/articles/2017-04-11/kkr-among-lyft-investors-at-7-5-billion-valuation-for-startup.

your new venture will compete. Ask yourself, these questions. What must I know about each of these potential competitors? How can I structure my findings in order to reach the most accurate conclusions about each competitor?

Researching the industry you are about to enter and your potential competitors in that industry is just common sense. Why would any entrepreneur not be willing to conduct this research and analysis prior to investing in a new business venture? Here are some specific questions to help guide your research:

1. What are the sources of any competitive advantages that the competitor demonstrates in the market? Does the competitor possess a unique set of skills and capabilities? Can these skill sets be legally replaced or replicated, and at what cost?

2. What strategies and tactics does the competitor demonstrate in the market niche? What are their stated objectives?

3. How has the competitor previously responded to significant market changes created by the interactions of the macroenvironment? How effective have these responses been?

4. How has the competitor previously responded to new ventures attempting to enter the market? Identify any strategies ranging from acquisition to other more competitive behaviors.

5. Does the competitor have the resources to mount a vigorous defense of its market position if a new entry challenges? What are these resources?

6. Does the competitor have any weaknesses that make it vulnerable? What, specifically, are these weaknesses?

7. How are the competitor's products or services positioned in the market in comparison with those the entrepreneur intends to introduce?

8. How would you rate each competitor's leadership?

9. Does the competitor have customers who are historically loyal to its products or services? If so, who are they and what percentage of the competitor's sales do these customers represent? (Even long-term customers can have unfulfilled needs. If you can cultivate clients from competitors based on your provision of innovative solutions, testimonials from these customers about why your solution is better than the status quo is a powerful marketing tool for any entrepreneurial start-up firm.)

10. Does the competitor have extremely loyal suppliers who might not be willing to supply the entrepreneur's firm if the competitor asked them not to?

11. How valuable to the competitor is the market niche that you wish to enter? How vigorously will the competitor defend this market niche? How would you evaluate the "cost/benefit" of attempting to enter the market niche?

12. Based on what you have learned about the competitor, how vulnerable will your new venture be to that competitor's response to your market entry?

Based on a positive analytical result from the questions posed in the competitor intelligence process, the entrepreneur must formulate a market entry strategy. The market entry strategy needs to recognize those critical components of all the competitors' products that generate superior performance. If the entrepreneur's products are superior to those of the competitors, the entrepreneur can compete on a "head-to-head" basis. Are there shared core competencies among the current market leaders? Will the new business venture be able to meet or exceed competitors on these capabilities? The new venture will also need to possess these core competencies, unless the entrepreneur anticipates a significant change in the market that will result in negating the importance of these core competencies, thus creating the need to replace them with others.

Reflect on the discussion of the characteristics of an industry, and remember the importance of many of the essential tangible and measurable conditions associated with success. Some of these strategic components include a large amount of initial capital, specialized equipment, and the achievement of economies of scale and operations, or having proprietary technology. In some market niches, a new business venture will fail if it ignores critical market realities.

Constructing a Competitive Profile Matrix

A *competitive profile matrix* needs to be constructed based on what the entrepreneur learns from the competitive intelligence analysis. The competitive profile matrix focuses

FIGURE 3.4 ■ Competitive Profile Matrix: An Example					
Critical Success Factor	**Relative Weight**	**Your Venture's Rating Score**	**Company 1**	**Company 2**	**Company 3**
Highly efficient low-cost production	.30				
Established and efficient distribution system	.20				
Innovative products	.20				
Competitive prices	.10				
High-quality product	.10				
Loyal customers	.05				
Excellence in management	.05				
Total	**1.00**				

on a critical set of factors, as well as on the relative impact of each factor on the achievement of success. This analytical tool allows for each firm to be rated and compared on all of these specific factors critical to success in this market niche. **Figure 3.4** provides an example of a competitive profile matrix.

If you apply evaluation process illustrated in **Figure 3.4**, the ratings for each critical success factor could be a maximum of 4 if the firm has a major strength on the specific success factor, of 3 if the firm has a minor strength, of 2 if the firm has a minor weakness, and of 1 if the firm has a major weakness. The score for each firm is then calculated according to the assigned relative weight of each factor. These weights are determined by an assessment of each factor's significance in impacting success in each targeted market niche. In other words, the score you assigned to each of the critical success factors is multiplied by the factor weighting that was assigned to that specific factor. The maximum score that a firm could earn in the example given in **Figure 3.4** is a 4.0, as the sum of the relative weighting numbers is 1.0.

The competitive profile matrix is just one additional analytical tool to assist the entrepreneur in the task of assessing the feasibility of a proposed new venture. The entrepreneur can determine the probability of success for the new venture in the targeted market niche based on a side-by-side comparison of competitors and can further the likelihood of this success by recognizing and employing the critical factors needed to flourish in that market niche.

Value Chain Analysis

Another analytical tool that sheds light on the viability of a business model is a very simplified version of *value chain analysis*. The focus of value chain analysis for an entrepreneurial firm needs to be on the relative cost advantages or disadvantages a new venture could encounter. A new venture's relative cost in comparison to that of competitors affects the firm's profit margin. In most markets, all firms have a similar value chain that is comprised of all the activities necessary to produce and deliver what it is selling and to service the customer base.

FIGURE 3.5 ■ Value Chain Analysis			
Total Sales Revenue			100%
Cost of All Supplies	10%		
Cost of Production	40%		
Cost of Marketing and Distribution	25%		
Customer Service Cost	10%		
Overhead Cost	10%		
Total Cost			95%
Net Profit			5%

Components of the value chain would normally include the cost of all supplies, production costs, marketing and distribution costs, customer service expenses, and all overhead expenses. Profitability is based on sales revenues that exceed the total cost that is incurred in creating and delivering the firms product or services. **Figure 3.5** is a simple illustration of the value chain; percentages have replaced actual dollars for the purpose of this illustration.

The objective of value chain analysis is to identify expenses and costs that can be reduced, resulting in a higher net profit. As an example, if a new venture possesses unique competencies that result in producing a product at an equal or higher quality than is standard but at a significantly lower cost, these superior production techniques, skills, or capabilities result in operating proficiencies that lower production cost and simultaneously increase the firm's profits.

Sometimes, firms lower costs by outsourcing noncore organizational functions, especially in the area of overhead items, to firms whose superior competencies in these areas allow the outsourcer to lower the entrepreneur's total cost and increase the firm's profits. An example might be a publisher outsourcing shipping and distribution. The entrepreneur should always be searching for a core competency that the new venture can create, as these can produce a competitive advantage. If the firm's core competencies are extremely difficult or impossible for competitors to duplicate, the new venture has the foundation for a lasting, sustainable competitive advantage.

Benchmarking

Another useful analytical tool used to determine whether a firm's value chain activities are competitive in comparison to those of its rivals is *benchmarking*. The benchmarking process entails attempting to measure the actual cost and efficiency of each component in the value chain in an attempt to identify specific superior actions or tactics, which are then termed *best practices*. Benchmarking involves the entrepreneur using the same sources of information employed in the competitive intelligence process. Competition requires that every firm continually search for improved operational technologies and methods that will achieve lower cost, superior performance, or both.

When entrepreneurs conduct value chain analysis and benchmarking prior to entering a market, they might be able to determine that the unique capabilities and core

Mike Lindell is a highly successful entrepreneur who has traveled a difficult path on his way to success. Mike was a heavy drug user before turning his life around. Today, you cannot watch television without seeing one of his commercials for MyPillow. Lindell developed his product in 2000. He sold his product at trade shows and state fairs. Above all, Lindell and his family believed deeply in the product, and his confidence in it motivated his drive to succeed. As an example, he ordered 30,000 plastic bags with the company logo printed on each before the final prototype was completed.

Cash flow was an issue, as most start-up firms discover. In response, he mortgaged the family home to obtain enough funding to continue. The product, MyPillow, is the result of 90 different trials before it satisfied the founder. Actually, Lindell went on to invent the machine that automatically fills his pillows. In 2011, the *Minneapolis Star Tribune* published a feature article on Mike Lindell and MyPillow, resulting in a surge of sales. He expanded his advertising from print media to the infomercials now shown nationwide.

The bottom line: MyPillow today has sales of over $280 million, and it had sold more than 26 million pillows by early January 2017. The firm employed over 1,400 people in its home state of Minnesota in the spring of 2017.

Sources:

The Mike Lindell Story—An American Dream, directed by Joe Brandmeier (New York and Los Angeles: LightBeaMedia, 2016), documentary, 59 min.

Patrick Kennedy, "MyPillow Lays Off 140 Workers Because of Slower Sales," *Minneapolis Start Tribune*, April 25, 2017, http://www.startribune.com/mypillow-lays-off-140-workers-because-of-slower-sales/420422463/.

Josh Dean, "The Preposterous Success Story of America's Pillow King," *Bloomberg Businessweek*, January 11, 2017, https://www.bloomberg.com/businessweek.

competencies their firms possess will allow them to achieve an early competitive foothold. A firm's core competencies—those that apply to performance and the firm's markets—are the foundation upon which its competitive strategies and tactics need to be based.

CREATING YOUR BUSINESS MODEL

In the previous chapter and in this one, we have addressed the critical issues of the birth of an idea for a new product or service; the application of creativity and innovation; the analytical evaluation of an idea to determine if it is a viable opportunity; the assessment of the opportunities created by the interactions of the components of the macroenvironment; the assessment of the industry in which a new product or service might compete; the competitive behaviors of industries; and, finally, the assessment of competitors. Now the entrepreneur must create a business model based upon the results of this comprehensive analysis. The new venture's business model will be based on the findings from all of the analyses. The business model needs to be unique and not simply a copy of a competitor's model. Any venture's business model needs to be deeply rooted in the basic values and vision of that venture, as well as in its unique competencies and resources. The business model illustrates how the entrepreneur plans to enter the selected market niche after having assessed an amalgamation of its competitive components. Once the business model is established, the entrepreneur then formulates core business strategies. These strategies are themselves based on the analysis that has been previously completed. Effective business strategies address the characteristics and behavior of the targeted market niche, as well as assessments of the strategies and weaknesses of competitors. The critical and tangible components of market dynamics are the building blocks of strategy. The strategies of the entrepreneurial firm must be sufficient to meet the needs of the market customers in a superior fashion to that of the firm's competitors.

The Value of Strategic Thinking

Strategic thinking gives rise to how the entrepreneur's new venture will choose to compete. Strategic thinking requires the ability to understand all aspects of the competitive landscape. Thinking strategically helps entrepreneurs avoid becoming myopic and short-sighted, and it is the mental foundation upon which the firm's strategic planning process is developed. The resulting strategic plan is used to integrate all components of the firm. Creating an effective business plan begins with the development of a clear vision for the business and the translation of that vision into the final mission statement. A mission statement addresses a series of essential questions, including the following:

1. What are the basic beliefs and values of the new business venture?

2. What are the products and services the firm plans to offer?

3. What are the purchasing characteristics of the specific targeted customers?

4. What are the specific needs and wants of the targeted customers that our product or services must satisfy?

5. How do our products or services meet or exceed the expectations of our targeted customer base?

6. How, specifically, does our product or service create value for the targeted customers?

Applying Critical Driving Forces

The firm's mission statement makes crystal clear what the business is and what market niches it is focused on. The mission statement also enables entrepreneurs to recognize and describe what are termed the *critical driving forces* of the new venture. Here are two examples of critical driving forces:

1. Unique or superior knowledge upon which the firm's products or services are based.

2. Detailed knowledge of the markets, customers, and their buying behaviors.

These driving forces serve to keep the entrepreneur focused on where the new venture has a competitive advantage, so this step serves to help and establish the scope of the business.

To ensure that the new venture maximizes its strengths and avoid its weaknesses, the entrepreneur develops an ***internal factor evaluation matrix***. This analytical tool allows for a focus on the firm's strengths that have the potential for the greatest impact on achieving successful market penetration and potential profitability. With the specific market niche in focus, what are the most critical strengths that must be present within the new business venture to achieve success? The internal factor evaluation matrix begins with the firm's key internal strengths and weighs the relative importance of each in the achievement of success.

Business Strategies

The entrepreneur has already developed a competitive profile matrix, which is revisited during the process of developing a business strategy in order to identify clearly each competitor's areas of weakness. Business strategies are normally most effective when they are focused on competitors' weaknesses. These strategies serve to lay out a roadmap that guides a firm to achieve its objectives. Effective business strategies are firmly rooted in the specific and highly focused application of the firm's unique core competencies to meet the measurable needs and wants of the targeted market niche the entrepreneur wants to penetrate. Distinctive market-focused competencies, then, are the foundation of the firm's success. A successful business strategy is comprehensive and integrates all of the firm's core competencies to focus on the key factors necessary for success in the market as the "point" of the competitive spear.

For new business ventures, the most effective business strategies are normally a combination of what are termed focus and differentiation strategies. The focused component of the firm's strategy is a recognition that the firm is attempting to gain initial penetration in a specific and possibly limited market niche. The differentiation component recognizes that successful market penetration requires that the product or service have unique capabilities that are superior to those of its competitors.

A ***focus strategy*** recognizes that not all markets are homogeneous. In any large market, there are normally many different segments or niches—each with different needs, wants, and characteristics. A focus strategy, as the name suggest, identifies the customers special needs, wants, and interest while offering them goods and services that meet or exceed these unique needs and wants. The products or services create value for a specific market niche. The differentiation strategy seeks to build customer loyalty by creating and distributing products and services that are unique. The ***differentiation strategy*** attempts to create superior value for the customer through making modifications in the product or service that result in valued uniqueness. One key to a successful differentiation strategy is that it is built on a distinctive competency of the firm. Also, the product or service differentiation must actually create value in the eyes of the customer, and customers must actually be able to afford to purchase the differentiated product or service. Typically, an entrepreneur can differentiate market offerings through producing a product or service that is of higher quality, has unique and valued features, or is more reliable and dependable. Another avenue to differentiation is for the firm to provide superior customer service.

To conclude, we have discovered that entrepreneurs research the market both to identify market niches in which their products or services will be successful and to develop strategies that best present their firms to those unique markets. This is the essence of the firm's business model. The business model is tangible and based on the firm's unique distinctive competencies that are capable of producing value for the market the firm serves. In a competitive world, the firm needs to have a business model that clearly communicates its uniqueness and value creation to its targeted market niches.

ENTREPRENEURIAL EXERCISES

The remainder of this chapter encourages you to complete exercises that allow you to apply the material in the chapter to a proposed business venture of your choosing. These practical exercises will help you determine whether your proposed business venture may prove to be a winner.

Entrepreneurial Exercise 3.1

Part 1

Please describe in detail the interactions of the macroenvironment that you believe will take place over the next five (5) years and what opportunities you believe these interactions will create during that time.

Major macroenvironmental forces, trends, and events that you believe will occur over the next five years include the following:

1.

2.

3.

4.

5.

Based on these predictions what do you see as potential opportunities?

1. New opportunity:

2. New opportunity:

3. New opportunity:

4. New opportunity:

Part 2

How do the new opportunities that you identified in Part 1 impact your proposed new business venture?

Entrepreneurial Exercise 3.2

Part 1

Please describe how cross impact analysis of the components of the macroenvironment and of their interactions has resulted in your identification of significant changes in market opportunities.

Part 2

Have the results of cross impact analysis and your consequent assessment of market changes affected your proposed business venture? If so, how? If not, why not?

Environmental Exercise 3.3

What are the primary research tools and measures that you plan to employ in scanning components of the macroenvironment?

1. Economic environment:

2. Technological environment:

3. Sociopolitical environment:

4. Demographic and lifestyle environment:

Entrepreneurial Exercise 3.4

Part 1

What is the industry or industry segment in which your proposed new business venture plans to compete? Please describe it in as much detail as possible.

Part 2

Using Michael Porter's five forces model guides the entrepreneur toward a measure of the competitive intensity of a proposed market. Please use this model to evaluate the anticipated competitive intensity in the industry or industry segment in which your business venture plans to operate.

1. New entry of competitors:

2. Bargaining power of buyers:

3. Substitute products or services:

4. Bargaining power of suppliers:

Part 3

List and describe the favorable and unfavorable characteristics of the industry.

Favorable	Unfavorable
1.	1.
2.	2.
3.	3.
4.	4.
5.	5.

Entrepreneurial Exercise 3.5

Based on a competitive analysis of the industry segment or segments in which you plan to compete, conduct an analysis of the ***three major competitors*** your research has identified. ***Please use the format below for each of the three competitors:***

Part 1

Competitor: _____

Estimated market share:

Competitor's nature:

Sources of competitor's advantages:

1.

2.

3.

Competitor's strategies:

1.

2.

3.

Competitor's historic ability to respond to changes in the market niche:

1.

2.

3.

Competitor's historic ability to respond effectively to new market entries:

1.

2.

3.

Competitor's resources that will allow it to respond effectively to new competitors:

1.

2.

3.

Competitor's weaknesses that might be exploited by a new market competitor:

1.

2.

3.

Quality of the competitor's leadership (please describe):

Competitor's top three existing customers based on their loyalty to the competitor:

1.

2.

3.

Entrepreneurial Exercise 3.6

Competitive profile matrix: please create a competitive profile matrix similar to that illustrated in **Figure 3.4**, and compare your proposed new business venture with your top three competitors, which you identified in Exercise 3.5.

Entrepreneurial Exercise 3.7

Internal factor evaluation matrix: please create an internal factor evaluation matrix for your proposed new business venture. Make sure the matrix allows for an assessment of your firm's key internal factors, those that will contribute to success.

Entrepreneurial Exercise 3.8

In this exercise, you will create your new business venture's business model.

Part 1

Describe in detail the business model for your new proposed business venture.

Part 2

How have you incorporated your values and beliefs into your proposed firm's vision and its mission statement?

Part 3

At this point in the evaluation of your proposed new business venture, how confident are you of the firm's success?

Part 4

Do you have any reservations about your proposed firm's success? If so, what are they? If not, why not?

NEW VENTURE MARKETING

*It is not the most intellectual of the species that survives;
it is not the strongest that survives; but the species that
survives is the one that is able best to adapt and adjust to the
changing environment in which it finds itself.*

Leon C. Megginson, paraphrasing Charles Darwin

*The aim of marketing is to know and understand the
customer so well the product or service fits him [or her] and
sells itself.*

Peter Drucker

*A business has to be involving; it has to be fun, and it has to
exercise your creative instincts.*

Richard Branson

CHAPTER LEARNING OBJECTIVES

Upon completion of this chapter you will be able to

Explain how customer's buying practices can impact new business ventures

Summarize the market segmentation steps

Compare the different marketing strategies and their potential impact

(Continued)

(Continued)

Describe the stages of a product's life cycle

Discuss the Internet's effect on place strategies

Evaluate the benefits of the different pricing strategies

Identify the main promotion strategies

CUSTOMERS AND THE MARKET

Chapter 2 detailed the analytical process involved in screening potential opportunities in specific market segments or niches, ones in which the entrepreneur's product or service has the potential to be successfully adopted. In Chapter 3, the entrepreneur assessed the nature of competition in those market niches and learned to profile current and potential competitors. Based on the analytical assessments conducted in these chapters, the entrepreneur was able to develop a unique business model. This chapter will extend the analysis from the previous chapters and focus on the specific market-oriented strategies and tactics that will result in the generation of needed revenues.

Getting to Know Your Customers—Some Fundamental Questions

The questions that need to be answered by the entrepreneur are normally very basic and fundamental. These questions include, but are not limited to, the following:

1. Will high "switching cost" be a barrier that must be overcome? Can these invisible costs be estimated, and, if so, what are they? Do they erect a difficult barrier to be overcome?

2. To what degree is price a critical component of the targeted customer's decision process? What are the market's existing "price points"?

3. What, if any, do the targeted customers have in common? When these common characteristics are identified, how will the new venture's marketing strategies focus on them?

4. How do the various targeted customer groups measure value creation and benefit? Describe how these measures are similar or different among customer groups.

5. Can these measures of value creation and benefit be quantified? If they are quantifiable, can the value creation and benefit of the firm's products or services be compared to those of competitors? How do they measure up?

6. What are the components of tangible or intangible product or service superiority that the targeted

customers use to guide their buying behavior? Can the new business convert its "value proposition" into an effective selling proposition?

7. Is your business venture targeted at an entirely new market segment, or does your firm require that customers be "won away" from existing competitors?

An entrepreneur will need to develop detailed marketing strategies and tactics based on facts. Gathering and analyzing information about the market niche and the targeted customers requires conducting serious research—there are no shortcuts. Inaccurate assumptions about the motivational components that affect buyers' behavior or about any unique characteristic of the targeted customers will inevitably result in wasted organizational and marketing resources. The entrepreneur needs to focus a venture's normally limited marketing budget like a laser to achieve the greatest efficiency in reaching the market. Every marketing dollar that misses the targeted customer is very likely wasted.

"MARKET DISRUPTORS"

When the goal of the new business venture is to achieve market penetration in a niche with strong and established competitors, it is imperative to know the decision criteria of the targeted customers. What product or service criteria drive the customers' buying decisions? The new business venture must have both a superior product and service, based on the needs and wants of the customer, as well as the ability to demonstrate tangibly how the product or service will create customer value. In addition, it is critical for the new business venture to communicate effectively to the customer the psychological components of the product's superiority. Entrepreneurs consequently need to understand the targeted customers in enough depth to communicate effectively the ways in which the entrepreneurs' products or services create superior value for customers through meeting or exceeding their wants and needs. Is your firm's new product or service potentially a "market disruptor"? Market disruptors are products or services with the potential to "shake up" an industry completely. In many cases, such products or services have the potential to make the current products or services seem inferior, overpriced, or even obsolete. You can imagine that such products or services have exceptional potential but will, at the same time, attract intensive competitor response.

The last few decades have witnessed the introduction of many products or services that can easily be considered "market disruptors." Just consider tech companies such as Apple, Google, and Amazon. Retail giants now must match Amazon's unique blend of product diversity and delivery services. The lifestyle and technology changes discussed in the previous chapter have given rise to Internet shopping convenience. "Market disruptors" will send you clothes that are in your size and match your style and color preferences. Food can be delivered to your door eliminating the need for grocery shopping. Even automobiles can be ordered online and delivered to your home. Change is clearly happening at

Customer Buying Practice

1. **How long** have the targeted customers been buying their current product or service from the current provider?

    (People easily become creatures of habit and often make purchasing choices unconsciously.)

2. Are the new firm's products **available** in the same location or outlet where the targeted customers **currently** purchased the competitor's product?

3. What is the nature of the customer's **buying cycle** for the product or service? Does the customer purchase the product or service **weekly, monthly, yearly**, or on an even longer purchasing cycle?

the pace not previously experienced. Entrepreneurs whose products or services are "market disruptors" may ride this wave of change.

SWITCHING COST: A BARRIER TO ADOPTION

The initial barrier for a business to overcome is the tendency for the targeted customer to continue to buy from its current (and often) established seller. Motivating a customer to change from a competitor's product or service to new products or services entails overcoming the customers "switching cost." Switching costs, as the name implies, are the tangible and intangible costs associated with making a switch from the product or service that is normally purchased to a new product or service. Understanding this concept prepares the entrepreneur for the difficult task of persuading the targeted customer to adopt the new product or service. Target customers simply do not automatically switch products or services because the entrepreneur believes that the new products or services on offer are superior. The box above shows some questions that need to be asked and answered to evaluate the customer's buying practices.

Answers to these customer buying questions and others specific to the entrepreneur's marketing challenge will serve to establish the problems that must be researched in detail to identify possible solutions. Without a detailed assessment of the answers to critical questions, the entrepreneur is likely to define incorrectly the true problems associated with the achievement of effective market entry and subsequently market the product or service poorly. This scenario in which little or no actual facts are collected regarding the targeted customer is unfortunately common.

MARKET RESEARCH AND MARKET SEGMENTATION

Entrepreneurs must strive to avoid confusing the true problems encountered in the product introduction stage. As an example, low initial sales might be due to a variety of factors. In most cases, the factors impacting the marketing problems are interrelated. Sales revenues fall short of expectations because the entrepreneur failed to predict the targeted customers brand loyalty or resistance to change accurately. The targeted customers are simply not willing to try the new product or service. In many cases, the existing market competitors have taken aggressive defensive actions designed to repel new market entries. In other cases, the target customers may be having difficulties finding the new product. Additionally, prices could have been set either too high or possibly too low, making the product seem "cheap" and therefore unattractive in the latter case. The greater the depth of knowledge about the targeted market niche, its customers, and the competitive responses to be anticipated from existing competitors the higher will be the likelihood that the firm's marketing strategy will be successful.

Market research can prevent you from attempting to enter a market niche that does not match well with the features of your product or service. That knowledge is power is an absolute truth. Market research produces market knowledge and will serve to encourage market entry or provide you with quantifiable warning signs. An analogy would be placing a bet at the tracks and consulting the information in the *Daily Racing Form*. Before placing a bet (making an investment), you can glean a complete history of horse; its breeding, size, and weight; its previous performance in similar races against comparable horses (competitors); the conditions of the track in which the horse has previously run; the performance of the jockey on this horse; the records of this jockey and horse at this distance; and whether this is a track or dirt race. Each of these pieces of information is a "fact"—not an opinion. If you would do this amount of analysis based on the "facts" presented in the racing form before you risked $2.00, why would you ever attempt a business venture without conducting significant market research to obtain the "facts" or without analyzing those facts in detail? Market research builds upon the analyses you conducted in Chapters 2 and 3.

One useful tool in market research is market segmentation. Market segmentation is the process of dividing the total market into meaningful and distinct customer groups based on their needs, wants, ability to buy, buying preferences, and other factors that would serve to isolate or distinguish the group members. One overlooked component of market segmentation involves first evaluating the size and scope of the segment. Is the targeted segment that is likely to be attracted to the firm's products or services actually large enough to sustain the new venture? Does the segment possess enough buying power for the new business venture to grow and sustain growth? The answer to these basic questions can provide insight into the viability of the business. There is no value in capturing the "lion's share" of a market segment that is insufficient to generated adequate sales and revenue to support the business.

Market research directly contributes to making business decisions that focus the entrepreneur's limited resources effectively on the specific characteristics of the targeted customer and on that customer's buying behaviors, both of which have been identified as relevant to the new business's products or services. Most new business ventures need to select strategies to focus on limited market segments or upon a single niche. Consequently, effective micro-marketing efforts can be built around the integration of geographic, demographic, and psychographic data. These types of data serve to define the targeted consumer and enhance the entrepreneur's understanding of the firm's market niche or market segment. The better the customer is understood the more accurately focused all subsequent marketing activities can be. The following are some of the absolutely essential types of data that need to be collected and analyzed in the development of effective marketing strategies:

Geographic data are statistics that identify where potential customers are located. They include measures such as the geographic scope of the market, the density of the population, and traffic patterns. It is also important to know if the population is primarily urban, suburban, or rural, as each population type would have differing purchasing behaviors.

Demographic data provide a profile of the personal characteristics that can be employed to assist in defining as accurately as possible the potential customers. Typically, a demographic analysis includes factors such as age, income level, gender, home address, working address, marital status, family status, occupation, ethnicity, religion, and nationality.

Psychographic data provide the entrepreneur with a customer profile based on social class, lifestyle, and personality traits. Personality variables are useful in further segmenting the market niche. Behavioral variables are extremely useful in the identification of targeted customer's attitudes and knowledge regarding the use of entrepreneur's products in order to most effectively tailor the marketing message to a specific targeted market.

The key to successful market research is to blend or integrate all of the findings into a detailed profile of the targeted customers. This ultimate customer profile allows the

Market Segmentation

Market research needs to focus on gaining a superior understanding of the targeted customer. This research needs to go well beyond the surface demographics of income, age, gender, and other standard descriptions of a population. The entrepreneur needs to capture the buyer's critical decision-making criteria, which may be both tangible and intangible. Understanding these criteria and how the customers recognized when products and services matched these criteria allows the entrepreneur to shape marketing communications.

The process of market segmentation is critical for the identification of the market niche that offers the new venture the greatest opportunities for success. The process of market segmentation can be summarized in the following steps:

1. **Identify the general market** to be segmented in search of a potentially viable market segment or niche.

2. **Identify the needs, wants, and capabilities of the buyers** in the market segments or niches identified.

3. **Attempt to segment the market** in search of the most attractive segment or niche for your firm's products or services.

4. **Evaluate the potential viability** of each segment or niche and how far its nature and characteristics are compatible with your firm's products or services.

5. **Evaluate the long-term attractiveness** of each potential market segment.

6. **Shape marketing strategies** in the support of the firm's competitive advantage.

7. **Establish a unique image and brand identity**, one supported by your assessment of market segmentation.

8. **Prioritize and focus the limited resources** of your firm after considering the results of this market segmentation process.

entrepreneur to develop and deliver a sharper micro marketing strategy. The entrepreneur's understanding of the makeup of the total potential customer base contributes to the creation and implementation of the firm's total marketing effort. Here are some steps to take when planning that marketing effort.

First, consider the financial cost associated with investing in entering each market segment, as well as the level of financial risk associated with failure. Next, select the market segment or segments compatible with your risk-reward calculation. Once a market segment has been selected, carefully position your product or service to "stand out" in it. Emphasize your product or service's value proposition. Communicate the value proposition in as many ways as possible to the selected market segment. Last, ensure that all components of the firm's marketing plan and its tactics are appropriate to the market segment selected.

Your marketing plan, as you can see, will need both to clearly identify and define the targeted market niche and to integrate all components of the marketing strategies and tactics to achieve maximum effectiveness.

ENTREPRENEURIAL SPOTLIGHT
LISA WANG—SHEWORX

Building on her great success and experience as a world-traveled gymnast, Lisa Wang founded SheWorx, a leading global firm designed to empower female entrepreneurs by providing them with "actionable business strategies and access to top investors." According to the *Wall Street Journal*, "In her continuing mission to elevate the lives of millions, Wang has made headlines by galvanizing female entrepreneurs and lending her voice to empowering women leaders." SheWorx has empowered over 20,000 female entrepreneurs to build and grow successful businesses.

Wang offers a strong and positive message that consistently encourages female entrepreneurs to ignore those persons who believe that their ideas are flawed or doomed to failure. She stresses that only the entrepreneur knows what success means on a personal level. SheWorx encourages female entrepreneurs to have a clear vision of what they wish to achieve and know clearly what their values are, as well as their strengths and weaknesses. She encourages female entrepreneurs to be careful in the selection of those around them. Positive people, with the appropriate skills, are always a benefit. Once you are ready to start a venture, she says to "charge forward with all of the energy and tenacity required to turn your dreams into reality." Her goal is the creation of a global community of successful female entrepreneurs.

The SheWorx Foundation provides entrepreneurial education to empower high school and college women to gain the skills necessary to become successful and become a force in the next wave of leadership.

Sources:

1. "About," Lisa Wang's website, https://www.lisawang.co/about/.
2. "SheWorx Co-Founder Takes On Gender Bias in Fundraising," *Wall Street Journal*, March 10, 2017, https://www.wsj.com/articles/sheworx-co-founder-takes-on-gender-bias-in-fundraising-1489149010.
3. Lisa Wang, "11 Easy Ways to Be More Successful," *Fortune*, January 6, 2016, http://fortune.com/2016/01/06/11-ways-to-be-more-successful/.

EFFECTIVE MARKETING STRATEGIES

Steps in the Marketing Plan

1. Identify and define, as clearly as possible, the potential target market niche for your product or service. Is the niche of adequate size and buying power to be profitable?

2. Conduct detail market research to determine

   a. The demographics of the targeted customers and their motivation in making their purchasing decisions;

   b. The size and scope of the current competitors in the target market niche;

   c. The potential level of customer loyalty to these competitors and the barriers, or switching costs, to be overcome before the targeted customers will purchase your products or services;

   d. Potential customers' level of "price sensitivity"; and

   e. The purchasing capabilities and behavior patterns of potential customers (Where and how do they make purchases? How often do they make purchases?).

3. Based on what your research has provided you, determine your "unique selling proposition."

4. Based on research, begin to create a marketing strategy that addresses the realities of the market. Consider the product or service itself, where and how it is sold, its price, and how it can be promoted to the targeted customer niche. How will these four components of a marketing strategy be integrated effectively?

5. Know the current and anticipated life-cycle position of the product or service within the market niche you are entering. (Is the product or service new, ascending in sales, stable, or possibly in decline?)

6. Determine an effective pricing strategy for introducing your product or service to the market niche How "price sensitive" are the customers in proposed target market?

7. Plan how and where to sell your product or service. Have you created an effective distribution system?

8. Decide on the most effective and affordable promotion strategies and tactics for your new product or service.

Effective marketing strategies require an entrepreneur to focus on anticipated customers while remaining a viable competitor in a dynamic market. A firm's marketing strategies cannot be developed in a vacuum. The dynamics of the competitive environment must be understood in order for the entrepreneur's marketing strategies to be implemented effectively. The profile of the customer base becomes the critical target that every component of the marketing strategy needs to be focused on. Successful ventures always create and reinforce a positive customer orientation. The attitudes and behaviors of every employee in the business must communicate a desire to be aggressively proactive in their relationships with customers. The firm's behavior must display a total commitment to delivering superior service, resolving every difficulty, and making every customer feel that the business is genuinely concerned about him or her as an individual. These concepts apply just as much in a business-to-business (B2B) relationship as in a typical business-to-customer one.

The products and services must achieve a level of quality that impresses their target customer. Quality is a significant source of creating a distinctive competence for a business. Quality is more encompassing than the products or services as it includes every aspect of the business and its ongoing relationship to every customer. Quality is never an accidental outcome. Successful firms measure every aspect of their relationship with their customers. Entrepreneurs must understand how their customers measure quality. Quality criteria can include any or all of the following elements and usually relate to the customers' experience of *both* the product or service *and* the behaviors of the firm:

- Reliability or dependability
- Durability
- Ease of use or operation
- Responsiveness to customer complaints
- Empathy from the seller to customers having problems
- Relationship based on trust and respect

A new business must take extraordinary steps to ensure that it can successfully match or exceed the quality of its competitors' products or services. In almost every market, the issue of product or service quality is a tangible barrier. One absolute "kiss of death" is marketing promises of quality that cannot be met by the new firm's products or services. New businesses generally depend on positive word-of-mouth referrals. When customer comments are positive, the impact on new sales can be dramatic, but when negative, these comments can result in a significant, and often immediate, decline in sales.

Innovation

Innovation can often be a market advantage for new firms. Entrepreneurial firms should possess the organizational and managerial flexibility to identify new opportunities quickly and respond to customers' changing needs faster than larger and more bureaucratic competitors. Innovation is measured by the degree to which a firm can produce new products or services in response to changing customer needs. Innovation must be an internalized organizational value. An entrepreneur must skillfully focus the firm's efforts on searching for new potential opportunities—times when innovation in its products or services may result in producing what is termed "first mover" strategic advantage. As mentioned earlier in the chapter, innovation can become the driving force behind new products or services that become market disruptors. These market disruptors have the potential to reshape the marketplace and skyrocket a firm into a market leadership position.

Convenience

In some market segments, the key customer demand is convenience. The product or service offering of the new business might be similar to those of competitors yet meet the customers' need and desire to make purchases at the most convenient location. Failure in the research to identify this important customer buying requirement can lead a new entrepreneur to select a business location that is not convenient, or not more convenient than the locations of competitors. The result of an inappropriate location is often a slow death because the business attracts only a marginal customer base. Some of the proactive steps an entrepreneur can undertake before selecting a location are outlined in the box "Select a Convenient Location."

Select a Convenient Location

1. Determine the **traffic patterns** of potential customers.

2. Select a location with **easy access and exit**.

3. Determine **the hours** that customers shop.

4. Ensure that all **business transactions** can be conducted quickly, efficiently, and politely.

Speed

Speed in response to customers' needs has become another competitive weapon that favors smaller, responsive firms. In business-to-business (B2B) ventures, companies are attempting to reduce cost and avoid the added risk of holding inventory by selecting suppliers based on their ability to respond with what is needed, when it is needed. For these businesses, dependability and delivery may be more valuable than a lower price. The same can hold true for other customers, a person buying a personalized T-shirt as a gift, for example. In these cases, speed is the value creator for the customer and therefore an opportunity exists for an entrepreneur who offers solutions that cater to this customer requirement of getting purchases quickly.

Customer Satisfaction

Finally, one often-overlooked component of effective marketing is simple customer satisfaction. Once a business has a customer, it is imperative to ensure that every effort is made to protect the relationship with that customer and retain her or his business. It is less expensive to retain current customers then to find replacements. What would motivate an established customer to switch suppliers? In some cases, the product or service of a competitor might better fit the customer's needs, but often it is the way the customer has been treated by a current supplier that is the determining factor. Customers will simply not tolerate rude, discourteous, inept, or incompetent employees. Customers will complain, or what is worse, they will not. They will simply stop

Spotify

Following early entrepreneurial ventures beginning at age 13, Swedish-born serial entrepreneur Daniel Ek began developing Spotify in 2006, as a paid music service for subscribers. It launched in Sweden in 2008. As Ek tells it, the idea struck him when Napster ran into legal difficulties over illegal downloading and ceased operations for a time: "The only way to solve the problem was to create a service that was better than piracy and at the same time compensates the music industry—that gave us Spotify." Since its beginning, Ek has developed and forged strong, strategic industry partnerships enabling the development and deployment of a music-streaming service that, as of March 2018, has 75 million subscribers in 65 countries. Through the utilization of a monthly subscription service fee, Spotify has disrupted traditional over-air music services by providing a more personalized form of music entertainment for users around the globe. As a result of the execution of this daring vision, Ek's company was estimated to have reached a market valuation of about 28 billion in April 2018.

Sources

1. R. Neate, "Music Website Spot-On for Fans and Industry," *The Daily Telegraph*, February 18, 2010.

2. "Company Info," Spotify website, https://newsroom.spotify.com/companyinfo/.

3. Bloomberg, "Spotify Stock Goes Public, Giving the Streaming Music Giant a $30 Billion Market Cap," *Fortune*, April 3, 2018, http://fortune.com/2018/04/03/spotify-stock-market-cap-ipo-direct-listing/.

doing business with firms in response to poor treatment. Treating customers competently and courteously must be an internalized employee value demonstrated by every employee, every day, and with every transaction. It is almost never the business owner who treats the customer poorly. Nevertheless, it is the owner's responsibility to see that customers are satisfied. Customer satisfaction must be a hallmark of the business. Every employee, at every level of the business, needs to practice superior service in every customer interaction. Employees with bad attitudes and those who treat others with indifference generate negative feelings from all with whom they come into contact. The answer is to hire the right employees and train them to always demonstrate positive and courteous responses in dealing with every customer. Every employee represents the business. Consequently, it becomes essential in the competitive environment to ensure that employees are trained to

- listen for additional ways the business can provide value for the customers,

- listen to every customer and attempt to uncover any specific problems that customer may be having, and

- encourage the customer to provide very specific feedback as to the performance of the firm's products or services.

The entrepreneur needs to set high standards and expectations for superior customer service. When the employees deliver on the owner's expectations, their performance should be recognized and rewarded.

The payoff for superior market research is knowledge that allows for the creation of market-driven and customer-focused marketing strategies. These marketing strategies should lead to actions that reinforce the value-adding capabilities of the firm, its products, and its services. Only in-depth market research reveals an expanding understanding of how the firm's external environment continually reshapes the market niche and the customer's expectations. Customer value can only be enhanced when the entrepreneur clearly understands the nature of the targeted customer's needs, buying preferences, and behaviors. Discovering specific and detailed knowledge of what the target market values in the products and services it purchases *is* the process of value determination. Specifically, value determination is the result obtained by market research that accurately identifies the detailed nature of targeted customers and what they value; it also focuses on how well the new firm and its competitors actually deliver the value that customers seek. This knowledge allows the new firm to construct an effective marketing strategy. That the new business can satisfy its customers' needs and excel at creating customer value is absolutely critical to its survival. The new business must skillfully implement an initial market penetration strategy to gain and secure a competitive advantage through its strategic actions; at the same time, it must be prepared to cope with the competitive backlash from the market's existing competitors. In reality, the new business must be strategically operating on the offensive and defensive simultaneously.

FIGURE 4.1 ■ Essential Components of a Marketing Plan

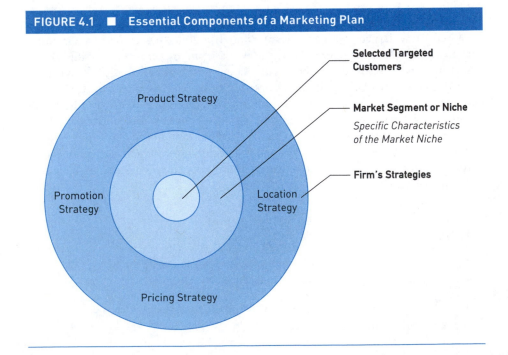

COMPONENTS OF A MARKETING STRATEGY

Figure 4.1 serves to help the entrepreneur visualize how the elements of the marketing strategy reinforce one another. At the center is always the selected customer base that market research has identified, both quantitatively and qualitatively, as being an appropriate target group. The next ring in the model is the market niche where targeted customers can be found; included here are also all the specific and unique characteristics of that market niche. The outer ring is composed of the four essential components of an integrated marketing strategy: product strategies, place strategies, pricing strategies, and promotion strategies. Each of these component strategies must reinforce the others in ways that generate superior marketing outcomes.

PRODUCT STRATEGIES

Product strategies will vary significantly based on the nature and characteristics of the market niche. The entrepreneur must have a clear understanding of what customers perceive as the benefits of the new venture's products or services, of how these create value for customers. Also, it is important to have a measure of the targeted customers' perceptions regarding the quality of these products or services. The entrepreneur needs to determine, for example, if a product's benefits can be easily duplicated or matched by current competitors. If these benefits are easily matched, the entrepreneur has a limited "window of opportunity" to gain a competitive foothold in the market niche. Product strategy needs to be based in reality. Does the product, when compared to the products of competitors, actually produce measurable superiority? If so, how long will it take competitors to identify the sources of the new product's superiority? Once these have been identified, how long will it take competitors to respond with a similar or superior product?

Product strategies normally evolve as the business travels through the various stages of its product's life cycle. **Figure 4.2** illustrates the course of a product's life cycle and the normal sales and profit at each stage. Tracking both sales and profitability allows the entrepreneur the opportunity to take proactive steps to introduce new product offerings prior to the profits being diminished significantly.

Product Life Cycle

Development Stage

The actual length of each stage in the product life cycle can vary widely based on the sustainability of the market and the competitive behaviors of other sellers. As the name implies, the "development stage" is where new products or services are created. The firm has no sales at this stage. It is critical for the firm to bring the product to market in a timely fashion. Expenses can grow rapidly, and the firm's "financial resources burn rate," or the amount of cash expended prior to the firm earning profits to cover all expenses, must not exceed its reserves. Additionally, the entrepreneur must focus on producing a

FIGURE 4.2 ■ **Product Life Cycle Stages**

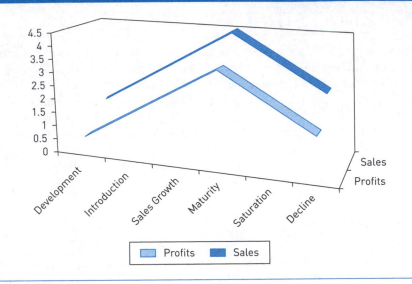

product that is market ready. There needs to be a careful measurement of the progress being made toward product introduction. Without well-defined performance metrics, the entrepreneur can easily confuse actions with accomplishments. Deadlines for each step in the new product development must be rigorously tracked, and when negative deviations are identified, actions must be taken quickly to make the needed corrections. Many new businesses never see the light of day because the entrepreneur underestimates both the time and money necessary to create a product that is "market ready." Some individuals working at the development stage strive for perfection, as opposed to market readiness, and spend their time and money in search of that "perfect" product or service. As a result, the resources are expanded but the final product is never created. The new venture fails before its product or service is offered to the market.

Introduction Stage

The introduction stage is critical for the entrepreneur, as a firm seldom gets a second chance to make that initial impression with the targeted customers. High levels of initial acceptance are a rarity. The new product introduction must be completely coordinated, therefore. All marketing activities must be fully integrated and supportive of the product introduction. Anticipated customers must be closely monitored to evaluate their product acceptance behaviors. If sales targets are not being achieved, it is essential that the entrepreneur determines the cause and quickly adjusts the marketing strategy. Normally, the costs of marketing at this point in the product life cycle are high as a percentage of revenue. Sales resistance must be met with an open mind, be understood, and adjustments made rapidly. Too often, businesses fail when the entrepreneur stubbornly blames the market for unacceptable sales instead of making every effort to learn the actual underlying causes of poor sales. Low sales lead to a lack of adequate profitability that often causes the entrepreneur to panic. That panic may result in the product price being lowered unrealistically in an attempt to increase sales. The lower price could earn additional sales but destroy the firm's profit potential and accelerate the burn rate of the firm's financial resources.

Growth Stage

If the new venture achieves adequate sales and profitability, the product enters the sales *growth stage.* In this stage, the marketing plan must focus on positioning the product for accurate evaluation by the targeted market niche. Market penetration must be achieved for growth to occur. Product acceptance needs to be evaluated through sophisticated market research methods. The more accurately the entrepreneur is able to determine the primary product characteristics that motivate the customer to purchase the product, the more effective the firm's marketing strategies will become. When a successful business experiences an extended sales growth stage, the entrepreneur has the opportunity to earn substantial profit. This profit can be reinvested in the creation of other products, which may be modifications of the original product or stand-alone new products. Some of these activities and events, for example, investing in product development and experiencing extended sales, often began in the introduction stage of the product life cycle. During the sales growth stage, however, profits rise and the firm attracts new competitors. Marketing strategies must focus on both retaining existing customers and attracting new customers.

Maturity and Saturation Stages

Eventually, the product life cycle enters the *maturity stage.* Competition becomes intense in the maturity stage, resulting in profits that normally decline even though sales remain positive. The entrepreneur can always anticipate that attractive profit margins will attract new and aggressive competitors. Price pressures normally result in a decline in profitability during the saturation stage of the product life cycle, which normally finds sales to be high yet declining. Profits remain positive but continued to decline. This is the final trigger that informs the entrepreneur that innovation must occur rapidly. The profitability of the original product is in final decline, and new products need to be introduced. The final stage in the product life cycle is *decline.* Sales often experience drastic decline during this stage, and profits may no longer exist. Some products in decline continue to sell, however, but this usually occurs only when the majority of the firm's competitors exit the market. For most firms, their focus at this stage needs to be on marketing new products.

PLACE STRATEGIES

Place or location strategies have expanded over the past few decades as technology provides entrepreneurs with the opportunity to serve a global market from a simple home-based business. To be competitive, an entrepreneur needs to have products where the customers wants to purchase them and expects to find them. The channels of distribution have themselves become increasingly complex, as even small entrepreneurial firms attempt to serve an international market.

Direct Sales Locations

For some new business ventures, such as brick and mortar retailers relying on in-store customers, finding a convenient location becomes an immediate critical issue. Having a poor physical location will result in insufficient sales and inadequate revenues. Any firm that depends on direct sales needs to ensure that customers can easily locate the business, that they view the location as being in a "safe" neighborhood, and that they have ease of entry and exit. The location needs to allow for adequate signage so that the business can be easily found. All of these criteria sound simple and obvious, yet consider the number of retailers whom you know have failed due to an inappropriate or ineffective location. In a highly competitive market, it is essential to ensure that your location fits the needs of your targeted customers and their buying behaviors.

Professional businesses need to have a location that is compatible with their services and with their desired image. The location and the overall appearance of the business must reinforce the professional nature of the business. The entrepreneur must also select a distribution channel for products. Many businesses have opted to sell directly to the customer with online engagement supplemented by sophisticated and dependable logistic support. This combination allows a new venture to market its products globally and have confidence that its products will be delivered to the customer in a timely fashion. This distribution method eliminates wholesalers and retailers, and consequently provides the entrepreneur with a potentially greater profit margin. As the new venture grows, some additional expenses for direct selling do occur. Inventories must be maintained, and staff may need to be added to address customers' questions and scheduled shipments.

Direct Electronic Marketing

Today's entrepreneur has the opportunity to reach potential buyers worldwide. The creation and management of a website for an emerging new business can help an entrepreneur reach market niches that were virtually unrecognized and unsearchable a decade or so ago. The marriage of global market research and electronic technology allows an entrepreneur access to customers worldwide. Success is achieved through the entrepreneur's detailed and sophisticated market research, which not only results in the identification of potential customers but also allows for the determination of the customers' buying behaviors; their unique product or service preferences and taste; and their government's regulation of electronic commerce, currency, and payment issues—not to mention allowing for the determination of the best way to deliver the product to these customers. Direct electronic marketing requires these factors to be addressed prior to the start of the marketing effort. Once these issues and others have been resolved, the entrepreneur can evaluate what international markets will be the most promising.

Although this model of direct sales to customers might fit many businesses, it will not produce the required results if the customers are unable or unwilling to order online or through a catalog. When the customer desires to see and touch the product before making a purchase decision, a physical location is needed. One option is selling through large volume retailers, but this strategy may result in a smaller profit margin as you must negotiate with potential sellers that have enormous buying power. The up side can be the achievement of a potentially global reach through global partners. Consider the sales that can be obtained through selling the firm's products through Walmart, Target, or another mass retailer. In this situation, the entrepreneur must consider the much lower price that the firm will receive while correspondingly considering the potentially extraordinary number of units these mass-market retailers can achieve. As an example, direct sales via the Internet with a profit margin of $10 per unit can produce a profit of $100,000 based on the sale of 10,000 units. Selling to mass marketers might result in a much lower net profit per unit, say of only $2 per unit, but the mass marketers could purchase and sell 500,000 units, resulting in a $1 million profit for the new venture. If an entrepreneur has the opportunity to sell to a mass marketer who has the capability to sell a very high volume, the entrepreneur might be able to earn a superior net profit.

Entrepreneur to Distributors and Wholesalers

Some industries traditionally market their products through distributors. This is common for industrial goods that have long purchasing cycles but that make profits through the sale of services. Think of dishwashers or cars. In these cases, both the product producer and the authorized distributors promote the product to the final customer, but the sales and services are delivered by the distributors. The distributor buys the product from the manufacture, holds it in inventory, and sells it directly to the final user (buyer). As you can see, contracting with a reputable distributor is absolutely crucial if you are a new entrepreneur in this sort of circumstance.

In many cases, a manufacturer will sell to distributors through an exclusive marketing agreement. The manufacturer's desire is to form an agreement with absolutely the best distributor in a territory. In this way, the manufacturer is confident that the established and well-respected distributor will sell the product effectively in that distributor's specific territory. Both the manufacturer and distributor benefit from this type of exclusive distribution agreement. The manufacturer's product benefits from the reputation and established market relationships of the distributor. This manufacturer-distributor marketing channel is very often the most effective means for a small firm wishing to enter a market in a foreign country. The manufacturer knows its product and all of that product's capabilities but is unaware of the unique marketing barriers that are likely to exist in a foreign country. In this situation, the distributor selected must be honest and have integrity. It must also have specific knowledge of government regulations, of how to resolve any importing issues quickly, of the customers who could realistically be potential buyers, and of which customers can be expected to meet their financial obligations. When the entrepreneur does not know the buying behavior of the customers or how business is conducted in a particular place, the use of the distributor is generally a wise marketing choice.

What an entrepreneur must absolutely avoid is offering a product for sale through a distributor or retailer and then offering to sell the same product directly to the customer at a lower price. This type of distribution channel conflict will inevitably create a hostile environment. No distributor or retailer will accept a situation in which the manufacturer attempts to "cannibalize" distributors' profits by selling directly to consumers at a lower price.

When entrepreneurs choose to sell through a wholesaler, distributor, or retailer, they must always recognize that their reputation and that of the product will be affected by the behaviors of all those involved in the marketing process. If the retailer is unethical, provides poor service, or behaves inappropriately, the reputation of the product can be damaged. Selecting ethical, efficient, and trustworthy firms to assist in the marketing of products must be taken very seriously.

Factors to Consider: Setting Price

- The current forces of **supply and demand** in the targeted market

- The price and price-related **policies and strategies** of market competitors

- The overall **economic conditions** currently occurring in the targeted market

- The **desired image** of the product

- The known **price sensitivity** of the targeted customers

- The seasonal or cyclical **market fluctuations**

- The psychological factors affecting customers' **buying behaviors**

- **Credit terms** and all purchasing discounts

- The **projected core required sales** volume

PRICING STRATEGIES

Initially, pricing strategies are normally a creative blend of art and science, with an emphasis on the art. Most entrepreneurs do not understand the intricacies of pricing strategies. Too often, product price is set based on unsubstantiated assumptions or false beliefs about the buying behaviors of the targeted customers. Without a thoughtful analytical assessment of the potential implications of the product's pricing, haphazard policies can be followed, policies that result in inadequate profitability and disappointing sales.

Product Value and Price

Pricing is the entrepreneur's opportunity to place a monetary value on a product or service. Competitive behaviors in the marketplace are what actually determine the final worth of a company's products or services, and this competition overwhelmingly influences what customers might be willing to pay. An entrepreneur usually hopes that pricing also serves to convey a psychological signal to the targeted customer. A higher price is designed to convey a message of product superiority. A competitive price might signal greater customer value for the price. The product price needs to be compatible with the customer's determination of the product's value. Customers determine if your product is worth the price that you attempt to charge. The closer the entrepreneur sets the product price relative to the customers' actual measure of value, the closer to the entrepreneur's sales forecast the firm is likely to come. For most products, a firm will settle on an acceptable "price range" after researching the market and considering its own circumstances. However, when there is no product differentiation and a product is viewed as a commodity (think lumber), external factors are often foremost in setting prices. In situations where there is no product differentiation, the product is viewed as a commodity. Outside groups often grade commodities, and the price for those products is universal. The more effectively the entrepreneur can differentiate a product through its superior performance, ease of operation, durability, dependability, or any other value-adding characteristic, the higher the price the product might be able to capture. Product value needs to be matched to price within a rather narrow range. The challenge is to evaluate the many products and market factors that impact the targeted customers' willingness to buy. The factors involved in setting product price include the total cost of the product, which comprises design, manufacturing, marketing, overhead, and other pertinent costs.

Value-Based Pricing

A second price strategy is **value-based pricing**. This pricing strategy attempts to quantify the value generated by the product for the customer. The customer is the sole arbitrator of the value of the product. What a customer is willing to pay is determined by an estimation of the perceived value of the product in comparison with the perceived value of all other similar products in the market. A value-based pricing strategy, then, searches for an answer to this question: "What will customers actually pay for this product?" In many cases, this search process is a trial-and-error effort. There is no specific formula on which value-based pricing can be based. Additionally, the product price is dramatically influenced by the firm's ability to market the product in ways that clarify its actual value-creating features. The customer must be able actually to recognize the value-creating features of the product in order to value them correctly. Many successful entrepreneurs attempt to gain valuable insight into setting prices through employing external reviewers. Focus groups can be formed with individuals who are qualified potential buyers of the product. These group members are shown the product and each of the product's features is demonstrated. The focus group members are asked to evaluate the product and its features and what they might be willing to pay for the product. Focus groups provide valuable insight into how the market might evaluate the relative importance of a product's features. These groups can also provide the entrepreneur with an assessment of the price range for the new product.

Marketing communication and sales techniques that fail to detail how the product generates value for the customer will result in a lower perceived value of the product in the eyes of the customer. With the assistance of a wide variety of Internet-based product evaluation services, today's customers can access the opinions of professional product researchers as well as the opinions of ordinary buyers. Every business must recognize that its products will be evaluated and reviewed. Customers purchasing very expensive products tend to seek verification of their choices through consulting the evaluations made by professionals, friends, or peer groups. Value-based pricing is now, more than ever, based on objective, professionally researched product evaluations.

Cost-Based Pricing

Although product price must be set relative to all of the previously discussed criteria, it must also accurately reflect the actual cost of the product, so the entrepreneur can avoid selling at a loss and earn a reasonable profit. Pricing strategies must be flexible enough to incorporate changes that stem from both external and internal environmental factors, as well as from the market's competitive behaviors. Internally generated factors most often influence product prices because of changes to a product's total cost. A **cost-based pricing strategy** typically employs a percentage markup based on the total cost of the product. This pricing method is simple and easy to implement. An example can be found in the retail industry; following industry standards, a bookseller, for instance, sets the price of a book based on a fixed markup of say 50% of the price from the publisher. The entrepreneur hopes that this product and the retailer's inventory will sell at the initial price, but when it does not, the retailer normally marks down the inventory by a series of fixed percentages until the inventory is sold. See **Table 4.1** for an illustration of this process.

In this example, the entrepreneur's pricing strategy was to sell as many units of the product at the initial 100 percent markup, but when 20 percent remained unsold after 180 days, the price was cut to $75. After 240 days, all but 50 units remained, so the price was reduced again from $75 to $60 per unit. This price reduction resulted in the sale of 40 units. After 360 days, the remaining 10 products were sold at cost. The retailer in this example employed a cost-based pricing strategy that was very systematically adjusted based on the time the product was in inventory. In this example, the entrepreneur's pricing policy employed a standard time-sales discount mode.

TABLE 4.1 ■ Cost-Based Pricing, Markup, and Revenue Generation Over Time						
Days	Number of Units in Inventory	Number Sold	Cost per Unit	% Markup	Price	Revenue
1–180	1,000	800	$50	100%	$100	$80,000
181–240	200	150	$50	50%	$75	$11,250
241–360	50	40	$50	20%	$60	$2,400
After 360	10	10	$50	0%	$50	$500
					Total Revenue	$94,150

Note: Total Cost of 1,000 units, 1,000 × $50 = $50,000

Price Sensitivity

Price sensitivity is determined by attempting to measure the customers' willingness or unwillingness to pay a higher price for the firm's products. The entrepreneur must attempt to estimate the sources of price sensitivity that exist in the targeted market niches. **Figure 4.3** shows the percentage of buyers who would purchase a product at various price points, and it demonstrates that there is extreme price sensitivity in the surveyed market niche. Given this very limited market at the "top-end" price, the entrepreneur will very likely fail to gain needed sales if the product is priced above three dollars.

Purchase Probability Analysis

The results demonstrated in **Figure 4.3** are termed a **purchase probability curve** and suggest that a large number of the targeted customers surveyed would be buyers at three dollars or less but only a small percentage would be willing to pay more than three dollars. Note the curve that would result if one were to connect the tops of the bars in **Figure 4.3**.

Figure 4.4 presents another purchase probability curve and illustrates that about 50 percent of the targeted customers surveyed would pay up to six dollars for the product. The value of such research is that an entrepreneur can attempt to set a price point for the product that is estimated to generate the highest revenue. As an example, let's say that market research identified that there were 100,000 persons who could become potential customers in two specific market niches. All 200,000 were surveyed to determine the price sensitivity in each market niche, and the results of those two surveys are presented in **Figure 4.3** and 4.4, respectively. The first survey indicates that 80 percent would pay $2.00 for the product (**Figure 4.3**). But in the other market niche, 50 percent of those surveyed would pay $6.00 (**Figure 4.4**). Therefore, the entrepreneur can estimate the following net revenues in each of these market niches:

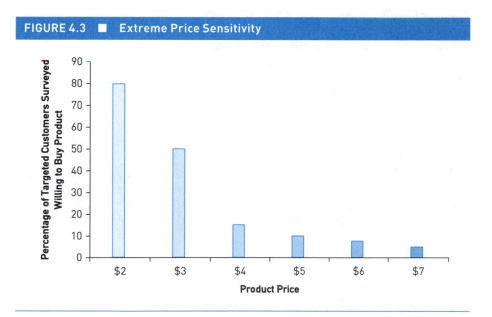

FIGURE 4.3 ■ Extreme Price Sensitivity

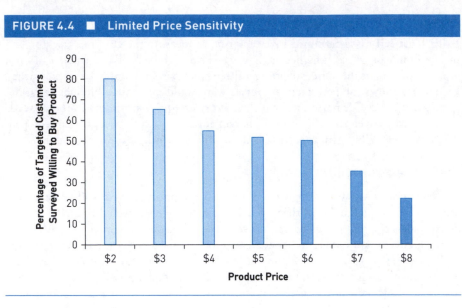

FIGURE 4.4 ■ Limited Price Sensitivity

Market Niche Having Extreme Price Sensitivity

Net Revenue = Sales × Price
= 80% of 100,000 units × $2.00/unit
= 80,000 units × $2.00/unit
= $160,000.

Market Niche Having Limited Price Sensitivity

Net Revenue = 50% of 100,000 × $6.00/unit
= 50,000 × $6.00/unit
= $300,000.

Under a scenario of price insensitivity, the entrepreneur would set the price at a higher level. In fact, $6.00 would be the optimum price as a $7.00 price would attract only 35,000 buyers and produce net revenue of $245,000.

This technique can be made more sophisticated by presenting the survey or focus group members with additional options for their answers. Measures of buyer intention can pose questions such as this:

If the product is sold for "x" dollars what would you do?

- Definitely would buy

- Probably would buy

- Not sure if I would buy

- Probably would not buy

- Definitely would not buy

The entrepreneur can then estimate the percentage of customers who indicated that they would probably buy and the percentage of customers who were undecided but who could eventually buy the product. These percentages, added to the percentage of customers who said that they definitely would buy, gives an estimate of the percentage of targeted customers in the survey who would buy at various price points:

Definitely would buy—40% positive response rate

Probably would buy—80% of the 20% or 16% positive response rate

Not sure if would buy—50% of the 20% or 10% positive response rate

With a response of 1,000 targeted customers in the survey, the entrepreneur would expect to sell the products to 66 percent of the targeted customers (40% + 16% + 10%).

Though "real world" scenarios are more difficult to predict with accuracy, such techniques assist an entrepreneur attempting to set the price of a product in a way that achieves the most favorable revenue outcome.

The most difficult pricing decision occurs when a new venture begins because the entrepreneur often has no previous precedent on which to base a pricing decision. If the price is set excessively high in an attempt to earn a large profit in order to break even quickly, a low sales volume could result in insufficient revenues, and, instead of earning a high profit, the business will be in jeopardy. In the contrary direction, a price that is too low may prove to generate insufficient revenues to cover the firm's total cost. Even worse, once a low price is recognized by the customers in the market, it is difficult to increase the price without a backlash. Customers might feel that they were originally deceived. They could experience the increase in price as a "bait-and-switch" pricing scenario that lured them in with false promises, and customers might feel that the firm's pricing strategies are less that ethical.

"Follow-the-Leader" Pricing Strategy

In many situations, a new business sets prices in line with those of existing competitors. This is termed a "follow-the-leader" pricing strategy. For some new businesses, this pricing strategy seems to be market tested, conservative, and secure. Matching competitors' prices, however, may result in underpricing a product that has recognizable superior features. As discussed previously, attempting to increase prices at a later date may not be acceptable to the initial customers despite the fact that the product creates superior value. A second possible negative outcome of a "follow-the-leader" pricing strategy is the potential reality that competitors are setting their prices based on a much lower cost structure. The established competition will likely be producing products in much higher volume and, due to economies of scale, have lower unit cost.

Established competitors may also be operating with equipment whose cost has been fully depreciated over time. An entrepreneur must be aware of a competitor's capability of pricing its product way below current market price. A competitor who has a lower cost structure and then chooses to lower its product price can place a new business at a significant short-term disadvantage. Such a competitor's pricing strategy may have the effect of setting a market price that is actually below the new firm's cost. The established competitor can still earn a small profit while the new business will be unable to earn any profit at the lower price. Pricing strategies are one of the areas of marketing where established competitors can have the greatest impact at crippling new market entries. Think back to what you have read about a new firm's financial "burn rate." If sales revenues are not producing profits, yet money is continually spent, the financial stress created by unprofitable sales will limit the life expectancy of the new business.

Market Penetration Pricing Strategy

In an attempt to gain quick market acceptance and achieve an extensive distribution in the market, a firm may choose to set a low initial product price. The strategy is to achieve very rapid customer acceptance and quickly earn a significant market share. Successful market penetration strategies normally require heavy advertising and product promotion to ensure that customers are aware of the product. In some cases, every identifiable potential customer receives introductory coupons. These activities are expensive and put the business in financial jeopardy if the strategy fails.

All of these potentially negative scenarios emphasize why establishing an effective pricing strategy is so difficult but so critically important. Pricing should never be a last minute decision. The entrepreneur needs to investigate thoroughly the behaviors and buying patterns of the targeted customers and the most likely competitors' responses to various pricing strategies. Then, the entrepreneur needs to select a product price that achieves a balance among the following essential marketing objectives:

Pricing Objectives

Gain market acceptance	Ensure that the business earns a sufficient profit to justify the entrepreneur's investment
Meet or exceed customers' expectations	
Earn a satisfactory market share that can be expanded over time	

Product pricing is a way that a new business venture "puts a stake in the ground." Pricing gets everyone's attention, especially the attention of market competitors.

PROMOTION STRATEGIES

One common error made by first-time entrepreneurs is to ignore the need for the promotion of the business and its products. Consequently, the market never hears the story about the firm's great new product or service and fails to make the anticipated purchases. A common cause of failure is the entrepreneur's misguided belief that "the product will sell itself." Promotion strategies involve three fundamental functions: advertising, product or business promotion, and personal selling. The entrepreneur must ensure that each of these three key components reinforces the strategic efforts of the others. Here again the entrepreneur discovers that the research conducted previously to identify and classify the targeted customers pays handsome dividends. An effective promotion strategy will address the following questions:

- What image of my business do I wish to present consistently? What type of business professionals are we? (Answers stress values, mission, products and services, and overall respect for the customers.)

- Is our promotional material clearly focused on having a positive impact on our customers?

- How do our products or services enhance value for our customers? Do our promotional efforts reinforce this "value creation" message?

- Have we correctly determined the best methods of communicating with our target markets?

- Have we made it clear in all of our promotional materials how to reach us and make a purchase?

Advertising needs to be built on the essential functions outlined here, and it should be expected to produce specific and measurable outcomes. The entrepreneur can only assess the value of her or his investment in advertising through the measurement of its outcomes. Does the advertisement "trigger" a purchasing decision? If not, the advertisement failed.

Messaging the Market

By the mid-1960s, major product brands had become adept at influencing consumers with advertising. Beginning in the 1940s, glossy magazine ads portrayed corporations as benevolent sources of goodwill and authority, as was reflected clearly in the smiling faces of the glowing celebrities and wholesome models endorsing or representing products. Positive "word-of-mouth" advertising has always been an effective marketing tool, and companies have often resorted to publishing customer testimonials alongside the toothy grin of a particularly appealing model. What, you ask, do these facts have to do with marketing using social media? Very similar strategies are used in traditional and social media marketing: strong visuals and pithy phrases to attract interest; testimonials, reviews, and word of mouth (or "likes" and "shares," for example) to convince the consumer of product value, and even celebrity endorsements or product spokespeople to create desire for the product. Indeed, marketing authorities have developed numerous methods of selling, which highlight the linkage among the essential components that influence the customer's purchasing behavior. These remain similar across various media.

Promotion strategies and tactics must be initially effective at drawing the potential buyer's attention. The second step is the creation of interest in the product. Step 3 is exciting the customer in a way that produces a serious desire to own the product. Step 4 is the action phase in which the customer makes the purchase, or decides not to. The product will be positioned to achieve sustainability and possibly customer loyalty if the initial purchaser becomes a repeat buyer. Today, one of the most powerful media for reaching the firm's intended market niche is social media. Social media platforms, such as Facebook® and Twitter®, have powerful market outreach tools for entrepreneurs. Potential customers who may be turned off by traditional advertising have a higher level of trust in what they read through social media.

"Brand Evangelist"

With the advent of the Internet, online commerce, and, finally, social networks, highly connected groups of individuals can influence brand strategy like never before. Social media enables customers to have a largely uncensored and uninterrupted dialogue about products, services, brands, and events. Companies with large audiences and those who are building a customer base in the open market must adapt to become both content providers and highly responsive to consumer needs and competitor strategies. Customers are now more vocal than ever before, and there is no shortage of forums in which they can vent their internal angst or joy about an entrepreneur's best (or worst) efforts. This is certainly not all bad for entrepreneurs. In fact, effectively identifying highly connected individuals who can act as brand evangelists is a very savvy means of promoting products, services, or events—rewarding these individuals, who then serve as an information hub for many other people, and creating a symbiotic relationship among customers and sellers will be the hallmark of successful brands of the future. Social networks allow for the rapid assimilation of information across the Internet and, indeed, across the world. The information passed through social networks in the form of customer feedback cannot be underestimated, and effective brand managers and marketers can take brand popularity within a social network and turn it into real profits.

Promotional Activities

Promotions can take the form of a very wide range of events, from lottery-type giveaways to the support of community events. These promotional activities are intended to draw attention to the firm and its products. The support of high-profile, compelling events that address recognized societal and health issues can gain the firm and its products a great deal of positive recognition. Organizations such as the United Way or the Boys & Girls Clubs of America have large bases of supporters who recognize businesses that reach out to support "their" causes, and these organizations may therefore support the company and purchase its product or service. Many local and even regional events can be relatively inexpensive to support.

Traditional Advertising Mediums

Newspapers

Newspapers have experienced a decline in use over the past few decades, but they can be valuable when the newspaper's circulation corresponds to your targeted market. Here are some of the advantages of using newspapers for marketing:

- Selected geographical coverage
- Flexibility
- Timeliness
- Relatively low costs
- Prompt responses

Of course, newspaper advertisements also have disadvantages:

- Wasted readership
- Reproduction limitations in quality
- Lack of prominence
- Declining readership
- Short ad life

Radio

Although newspapers offer blanket coverage of a region, radio permits the advertiser to appeal to a specific audience over a broader region. By choosing the appropriate station, program, and time for the radio ad, an entrepreneur's firm can reach virtually any market it targets. Here are some of the advantages of radio ads:

- *Universal infiltration:* Virtually every home and car in the United States is equipped with a radio
- *Market segmentation:* Radio advertising is flexible and efficient because it can be directed toward a specific market within a broad geographic region.
- *Flexibility and timeliness:* Radio commercials have short closing times and can be changed quickly.
- *Friendliness:* Radio ads are more active than ads in printed media because they use the spoken word to influence customers.

Radio advertisements also have a number of disadvantages:

- *Poor listening:* Radio's intrusiveness into public life almost guarantees that customers will hear ads, but they may not listen to them.

- *Declining audience:* Discretionary and on-demand services are cutting into radio's market share.

Trade Shows

Trade shows are often the best way for a new business to meet potential customers in an environment where the firm's products can be compared to those of its competitors. Start-up firms with limited financial ability to employ a large sales force can benefit from participating in trade shows. Trade shows are a natural marketplace. Buyers and sellers are together in a setting where products can be demonstrated and critically evaluated by the buyers. Buyers can ask questions that are critical to their buying decisions. Sellers can give their best sales pitches and can demonstrate the product features that customers indicate are important. Deals can be made with customers whom the sellers would not normally encounter.

Television

In advertising dollars spent, television ranks second in popularity when all media are compared. Although the high cost of nation TV ads precludes their use by most small businesses, local spots can be an extremely effective means of broadcasting the small advertiser's message. Television offers a number of distinct advantages over other media:

- *Broad coverage:* Television ads provide extensive coverage of a sizable region, and they reach a significant portion of the population.

- *Visual advantage:* The principal benefit of television is its capacity to present the advertiser's product or service in a graphic, vivid manner.

- *Flexibility:* Television ads can be modified quickly to meet the rapidly changing conditions in the marketplace.

- *Design assistance:* The television station from which the entrepreneur buys the airtime may be willing to offer design assistance very inexpensively.

Television advertising also has several disadvantages:

- *Brief exposure:* Most television ads are on the screen for only a short time and require substantial repetition to achieve the desired effect.

- *Clutter:* Because the typical person sees 2,700 advertising messages a day, a television ad can easily become lost in the tremendous number of ads broadcast over the air.

- *"Zapping":* Zappers, television viewers who flash from one channel to another, especially during commercials, pose a real threat to TV advertisers. Zapping means that TV advertisers are not reaching the audiences they hope to reach.

- *Costs:* TV commercials can be expensive to create and broadcast. A 30-second ad can cost several thousand dollars to develop, even before the owner purchases airtime.

Magazines

Another advertising medium available to the entrepreneur is the magazine. Most of the magazines printed today are special-interest publications; very few general-interest, mass-circulation periodicals remain on the market. Currently, there are special-interest magazines covering photography, fashion, yachting, cooking, hunting, fishing, gardening, and many other topics. These special-interest publications permit small advertisers to pinpoint their advertising target and to appeal to a specific need in that market.

Magazine advertising offers several advantages:

- *Long lifespans:* Magazines have a long reading life because readers tend to keep them longer than they do other printed media.

- *Multiple readership:* The average magazine has a readership of 3.9 adults, and each reader spends about one hour and thirty-three minutes with each copy. Many magazines have a high pass-along rate—they are handed down from reader to reader.

- *Targeted marketing:* By selecting suitable special-interest periodicals, entrepreneurs can reach customers with a high degree of interest in their goods or services. Such customers are likely to be more receptive to advertising messages.

- *Ad quality:* Magazine ads are usually of high quality. Photographs and drawings can be reproduced very effectively, and color ads are readily available.

Magazines also have several disadvantages:

- *Costs:* Magazines can be either local or national in their coverage, but national magazines are not practical advertising vehicles for the typical small business.

- *Long closing times:* For a weekly periodical, the closing date for an ad may be several weeks before the actual publication date. A monthly magazine may require an ad to be in a few months before the front-cover date.

- *Lack of prominence:* The effectiveness of a single ad may be diminished because of a lack of prominence. Positioning, therefore, is critical to an ad's success.

Direct Mail

Direct mail, which has always been a popular method of advertising, uses tools such as letters, postcards, catalogs, discount coupons, brochures, and many other printed advertisements mailed to homes or businesses. Direct-mail marketers sell virtually every kind of product imaginable.

Direct mail offers a number of advantages to the entrepreneur:

- *Selectivity:* One important advantage of direct-mail advertising is its ability to tailor the message to the advertiser's target. The presentation to the customer can be as simple or as elaborate as necessary.

- *Reader attention:* With direct mail, the advertiser's message does not have to compete with other ads for the reader's attention.

- *Rapid feedback:* In most cases, the ad generates sales within three to four days after it is received.

There are some disadvantages to direct mail:

- *Inaccurate mailing lists:* If the mailing list is inaccurate or incomplete, advertisers will be addressing the wrong audience and alienating customers with misspelled names. The result is that the advertisers are throwing away their advertising dollars.

- *High relative costs:* Direct mail has a higher cost per thousand than does any other advertising medium. Relative to the size of the audience reached, the cost of designing, producing, and mailing an advertisement via direct mail is high.

- *High throwaway rate:* Direct mail advertisements are often called junk mail, and many recipients give them only a cursory glance before throwing them away; but they become junk mail primarily because the advertiser selected the wrong audience or broadcast the wrong message.

Directories

Directories are an important advertising medium for reaching those customers who have already made purchasing decisions. The directory simply helps these customers locate the specific product or service they have decided to buy. Directories include industrial or trade guides, buyer guides, annuals, catalog files, and yearbooks that list various businesses and the products or services they sell.

Many organizations publish more specific trade directories that are organized on the basis of the industrial category or that provide listings by product groups or geographic location. In many cases, a simple listing of names and addresses is free, but many businesses elect to purchase a bold listing—a listing printed in heavy black type—to make their names more prominent. Some directories offer paid display advertisements that permit businesses to elaborate on their operations and on the products or services they sell.

Directories offer several advantages to the small advertiser:

- *Prime prospects:* Directory listings reach customers who are prime prospects because they have already decided to purchase an item or service. The directory just helps customers find what they are looking for.

- *Long life:* Directory listings usually have long lives. Many directories are published annually.

Nonetheless, there are certain disadvantages to using directories:

- *Lack of flexibility:* Listings and ads in many directories offer only a limited variety of design features. Entrepreneurs may not be as free to create unique ads as they are in other printed media.

- *Obsolescence:* Because directories are generally updated only annually, some of their listings become obsolete. This is a problem for the small firm that changes its name, location, or phone number.

In choosing the directory, the entrepreneur should look at several features:

- *Completeness:* Does the directory include enough listings so that customers will use it?

- *Convenience:* Are the listings well organized and convenient? Are they cross-referenced?

- *Evidence of use:* To what extent do customers actually use the directory? What evidence of use does the publisher offer?

- *Age:* Is the directory well established, and does it have a good reputation?

- *Circulation:* Do users pay for the directory, or do they receive complimentary copies? Is there an audited circulation statement?

Personal Selling

Personal selling is too often overlooked as a critical component of a firm's marketing strategy. For the sale of industrial products, the relationship between buyers and seller created through the salesperson is often key. The face of the salesperson becomes the face of the business. Exceptional salespersons are often legendary in an industry. This deep level of trust and commitment between seller and buyer is often based on tangible events, times when the salesperson helped the customer resolve a serious problem. The salesperson builds a bond with customers. Over time, the conversation with a client is more directed toward "How can I help you?" rather than "What can I sell you?" The most effective salespeople represent your business so as to create a positive and mutually beneficial relationship with customers. The effective salesperson communicates to a corporate client, for example, the desire to become a partner in improving that client's profits. Over time, this message is what you wish the customers to hear and believe. Becoming that partner adds longevity to the sales relationship.

Personal selling is powerful because it allows for a face-to-face interaction with a potential customer. The personal sales process involves reinforcing with customers how the product creates benefits for them. The most critical benefits for the specific customer can be emphasized by the salesperson, as can examples of positive outcomes. The salesperson can clearly tailor the firm's value and sales proposition to each customer's situation. Another major value of personal selling is that it enables a firm to address any customer concerns immediately. Only personal selling allows for this immediate and ongoing adjustment in the delivery of the marketing message. An advertisement is not able to listen and respond. When customers have a very high level of comfort with and respect for the firm's salesperson, a significant barrier has been erected against competitors. The characteristics of individuals who are highly effective salespersons include the following:

- *They never fail to ask for the business.* Effective salespersons are "closers." They identify when a customer is ready to buy and remind that customer that they have asked for his or her business. They always want to make a sale!

- *They are extremely effective listeners.* They concentrate on what the potential customer is saying in an attempt to shape the product's value and sales proposition to address, as specifically as possible, the potential customer's needs.

- *They remain alert to sales opportunities and have the ability to focus their efforts on accounts with a high probability of "closing."* They have a sales plan that lays out where they should invest their time and efforts. They are self-managers.

- *They are empathic to the customer's needs while being personally enthusiastic about the product and the firm.* They are self-motivated.

CONCLUSION

A firm's marketing strategies must be based on detailed and accurate market research that uncovers the actual needs of the customers targeted by the entrepreneur. In this way, the new business venture can focus its products more accurately. Marketing strategies need to be market driven and customer focused. The firm's overall marketing strategy is comprised of four integrated strategic components; product strategies, place strategies, pricing strategies, and promotion strategies. The successful integration of these critical strategic components allows the new venture to be both more effective at meeting customers' expectations as well as efficient in that process. The firm will always need to establish and monitor specific success metrics for each of its marketing strategies. Marketing links the entrepreneur with the customer in tangible ways. Without marketing, an entrepreneur might have a great product or service that nobody knows exists.

ENTREPRENEURIAL EXERCISES

Entrepreneurial Exercise 4.1

Market research provides you with the needed information to evaluate accurately and understand your targeted customers. It is also absolutely essential in the development and implementation of effective marketing strategies and tactics. After you have conducted this necessary market research, what, specifically, do you know about the following aspects of your targeted customer?

1. Demographics of the targeted customers?

2. Buyer motivation?

3. Current competitors?

4. Your targeted customers' level of customer loyalty to current suppliers?

5. Estimated "switching cost" that each customer might experience to adopt your product?

6. Location at which customers purchase competitors' products?

7. The "price sensitivity" of targeted customers?

Entrepreneurial Exercise 4.2

Building on your defined business model and on the detailed description of your product or service, please write a "unique selling proposition" that communicates your product or service's "value proposition."

Product/service:

Unique selling proposition:

If you have more than one product or service, please repeat this exercise on a separate sheet of paper for each product and service.

Entrepreneurial Exercise 4.3

Part 1

Please describe, in detail, your new business venture's product strategy that will be a part of your overall marketing strategy.

Part 2

Please describe, in detail, your new business venture's place strategy that will be a part of your overall marketing strategy.

Part 3

Please describe, in detail, your new business venture's pricing strategy that will be a part of your overall marketing strategy.

Part 4

Please describe, in detail, your new business venture's promotion strategy that will be a part of your overall marketing strategy.

Part 5

Please describe how you will successfully integrate these four proposed strategies—your product, place, pricing, and promotion strategies—into a unified and highly focused overall marketing strategy.

Part 6

Do you anticipate any difficulties in the implementation of your firm's marketing strategy? If so, what are they, and how can these difficulties be overcome? If not, why not?

Entrepreneurial Exercise 4.4

Part 1

Where currently is the product life cycle of the market niche in which you plan to compete?

Part 2

In what way does the position of the market niche in the product life cycle impact your ability to effective achieve market entry?

Part 3

How, specifically, will the current position of your product within the product life cycle influence each element of your overall marketing strategy?

Entrepreneurial Exercise 4.5

Part 1

What will be your initial pricing strategies and tactics to ensure that you can achieve market entry effectively and adequate market penetration? If these pricing strategies and tactics fail, what is your" back-up plan"?

Part 2

Based on your market research, how would you describe the sensitivity to price of your targeted customers as a component in their purchasing decisions?

Part 3

Do you anticipate that your firm's total cost of producing and marketing your product will be competitive with those of your competitors? If not, what do you anticipate the current competitors' pricing behaviors are likely to be? How effectively can the current competitors employ aggressive pricing tactics to impair your market entry strategies?

Entrepreneurial Exercise 4.6

Part 1

What are your current plans and strategies for product distribution? How was this strategy arrived at?

Part 2

Please list the positive and potentially negative outcomes of your product distribution choices.

Positives	Potential Negatives

Entrepreneurial Exercise 4.7

Part 1

Discuss, in detail, the specific promotion strategies and tactics you plan to employ in the initial market entry phase of the business.

Part 2

How will each of these promotion components be integrated to achieve maximum market impact?

Part 3

How do you plan to employ social media in the promotion of your product and your firm?

Entrepreneurial Exercise 4.8

Part 1

What role, if any, will personal selling play as a component of your firm's marketing plan?

Part 2

Please list what you believe are the key characteristics of an ideal salesperson for your firm and its products.

5

THE FINANCIAL PLAN

Accountants are the witch doctors of the modern world and willing to turn their hands to any kind of magic.

Charles Eustace Harman (1894–1970), British judge

The pen is mightier than the sword, but no match for the accountant.

Jonathan Glancey

CHAPTER LEARNING OBJECTIVES

By the end of this chapter you will be able to

- Explain the components of an effective financial analysis
- Describe the different basic financial statements
- Create a sample breakeven analysis
- Summarize the results of a financial ratio analysis
- Compose a financial statement using the financial ratios and formulas

BY THE NUMBERS

After you determine the business model's possible viability and select what seem to be the most appropriate marketing strategies, your next step is to create the firm's financial plan. The financial plan serves two critical functions. First, it informs the entrepreneur about the financial health of the business, internally, and indicates specific financial problems.

Second, it communicates the firm's financial viability to potential investors and lenders, who will be keenly aware of financial documents and who will scrutinize them in depth before acting.

There is one almost universally true reality: potential investors and lenders will be highly skilled at reading and interpreting the financials of a proposed new venture. An entrepreneur must become aware of the investors' expectations in this section of the business plan. Investors may never be as knowledgeable about your product or service as you, but they are keenly aware of what the financials are telling them about the potential level of risk associated with your business venture, and about its potential profitability and financial viability. Consequently, the financial management section of the business plan must be as accurate and complete as possible. Investors expect that your business plan will include the following financial analyses and statements:

- An accurate assessment of the new venture's start-up expenses

- The "burn rate" of cash prior to the point at which cash from sales revenues covers cash flow

- An estimate of the time it will take to reach a "liquidity event" or a payback of the monies invested

- A pro forma balance sheet

- A pro forma income statement

- A breakeven analysis

- A financial ratio analysis

- A cash flow analysis

A venture's financial plan must provide evidence of a well-defined revenue model that shows the firm generating revenues that are adequate enough to produce a free cash flow and an acceptable level of profitability.

FINANCIAL ANALYSIS

Financial analysis needs to include an accurate determination of all start-up costs or expenses for the new venture, as well as an assessment of when financial breakeven is forecasted to occur. The specific nature of the proposed business venture clearly influences the amount of money that must be expended to get the business started. As an example, a proposed new product that is manufactured will normally require expenditures to design and produce a prototype for final commercialization and expenditures for the acquisition of production equipment, of a materials inventory, and of all the necessary office support equipment. Start-up costs also include other expenses, such as a cash reserve necessary to pay for rent, insurance, utilities, and, of course, employee compensation.

In contrast, a small retailer will need to lease a building, purchase needed fixtures and displays, and stock the shelves with inventory. The specific costs and expenses that your proposed business is likely to incur are identified by category, and the amounts needed are determined through research. **Figure 5.1** is a listing of possible generic costs or expenses that need to be determined in order to develop an accurate estimate of the firm's start-up cost. **Figure 5.2** allows the entrepreneur the opportunity to identify the specific months when each cost or expense will be due. These two exercises provide the entrepreneur the opportunity to develop a realistic view of the new business venture's initial and continuing expenses. Many firms quickly discover that large start-up expenses require the entrepreneur to raise disproportionally large amounts of cash to meet them. It is important to remember that undercapitalization is a significant cause of early-stage business failure. Accurately assessing your total start-up cost helps you avoid finding yourself unable to get your business off the ground in a timely manner because you are forced to find additional capital. Investors will feel deceived if you fail to meet your projected performance milestones because you lack the needed cash. In their view, your inability to estimate the start-up cost for the business accurately is a measure of your incompetence as an entrepreneur. Entrepreneurs often make unrealistically optimistic assumptions about the start-up expenses they will incur, and they can misjudge the timing of the receipt of sales revenues. Most experienced entrepreneurs recognize that, for these reasons, it is imperative to include a contingency factor when determining the start-up and revenue projections.

FIGURE 5.1 ■ Possible Start-Up Costs and Expenses	
Item or Category	**Estimated Costs or Expenses**
Lease or Rental Costs	
Costs of Production Equipment Costs of Office Equipment	
Facility Improvement Expenses	
Estimated Wages, Salaries, and Benefits	
Professional Expenses (legal, accounting, engineering, etc.)	
Marketing Expenses	
Regulatory Expenses (permits, licenses)	
Insurance Costs	
Estimated Utility Costs	
Estimated Tax Liabilities	
Interest Expenses on Outstanding Loans	
Costs of Inventories	
Association Membership Dues	
Contingency Expenses Allowance	
Other Costs Specific to Firm or Industry	

Consider a new venture that will require a number of months to move from its operational prototype to a fully functional commercial product. Businesses often face an extended time period prior to a product's ability to be marketed and earn revenues, making it crucial for the entrepreneur to assess these extended expenses carefully. The firm's "burn rate" of cash prior to revenue generation will be addressed in greater detail later in this chapter in a discussion of the firm's "valley of death." Additionally, in the next

FIGURE 5.2 ■ Expenses Due Each Month for the First Six Months of the Firm's Start Up						
Items or Categories	**Months**					
	1	2	3	4	5	6
Fixed Expenses						
Equipment Expenses Facility Improvements						
Office Furniture, Technology, Equipment						
Variable Expenses						
Rent Lease Payment						
Wages, Salaries, Benefits						
Professional Services						
Marketing Expenses						
Utilities						
Insurance						
Taxes						
Government Expenses						
Inventories						
Interest Expenses						
Other Costs Specific to Firm or Industry						
Basic Financial Statements	$	$	$	$	$	$

chapter that deals with cash flow management, the operational realities of a deep "valley of death" will be examined.

Investors are reasonably concerned about the risk involved in firms with extensive "up-front" expenses and a "burn rate" on capital that significantly extends the time before revenues are being earned. Entrepreneurs will need to display a financial management plan that addresses these investor concerns.

The payback period is the length of time your financial analysis indicates it will take your business to generate cash, derived from sales revenue, to cover all expenses incurred in starting the new venture. The following formula is a crude measure of the payback period:

Payback Period

$$\text{Payback} = \frac{\text{Startup Expenses}}{\text{Net Cash Flow per Month}}$$

This formula becomes more complex when the investments are made in multiple stages or tranches (securities that can be split into smaller pieces and sold to investors). It is very common for investors to require the entrepreneur to accomplish specific performance targets prior to receiving additional funding. Consequently, the new venture's financial plan is linked to the entrepreneur's ability to demonstrate performance. Quickly, the entrepreneur recognizes that the firm's financial forecast must be accurate because the initial investment must be adequate to support the expenses linked to the achievement of the specified performance outcomes. It is critical to remember that, as the entrepreneur, you are making a commitment to the investors—you will employ their money in an efficient manner that results in meeting the promised performance targets or milestones. In future chapters, we will investigate how investors actually value a new venture.

BASIC FINANCIAL STATEMENTS

When the business is created, there are no existing financial statements or reports. Consequently, the entrepreneur will be required to create what are termed "pro forma" or projected financial statements. One of those important financial statements is the balance sheet.

Balance Sheet

The balance sheet is based on what is commonly termed the *accounting equation*:

Assets = Liabilities + Owners Equity (or net worth)

The term balance sheet is used because this equation must always balance. Any increase or decrease on one side of the equation must be offset by an equal increase or decrease on the other side. The left side of the balance sheet includes a list of all the firm's assets, which are everything that the business owns. Assets themselves are categorized as current, fixed, or intangible. Current assets consist of cash or items that can be converted into cash within one year or within the normal operating cycle of the business. Other current assets would include items such as inventories and accounts receivable. Fixed assets are comprised of items such as land, buildings, equipment, and furniture. As the name implies, fixed assets are long-term assets. Intangible assets include items that are valuable but not tangible. These assets would include items such as intellectual property in the form of patents and copyrights, as well as goodwill. The second section of the balance sheet lists the firm's liabilities. Liabilities are creditors' claims against the firm's assets. Current liabilities are the debts that must be paid within one year or within the normal operating cycle of the business. Current liabilities are items such as accounts payable and accrued wages and salaries. Long-term liabilities are the debts that come due after one year. Examples of long-term liabilities include notes payable or a mortgage. The third section of the balance sheet includes what is termed *owner's equity*, or the financial value of the owner's investment in the business. This section is also termed the firm's *net worth*.

Income Statement

The income statement, also known as a profit and loss statement, is designed to determine if the business earned a profit or possibly experienced a loss. The income statement begins with the firm's sales revenue and then deducts the operational costs not related to the capital investment during that period to determine whether there is a profit or loss. Income statements can be produced monthly, quarterly, or yearly. The income statement follows the activity of the firm over the period in question. This is the financial statement that produces what investors term *the bottom line*, or the record of net profit or loss that is the final residual of activity, which *is* found at the bottom of the income statement. Net income or loss is calculated through a series of deductions or subtractions beginning from the "top line," which shows the sales revenue. From this sales revenue are deducted returns and allowances for bad debts to obtain the *net sales revenue*. Deducted from net sales revenue is the cost of the goods sold, which is calculated in a series of steps: First, add the firm's beginning inventory and the value of all purchases made during the period in question, which gives the value of the goods available for sale. From the value of goods available is deducted the firm's ending inventory for that period. The result is termed the *cost of goods sold*. In order to determine the firm's gross profit, the cost of goods sold is deducted from the net sales revenue. Often the result is divided by the firm's net sale revenue to determine the percentage gross profit margin. The next step is to reduce the gross profit figure by all items that are identified as operating expenses and general administrative expenses. Operating expenses are the expenses that contribute directly to the manufacturing, marketing, and distribution of the product. General expenses will also be deducted from the gross profit number, as these expenses exist as part of the ongoing business. These expenses are unrelated to the product and exist even if no production takes place. They are indirect costs that are incurred in operating the business. Here is the process outlined:

Net Sales Revenue − Cost of Goods sold = Gross Profit

Gross Profit − Operating Expenses + General Expenses

= Net Income (or Loss)

Cash Flow Statement

The third essential financial statement for any business is the statement of cash flow. Cash flow management is so absolutely critical to the survival of new ventures that a separate chapter will be dedicated to its study. The statement of cash flows illustrates and highlights the changes in the firm's working capital that take place typically on a month-by-month basis. The statement of cash flow tracks both the sources of funds and the uses of funds. The sources of funds are net income, borrowed funds, owner's contributions, depreciation, and a few others. Depreciation is listed as a source of funds because it is a noncash expense that is deducted as a cost of doing business. Since the owner has already paid for the item being depreciated, it is depreciation in a source of funds. The uses of funds would include items such as the purchase of a plant and equipment, the repayment of debt, the dividends paid to investors, and so on. The difference between the total sources of funds and their uses is either an increase or decrease in the firm's working capital. Working capital equals current assets less current liabilities. The entrepreneur must watch carefully the changes in working capital because, without adequate cash to meet its liabilities, the firm may be forced into bankruptcy. Experienced entrepreneurs often use the phrase, "Cash is king"; they know that only cash can be used to meet financial obligations so that a firm remains solvent. Cash is king because you can only pay your liabilities with cash, not profits.

BREAKEVEN ANALYSIS AND THE PRO FORMA FINANCIAL STATEMENT

Breakeven Analysis

Breakeven analysis is conducted based on the new firm's start-up cost and the projected monthly expenses and projected revenues. These initial expenses are very often underestimated. Legal fees, building or office leases, equipment, inventories, supplies, licenses, tools, utilities, and initial staffing costs comprise a significant initial investment. In addition, the entrepreneur must normally maintain a capital reserve large enough to carry the business until revenues are sufficient to reach the point of breaking even. An effective financial analysis must identify, based on revenue and cost projections, how long it will take to reach breakeven, as well as how much money will be needed until that point is reached. This financial analysis is essential in assuring that the new venture has the capital that will be required to survive. The breakeven point is the level of operations at which a business neither makes a profit nor incurs a loss. When sales revenues equal expenses, the firm breaks even. By conducting a thorough and in-depth analysis of cost and expenses, the entrepreneur can estimate the minimum level of business activity required to keep the firm operating. These techniques can then be refined to project the sales revenues needed to generate the desired profit.

Constructing a breakeven analysis begins with determining which anticipated costs are fixed and which are variable in nature. Fixed expenses are those that do not vary with changes in the volume of sales or production. Examples would be rent and interest payments. Variable expenses vary directly with changes in the volume of production or sales.

Examples would be sales commissions and raw materials cost. To proceed, the entrepreneur uses the projected budget to estimate both the sales revenues and costs, which, as mentioned, are allocated based on whether they are fixed or variable. Next, the ratio of variable expenses to projected net sales is used to determine what percentage of every dollar of sales it takes to cover the variable expenses. What remains is the percentage of sales available to pay for fixed expenses. This portion of the sales revenue is called the *contribution margin*. The breakeven point, then, is determined by the following formula:

$$\text{Breakeven Sales} = \frac{\text{Fixed Expenses}}{\text{Contribution Margin}}$$

The entrepreneur can analyze the results of the breakeven calculation to assess if the contribution margin is sufficient to achieve the breakeven point in a reasonable time based on the projected sales forecast calculated in months. The longer it takes to produce sufficient sales volume to achieve the breakeven point the greater the firm's financial risk. Another analytical tool that can help the entrepreneur visualize this situation is termed "the valley of death."

When the new venture begins, its sales are normally far from adequate to cover expenses. Consequently, cash flow is negative and continues that way until the sales volume increases to the point at which sales revenues are sufficient to generate a positive cash flow. In **Figure 5.3**, that is point X. The entrepreneur must recognize that point X in this model is *not* the breakeven point. That point would not accrue financially until the negative cash flow experienced in area A is replaced by the positive cash flow experienced in area B. The firm's cash flow breakeven point is at point Z. (At point Z, positive cash flow equals the negative cash flow that occurred during the firm's initial operations.) What is critical for the entrepreneur to recognize and calculate is the length of time it will take for a firm to become financially solvent. The deeper the "valley" the higher the financial risk. In reality, what is happening is that expenses continue to accrue without any corresponding revenues for a considerable

FIGURE 5.3 ■ Valley of Death

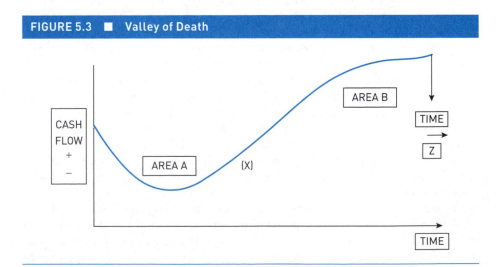

length of time. Much of the initial invested capital is placed at risk. Both the cash flow and the investment risk vary according to the type of new venture. For a retail business with a solid business model, the critical elements may be achieved in a matter of months, whereas a sophisticated technology-based new venture may take years to gain a foothold in its market niche and achieve sufficient sales. Investors are always concerned when the "valley of death" model indicates that the new firm's breakeven point is far into the future. The deeper the "valley" (i.e., the more negative the cash flow) and the broader the "valley" (i.e., the longer to breakeven), the riskier the business model is.

Analytical financial models serve to provide the entrepreneur with powerful evidence of the financial viability of a proposed business. Investors understand financial models and financial statements. They expect these models and statements to be accurate and realistic. All aspects of this early-stage "financial analysis" serve to determine accurately the total capital needed to achieve success. As mentioned previously, one of the greatest causes of new venture failure is inadequate capital.

Pro Forma Income Statement

When a new venture is seeking external funding, it will not have historic financial statements, so its accountants will need to develop projected financial statements. These projected financial statements are termed *pro forma statements*. The new venture's pro forma statements are based on a detailed budget for the business that would include all projections of revenue, cost, and expenses. Creating projected financial statements via the budgeting process allows the entrepreneur to answer critical questions such as this: Based on revenue and expense projections, can we anticipate what the firm's profits will be? The new venture produces pro forma financial statements that estimate the profitability and overall financial condition of the business over its first year of operation. Without historic financial statements to work from, the entrepreneur needs to use available financial data from sources such as the Risk Management Association's Annual Statement Studies®, which provide the entrepreneur with compiled financial data on thousands of firms broken down by industry and size.[1]

The creation of a pro forma income statement can be achieved by either a "top-down" or "bottom-up" method. The "top-down" method begins by the entrepreneur using the sales forecast developed in the firm's budget and then subtracting all forecasted costs and expenses until the profit or loss is determined. The "bottom-up" method is developed based on the entrepreneur's targeted net profit. The "bottom-up" method is most popular when the entrepreneur sets a net profit target and seeks to determine the volume of revenue that must be achieved to earn the targeted net income. A pro forma budget can also be employed to estimate the fixed and variable expenses. Again, the entrepreneur searches for objective data published by trade associations or the Risk Management Association (RMA) to determine what is the average net profit margin for a business of a similar type and size in this industry that entrepreneur wants to enter.

If the entrepreneur wishes to be able to earn $100,000 per year based on his or her invested capital and with an average profit margin of about 10%, determined from a reliable source, the following formula would be used to determine the necessary sales to meet the desired net profit:

$$\text{Net Profit Margin} = \frac{\text{Net Profit}}{\text{Net Sales}}$$

OR

$$\text{Net Sales} = \frac{\text{Net Profit}}{\text{Net Profit Margin}}$$

IN OUR EXAMPLE:

$$\text{Net Profit Margin of } 10\% = \frac{\text{Net Profit of } \$100,000}{\text{Net Sales}}$$

$$\text{Net Sales} = \frac{\$100,000}{10\%}$$

$$\text{Net Sales} = \$1,000,000$$

The remainder of the pro forma income statement can be constructed by again employing the industry- and size-specific statistics from a reliable and accurate source. In our example, the next financial calculation is the firm's cost of goods sold. Based on the appropriate statistics, the firm's estimated cost of goods sold will be 70% of net sales, or $700,000. Subtracting the $700,000 cost of goods sold from the $1,000,000 in net sales produces a gross profit of $300,000:

Net Sales	= $1,000,000	100%
Cost of Goods Sold	= $700,000	70%
Gross Profit	= $300,000	30% (Gross Profit Margin)

For the sake of simplicity, the firm's total additional operating expenses of $200,000 (20% of net sales) can be subtracted from the gross profit to produce a net profit of $100,000:

Gross Profit	= $300,000
Operating Expenses	= $200,000
Net Profit	= $100,000

The next logical step that must be taken is to evaluate, as objectively as possible, whether the firm's sales projections are dependable, logical, and realistic. In our example, $1,000,000 in annual net sales would require the new firm to sell, on average, $83,334 in products or services each month. Can the firm's targeted sales be achieved after considering the forecasted economic situation, potential competitor responses, industry-specific business cycles, and seasonal sales cycles? The entrepreneur should expect that any sophisticated investor will ask to see the firm's marketing plan in order to determine whether the monthly sales projections are realistic.

The pro forma income statement allows for an objective examination of the major financial components of the proposed business. It is important to evaluate the financial consequences of failing to meet the sales projections. Consider how failing to meet the sales projections would impact cash flow and the depth of the "valley of death."

Pro Forma Balance Sheet

The pro forma balance sheet sets out the firm's projected assets and liabilities. One critical issue is the amount of liquid assets that the business will need to meet its liabilities. The pro forma statement of assets includes the estimated requirements for cash, inventories, and fixed assets. Cash is absolutely essential, as discussed earlier in this chapter. A new business normally needs to have a cash balance sufficient to cover all operating expenses for at least one inventory turnover period. Cash needs to be adequate to cover expenses until accounts receivable are collected. When inventory is both expensive and slow to sell, there can be a lengthy time between when cash must be expended to pay suppliers and when the firm collects accounts receivable from sales. Fixed assets support the operations of the business and include such items as land, buildings, equipment, tools, and fixtures. Some of the fixed assets can be leased, but others must be owned. Fixed assets must be accounted for in the determination of the firm's start-up cost.

Figure 5.4 and **5.5** are examples of financial tools that serve to guide the entrepreneur in the estimation of monthly and start-up expenses and that assist in the construction of the pro forma balance sheet and income statement. They have been completed with projections from an imaginary new start-up business, Digital Dynamics, that is looking for investors.

FIGURE 5.4 ■ Balance Sheet—Digital Dynamics, Inc.

	ASSETS	
	calculations	results
Current Assets		
Cash		$300,000
Accounts Receivable (Less) Allowance for Bad Debts	$160,000 ($10,000)	$150,000
Inventory		$440,000
Prepaid Expenses		$10,000
Total Current Assets		**$900,000**
Fixed Assets		
Land		$200,000
Building (Less) Accumulated Depreciation	$320,000 ($20,000)	$300,000
Equipment (Less) Accumulated Depreciation	$210,000 ($10,000)	$200,000

(Continued)

(Continued)

	ASSETS	
	calculations	results
Furniture and Fixtures (Less) Accumulated Depreciation	$105,000 ($5,000)	$100,000
Total Fixed Assets		**$800,000**
Intangible Assets		
Patent		**$100,000**
TOTAL ASSETS		**$1,800,000**
		LIABILITIES
Current Liabilities		
Accounts Payable		$300,000
Short-Term Notes Payable		$150,000
Accrued Wages/Salaries Payable		$200,000
Accrued Interest Payable		$10,000
Accrued Taxes Payable		$90,000
Total Current Liabilities		**$750,000**
Long-Term Liabilities		
Mortgage		$400,000
Long-Term Payables		$350,000
Total Long-Term Liabilities		**$750,000**
TOTAL LIABILITIES		**$1,500,000**
Owner's Equity		
Common Stock		$300,000
TOTAL LIABILITIES AND OWNER'S EQUITY		**$1,800,000**

FINANCIAL RATIO ANALYSIS

Financial ratios offer feedback on how well a business is operating. They are, in effect, a financial early-warning system that detects emerging financial or operational problems so that the entrepreneur can take corrective actions. Thus, they enable financial management to become an ongoing and responsive process that positively influences decision making.

FIGURE 5.5 ■ Income Statement—Digital Dynamics, Inc.		
Net Sales Revenue		$4,000,000
Cost of Goods Sold		
Beginning Inventory Purchases	$2,100,000 $900,000	
Cost of Goods Available for Sale	$3,000,000	
(Less) Ending Inventory	($1,800,000)	
Total Cost of Goods Sold	$1,200,000	
Gross Profit Margin		$2,800,000
Operating Expenses		
Marketing and Advertising	$185,000	
Depreciation	$35,000	
Wages and Salaries	$440,000	
Travel	$50,000	
Entertainment	$30,000	
Insurance	$20,000	
Total Operating Expenses		$760,000
General Expenses		
Payroll Taxes	$15,000	
Utilities	$15,000	
Telephone	$20,000	
Postage, UPS, and Fed Ex	$40,000	
Total General Expenses		$ 90,000
Total Expenses		$ 850,000
Net Income		$ 1,950,000

Financial ratio analysis is also a form of financial control, allowing the entrepreneur to take the financial pulse of the business and guide it toward health. Financial ratio analysis can detect problems such as these:

- Declining sales
- Falling profit margins

- Increasing overhead expenses
- Growing levels of unsold inventories
- Unpaid and rising levels of accounts receivable

Ratio analysis is a method of expressing the relationship between two accounting elements, so it is a convenient analytical technique. These comparisons allow the entrepreneur to determine if the firm is carrying excessive inventory, experiencing disproportionally high operating expenses, has overextended credit, or is currently managing its debt payments properly, for example. As stated previously, tracking these ratios and responding to the "red flags" that indicate problems is essential to successful financial management.

There are twelve key financial ratios that should be evaluated on a regular basis. These twelve ratios are categorized in four major groups: liquidity ratios, leverage ratios, operating ratios, and profitability ratios. Liquidity ratios indicate whether the business is able to meet its maturing obligations as they come due. There are two measures of liquidity: the current ratio and the quick ratio.

ENTREPRENEURIAL SPOTLIGHT
BRAYTON WILLIAMS—BOOST VC

Brayton Williams cofounded Boost VC with Adam Draper in 2012. Boost is a technology accelerator that offers pre-seed venture capital funding. Boost has been exceptionally active and aggressive, investing in more than 75 blockchain companies and more than 60 virtual reality and augmented reality companies. Indeed, since its beginning in 2012, Boost VC has invested in more than 200 start-ups from over 30 countries, and the Boost portfolio has been able to attract $1 billion in follow-up investments. Boost VC is attracted to what Brayton calls "sci-fi" tech companies, and it divides its start-up investments into three sectors: virtual reality, blockchain, and "wild cards." In the virtual reality sector, Boost VC has invested in Mindshow, Kite & Lighting, Boom, Fearless, Alta, and Jump. In the blockchain sector, the following firms are benefactors of Boost investments: Aragon, Wyre, Etherscan, and Ripio. In the wildcard sector are Favor, Pillow, Kubos, Blockscore, Cobalt, and Mothership, for example.

Each year, Boost VC runs accelerator programs. The company invests up to $500,000 in exchange for 7% equity in the business. Boost offers the companies it invests in a physical place in which to live and work, an introduction to Boost's extensive network of technology firms, and advisors. Boost is committed to assisting these accelerator companies with the tools they need to succeed.

The most difficult financial capital to attract is what is termed "seed capital," as this sort of investment carries absolutely the highest risk. Boost VC is a unique venture capital firm blending an accelerator program and seed funding.

Sources:

1. "Profile: Brayton Williams," *Forbes*, accessed June 2018, https://www.forbes.com/profile/brayton-williams/.

2. "About," Boost VC website, accessed June 2018, https://www.boost.vc/about/.

3. "Companies," Boost VC website, accessed June 2018, https://www.boost.vc/companies/.

Liquidity Ratios

Current Ratio

The current ratio measures the firm's solvency by indicating its ability to pay current debts and liabilities from current assets. Here is the formula:

$$\text{Current Ratio} = \frac{\text{Current Assets}}{\text{Current Liabilities}}$$

Current assets are those that are capable of being converted into cash in the ordinary business cycle. Current assets are comprised of cash, notes receivable, accounts receivable, inventory, and short-term marketable securities. Current liabilities include short-term obligations that are scheduled to come due within a year. Examples are short-term notes, accounts payable, and taxes payable. The current ratio is the most commonly used measure of short-term solvency. The higher the firm's current ratio is the stronger its financial solvency and the greater its ability to cover short-term liabilities. One critical issue that needs to be addressed is the actual value of the firm's inventories. If the inventories are old and not necessarily saleable, their value may be overstated. The normal acceptable current ratio is 2:1. Current assets should be twice as large as current liabilities.

Quick Ratio

The quick ratio, often termed the *acid ratio*, is a much more conservative measure of a firm's liquidity. Quick assets are limited to cash, readily marketable securities, short-term notes receivable, and accounts receivable. This ratio excludes inventories, which may not be convertible into cash quickly. The quick ratio is calculated as follows:

$$\text{Quick Ratio} = \frac{\text{Quick Assets}}{\text{Current Liabilities}}$$

The normally acceptable quick ratio is 1:1. This is the most vigorous test of the firm's liquidity.

Leverage Ratios

Leverage ratios measure the financing supplied by the investors compared against that supplied by its creditors. These ratios are a gauge of the depth of the firm's debt. Leverage ratios highlight the extent to which an entrepreneur relies on debt capital to finance the firm's operations, and they also indicate whether capital growth is needed. When a firm is financed by debt capital, the entrepreneur's risk is higher as the holder of the debt can drive the venture into bankruptcy if not repaid as specified in the loan. Thus, leverage ratios, in effect, measure the degree of financial risk undertaken by the firm. When the firm's debt is disproportionably high relative to the investor's capital, an economic downturn can weaken the firm's financial stability because the firm will have difficulty paying the interest on debt. Correspondingly, when the firm is experiencing high levels of growth, lower debt will result in a higher return on equity. In other words, if an entrepreneur is able to get the business started with less capital from investors, he or she has retained a high ownership position in the business and therefore will have a higher return on invested equity. Leverage ratios include the debt ratio, the debt to net worth ratio, and the times interest earned ratio.

Debt Ratio

The debt ratio measures the percentage of total assets financed by the firm's creditors. The debt ratio is calculated in this way:

$$\text{Debt Ratio} = \frac{\text{Total Debt}}{\text{Total Assets}}$$

Total debt includes all current liabilities and any outstanding long-term notes and bonds. Total assets represent the sum of the firm's current assets, fixed assets, and intangible assets. A high debt ratio indicates that the creditors provide a large percentage of the firm's total financing. Entrepreneurs do tend to prefer using creditors' money to generate profits. However, they must be careful not to allow this ratio to get unbalanced in favor of excessive debt financing. If it does and additional funds are needed to address a financial problem, lenders are likely to be unwilling to lend, fearing that the firm already has excessive debt and the business might be unable to repay further loans.

Debt to Net Worth Ratio

The debt to net worth ratio also serves to express the relationship between the capital contributions from creditors and those from the firm's owners. This ratio compares what the business "owes" to "what it owns." It is again a measure of the firm's ability to meet its obligations to creditors and owners in case of business failure and liquidation. The debt to net worth ratio is calculated as follows:

$$\text{Debt to Net Worth} = \frac{\text{Total Debt}}{\text{Tangible Net Worth}}$$

Total debt is the sum of current and long-term liabilities. Tangible net worth is the owner's investment in the business less any intangible assets. The higher this ratio, the lower the degree of protection afforded to creditors if the business fails. A high debt to net worth ratio reduces the attractiveness of the firm to new sources of investment. A point of balance would be a ratio of 1:1, at which both creditors and owners have an equal position.

Times Interest Earned Ratio

The times interest earned ratio measures the firm's ability to make the interest payments on its debt. This ratio indicates how many times the firm's earnings are capable of paying the interest that is due on its debt. The times interest earned ratio is calculated as follows:

$$\text{Times Interest Earned} = \frac{\text{Earnings Before Interest and Taxes}}{\text{Total Interest Expenses}}$$

A high ratio would indicate that the firm would have very little difficulty being able to meet its interest payments on its outstanding loans. Potential lenders prefer firms with a 4:1 or higher times interest earned ratio. Debt in itself is not bad. In fact, when used carefully, debt allows a business to grow and reach levels of success that it might not have been able to obtain based on the internal reinvestment of earnings. Debt can become a destroyer of business, though, when interest payments become so large that a considerable proportion of the firm's earnings must be used to meet the loan payments, so insufficient monies exist to meet the firm's operational needs. Competitive advantage can be lost quickly due to the firm's inability to invest in the assets it needs to meet increasing market demands.

Operating Ratios

Operating ratios are analytical tools that provide the entrepreneur with an evaluation of the effectiveness of the operations of the business. The more effectively the firm uses its resources the higher the probability that it will meet profit objectives and generate internal capital for reinvestment. There are five key operating ratios: the average inventory turnover ratio, the average collection period ratio, the net sales to total assets ratio, the average payable period, and the net sales to working capital ratio.

23andMe

Seizing on the unmet desire of consumers to know more about their genetic heritage and their possible propensity for developing chronic diseases because of that heritage, founders Anne Wojcicki, Linda Avery, and Paul Cusenza began 23andMe in 2006. The company, which is named for the 23 pairs of chromosomes found in the human genome, began as a genetic testing service for individuals concerned about their risk for developing certain diseases, including Alzheimer's and Parkinson's. In 2013, the FDA put a hold on approving the company's health-related, direct-to-consumer genetic testing service, so 23andMe was selling only raw genetic data and ancestry-related results. By 2017, the FDA had authorized 23andMe to market genetic reports on personal risks for 10 conditions. 23andMe has now pivoted its business model to provide direct-to-customer information on what DNA says about a client's traits (e.g., hair loss), path to wellness (e.g., the impact of different healthy eating habits on weight), and ancestry, as well as providing information on whether a client is a carrier for certain inherited conditions or has an increased risk for certain diseases. The company has become a disruptive, low-cost service provider to consumers and has a 2018 market valuation of $1.8 billion (according to PitchBook).

Source:

1. See the pages titled "About Us" and "Health and Ancestry Service" from the company website: https://www.23andme.com/.

2. "23andMe, Inc. Granted First FDA Authorization to Market Direct-to-Consumer Genetic Health Risk Reports," *23andMe Newsroom*, April 6, 2017, https://mediacenter.23andme.com/press-releases/23andme-inc-granted-first-fda-authorization-market-direct-consumer-genetic-health-risk-reports/.

3. "23andMe: A Genetics House Call," *CNBC*, May 22, 2018, https://www.cnbc.com/2018/05/22/23andme-2018-disruptor-50.html.

Average Inventory Turnover Ratio

This critical ratio measures the firm's ability to sell its inventory (turn the inventory over). It is a measure of the number of times during an accounting period that the average inventory is sold. An acceptable inventory turnover ratio is very industry specific. As an example, a successful grocery store has high inventory turnover, whereas a furniture store's inventory turnover would be dramatically lower. The average inventory turnover ratio is a critical measure of the firm's management of its inventory. Inventory is almost always the largest component of a business's current assets, and its sale is the source of the firm's revenue. The average inventory turnover ratio is calculated as follows:

$$\text{Average Inventory Turnover} = \frac{\text{Cost of Goods Sold}}{\text{Average Inventory}}$$

This ratio indicates how fast the merchandise is moving through the business. The entrepreneur can further calculate the average inventory turnover ratio into the number of days in the accounting period. The result is termed *days' sales in inventory*. For example, imagine that the annual cost of goods sold in a year is $800,000 and that the average inventory value is $100,000. That would mean that, over the course of one year, you turned inventory over 8 times. You could further estimate the average number of days in this period that it took you to turn over inventory (365 days / 8 = 45.6). The better-managed businesses have an average inventory turnover that is higher than the industry's average. This is an objective measure that the firm's inventory is highly saleable and most likely supported by a sound pricing strategy. In contrast, low average inventory turnover in comparison to the industry's standard suggests a serious operational problem that may stem from stable or obsolete inventory or a poorly designed pricing strategy. The ability to sell a firm's inventory is always a critical factor in the firm's profitability and survival.

Sometimes, a firm's average inventory turnover ratio can be misleading. For example, a serious shortage of inventory due to errors in ordering and subsequently "stock outs" would present as a high average inventory turnover ratio. The cause could be an inefficient ordering system. Also, when sales are very seasonal, the ratio might suggest that turnover is too low, whereas what is actually taking place is good planning—the buildup of inventory purchased in bulk at a deep discount in preparation for the high-sales season. Financial analysts suggest that a favorable inventory turnover ratio depends on the type of business, the durability of its products, its size, its profitability, its method of inventory valuation, and other relevant factors.

Average Collection Period Ratio

This ratio informs the entrepreneur of the number of days the business takes to collect its accounts receivables. Accounts receivables are monies owed to the business but not yet collected. To evaluate the firm's management efficiency, you would compare this ratio to the industry's average, as well as to the firm's credit terms. This ratio requires a two-stage calculation. First, the receivable turnover ratio must be determined. That number is then used as the denominator in calculating the average collection period ratio.

$$\text{Receivables Turnover} = \frac{\text{Credit Sales}}{\text{Accounts Receivable}}$$

$$\text{Average Collection Period} = \frac{\text{Days in the Accounting Period}}{\text{Receivable Turnover Ratio}}$$

If the firm's credit terms are net 30 days, the buyer is required to pay for purchases in 30 days or less. When the average collection period extends a significant number of days beyond the allowed 30 days, the entrepreneur may be facing a variety of operational problems. First, the business may have failed to conduct a credit check on its customers to determine their credit worthiness. A proactive policy of verifying the credit history of each customer can help the firm avoid selling to customers who have a "track record" of not meeting their financial obligations. In many cases, the problem stems from a lax collection policy. The entrepreneur does not aggressively implement the terms of the sales contract. The firm's staff might not attempt to collect the outstanding accounts payable for many days past their due date. Once the customers recognize that little serious effort is being made to collect what they owe, some, not all, will take advantage of this lax behavior. Effective entrepreneurs set reasonable credit terms, often following industry norms, but strictly enforce the collection of all accounts payable. All entrepreneurs must aggressively implement a policy to collect what is owed their firms, or they undertake the role of financing customers through a lax, and expensive, credit policy. A striking number of entrepreneurs find it necessary to borrow money to operate while failing to collect efficiently the money owed to them.

Net Sales to Total Assets Ratio

This ratio, often termed the *total asset turnover ratio*, is a general measure of a firm's ability to generate sales in relation to its assets. It is a measure of the productivity of the business in the employment of its assets to produce sales revenue. The net sales to total assets ratio is calculated as follows:

$$\text{Net Sales to Total Assets} = \frac{\text{Net Sales}}{\text{Total Assets}}$$

This ratio is meaningful when it is compared to that of other firms of similar size in the same industry.

Net Sales to Working Capital Ratio

This ratio measures how many dollars in sales the business earns for every dollar in working capital. It is a measure of working capital efficiency. The net sales to working capital ratio is calculated as follows:

$$\text{Net Sales to Working Capital} = \frac{\text{Net Sales}}{\text{Working Capital}}$$

If this ratio is excessively low in comparison to those of similarly sized firms in the industry, the firm is failing to employ its working capital efficiently. In contrast, a ratio that is extremely high indicates an inadequate level of working capital to maintain a suitable level of sales. Growth is dependent on achieving an acceptable level of working capital. The net sales to working capital ratio serves to define the level of working capital required to support a higher sales volume.

Profitability Ratios

The two ratios comprising this final group are the ones most often used in discussing the competencies of management. These ratios provide a measure of the success of the business.

Net Profit on Sales Ratio

This ratio is often termed the firm's profit margin. The net profit on sales ratio is used to compute the percentage of the firm's sales that remain after all expenses and taxes. The profit margin is calculated as follows:

$$\text{Net Profit on Sales} = \frac{\text{Net Profit}}{\text{Net Sales Revenue}}$$

To evaluate this ratio meaningfully, the entrepreneur must consider the firm's asset value, its inventory and receivables turnover ratios, and its total capitalization. If a business has a low profit margin on sales but its inventory turnover is high, it may be capable of generating a competitive profit. As you can imagine, profit margins vary depending on the nature of the industry.

Net Profit to Equity Ratio

This ratio is also termed the *return on net worth ratio* and measures the owner's rate of return on investments. This is the most quoted financial ratio because it reports the firm's profitability and managerial effectiveness. The net profit to equity ratio is calculated as follows:

$$\text{Net Profit to Equity} = \frac{\text{Net Profit}}{\text{Owner's Equity (or Net Worth)}}$$

This ratio compares profits earned during the accounting period with the amount the entrepreneur and equity investors have invested in the business during that time. It could be considered the rate of return earned on the owner's investment.

The results of all of these critical ratios provide the entrepreneur with a performance scorecard that will assist in "fine tuning" the business. The entrepreneur strives to keep the ratios on the positive side of the model. Studying these ratios guides the entrepreneur to the sources of operational problems so that corrective actions can be implemented.

Figure 5.6 gives the results of a ratio analysis conducted on Digital Dynamics, Inc., whose pro forma balance sheet and income statement were presented earlier in the chapter.

FIGURE 5.6 ■ Ratio Analysis— Digital Dynamics, Inc.			
Ratio	**Formula**	**Calculation**	
Current Ratio =	Current Assets / Current Liabilities	$900,000 / $750,000	1.2
Quick Ratio =	Quick Assets / Current Liabilities	$460,000 / $750,000	.61
Debt Ratio =	Total Debt or Liabilities / Total Assets	$1,500,000 / $1,800,000	.83
Debt to Net Worth Ratio =	Total Debt or Liabilities / Tangible Net Worth	$1,500,000 / $300,000	5.0
Times Interest Earned =	Earnings Before Interest and Taxes / Total Interest Expenses	$1,950,000 / $10,000	195
Average Inventory Turnover =	Cost of Goods Sold / Average Inventory (AI) (AI = BI + EI / 2)	$1,200,000 / $1,950,000 (AI = $2,100,000 + $1,800,000 / 2)	.61
Receivables Turnover Ratio =	Credit Sales / Accounts Receivable	$400,000 / $150,000	2.66
Average Collection Period Ratio =	Days in Accounting Period / Receivables Ratio	365 / 2.66	137.2
Payable Turnover Ratio =	Purchases / Accounting Payable	$900,000 / $300,000	3
Average Payable Period Ratio =	Days in Accounting Period / Payable Turnover Ratio	365 / 3	121.6
Net Sales to Total Assets Ratio =	Net Sales / Total Assets	$4,000,000 / $1,800,000	2.22
Net Sales to Working Capital Ratio =	Net Sales / Working Capital (WC) (WC=CA–CL)	$4,000,000 / $150,000 (WC = $900,000 –$750,000)	26.6%
Net Profit on Sales Ratio =	Net Profit / Net Sales Revenue	$1,950,000 / $4,000,000	.48
Net Profit to Equity Ratio =	Net Profit / Owner's Equity (Net Worth)	$1,950,000 / $300,000	650%

CONCLUSION

Every entrepreneur needs to ensure that her or his financial plan is realistic, accurate, and provides the tools to enable the effective management of financial assets. When you seek investor financing, it is absolutely imperative to have "done your homework" on the financials. Investors will always inspect the financial statements and study your financial analysis in an attempt to evaluate the financial feasibility of your proposed business venture.

ENTREPRENEURIAL EXERCISES

Entrepreneurial Exercise 5.1

Start-Up Cost Estimate

Based on your proposed new business venture, please create a detailed list of all anticipated start-up costs:

Specific Item or Cost Category

1.	$
2.	
3.	
4.	
5.	
6.	
7.	
8.	
9.	
10.	
11.	
12.	
13.	
14.	
15.	
16.	
17.	
18.	
Total Estimated Start-Up Cost	$

Entrepreneurial Exercise 5.2

Six-Month Expense Projection

Once your proposed new business has started, when will the expenses of operating it actually occur? Some may be monthly, others quarterly.

Projected Expense Due Each Month	Months					
	1	2	3	4	5	6
I. Fixed Expenses						
1.						
2.						
3.						
4.						

II. Variable Expenses						
1.						
2.						
3.						
4.						
5.						
6.						
7.						
8.						
9.						
10.						
Total Estimated Monthly Expenses	$	$	$	$	$	$

Entrepreneurial Exercise 5.3

Breakeven Analysis and the Valley of Death

Part I. Based on your proposed new business venture, please construct your breakeven analysis.

Part II. Based on the financial analysis you have conducted about your new business, please construct your firm's "valley of death" diagram.

Part III. Based on your breakeven analysis and the "valley of death" diagram, what do you conclude about the financial viability of your business model? **Please be as specific as possible.**

Entrepreneurial Exercise 5.4

Please use the models presented in **Figures 5.4** and **5.5** to create an accurate pro forma balance sheet and income statement for your proposed new business venture.

CASH FLOW MANAGEMENT

Happiness is a positive cash flow.

Fred Adler

The fact is that one of the earliest lessons I learned in business was that balance sheets and income statements are fiction, cash flow is reality.

Chris Chocola

CHAPTER LEARNING OBJECTIVES

Upon completion of this chapter you will be able to

Explain the difference between cash and profits

Describe the cash flow process

List the methods for screening applicants

Recall the elements of a sales contract

Appraise an invoice statement

Compose a sample accounts payable policy

Explain how business can avoid a cash crunch

CASH AND PROFITS ARE NOT THE SAME

An entrepreneur must always recognize that cash and profits are not the same. Profit is the net increase in capital cycled through the business during its operations. Profits are an essential measure of operational efficiency. Profit is the product of subtracting all costs and expenses from net revenues. These profits are normally reinvested in additional inventories, new equipment, and other items; this reinvestment allows the business to grow.

Creditors, lenders, and employees cannot be paid in profits, only in cash. Cash is the money that flows through business in a continuous cycle without being tied up in any other asset. A business that is showing a profit on its income statement can still fail if it does not have cash to meet its financial obligations. Decreases in cash occur when the business makes purchases of inventories, parts, or materials for production. As discussed previously, cash outflow is high for new business ventures at the beginning of the cash flow cycle: there will be purchases for inventory and payroll and production expenses, and these will always lead the cash inflow that comes from collecting receivables. The reality is that, on many occasions, a business grows at a rapid pace, and it expends all of its cash—paying employees, managers, suppliers, and creditors—until cash is completely expended and the business is no longer able to meet its financial obligations. Banks, the normal source for loans, are reluctant to provide additional financing in this circumstance because their managers will see the entrepreneur as incompetent for allowing this cash crisis to occur. Without additional cash, the firm cannot meet obligations to creditors. When this occurs, creditors can file an action with the courts to force the business into bankruptcy in an attempt to recover some of the money owed to them. The bottom line is always the same: Cash is king.

CASH FLOW PROCESS

Chapter 5 briefly discussed the need for every new business venture to have a statement of cash flow. Cash flow management is critical and involves tracking the sources and uses of funds on, normally, a monthly basis. Cash flow is the volume of cash that comes into and goes out of the business during an accounting period. Cash is decreased when the business makes purchases of raw material and parts and pays wages and salaries. When material and human resources are combined, the business produces goods, which are held in inventory.

Cash and accounts receivables are collected when the business sells the inventory and the firm's cash balance increases. **Figure 6.1** illustrates the cash flow process. Accounts payable along with wages and salaries typically represent cash that leaves the business well before sales are made and accounts receivables are collected.

The significance of this lag in the cash flow process is best understood by examining a simple cash flow cycle for a retailer, as presented in **Figure 6.2.** In this example, a retailer paid its supplier on day 45 but did not receive payment from its customer until day 235. The retailer's cash is gone for 190 days, or in excess of six months.

The extended cash flow cycle is a potential contributor to a cash crisis, so a cash flow forecast that presents the realities of this cash cycle is an analytical tool that may help the entrepreneur avoid a cash crisis. Also, a cash flow cycle analysis and a cash flow forecast will allow the entrepreneur to demonstrate to a lender why, especially during slow economic times, additional lending capacity will be needed. It is critical to make the case for additional lending capacity before the money is actually needed.

FIGURE 6.1 ■ Cash Flow Process

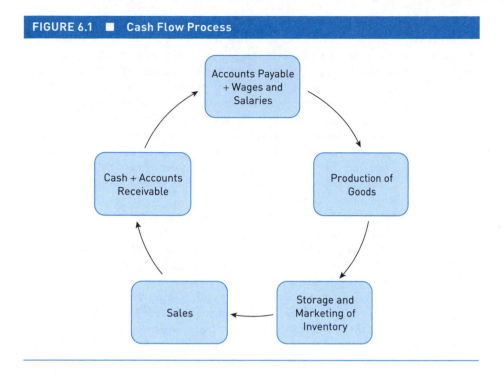

FIGURE 6.2 ■ Cash Flow Cycle

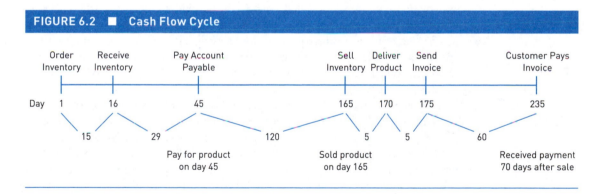

The Cash Budget

A firm's cash budget is the analytical tool that allows the entrepreneur to track the cash flow of the business on a month-by-month basis. With this tool, the firm's cash flow pattern can be estimated in advance, allowing for better control over the critically needed cash resource. Once established and fine-tuned, the cash budget is a simple financial tool that is easily updated. When fully implemented, the cash budget allows the entrepreneur to predict the amount of cash needed to operate the business without facing a cash crisis. The cash budget is based on the cash method of accounting. Cash receipts and cash distributions are recorded in the forecast only when the cash transaction is expected to occur.

The entrepreneur begins the development of the cash budget by deciding on the minimal cash that the business will always need. There is no "best" answer as to the minimum cash balance a firm should have because this minimum depends on issues such as the firm's cash flow cycle, the degree of seasonality and the number of distortions anticipated in the cash flow cycle, and the entrepreneur's "personal comfort" with what a cash minimum needs to be. Two firms with two different entrepreneurs, even in the same business, may select quite different minimum cash balances. The most reliable method for determining the most appropriate cash minimum is experience. Consequently, a cash budget for the first few years of operations is a work in progress. Experience allows the entrepreneur to "fine tune" the cash budget, always considering how the firm's growth or retraction will affect cash flow. Growth in sales, for example, will normally require an adjustment to the minimum cash budget.

The cash budget is based on the firm's sales forecast because sales revenues are the major source of cash flowing into the business. For existing businesses, the sales forecast is based on the firm's historical sales data. For new ventures, the sales forecast will usually lack historical sales data but should depend on market research and sales estimates based on the sales achieved by comparably sized businesses in the same market. This is normally the only way to estimate the new venture's initial sales forecast. It is crucial that this preliminary sales forecast is determined through good market research. How many potential customers is the new firm likely to attract? What will their average purchase size be? These estimates and the resulting sales forecast are employed both in the development of the cash budget and the firm's pro forma income statement.

The next step is forecasting cash receipts. Sales are made and recorded as either cash received or accounts receivable. Accounts receivable will be collected (the entrepreneur hopes!) but not immediately. This delay between sales and the actual collection of accounts receivable is a primary reason for tracking cash flows. To accurately assess the flow of cash in the business, the entrepreneur must initially estimate the collection pattern of accounts receivable and, when an accurate collection pattern is determined, modify this estimation.

The final step is the cash distribution forecast. Cash distributions are the payments of the firm's financial obligations such as rent, loan repayments, interest, operating expenses, overhead expenses, wages and salaries, and production costs. The key factor is the development of a cash disbursement pattern that is accurate. Entrepreneurs with new business ventures need to be sure that the start-up costs are included as a unique set of expenses, and it is wise to estimate expenses on the high side initially to avoid surprises.

Table 6.1 provides an example of a cash budget. Cash budgets should be developed that reflect what will "most likely" occur; many authorities also recommend that a new business venture create best- and worst-case budgets in order to evaluate the impact that differences in sales revenues, collections, and expenses would have on the firm's cash situation. In the "most likely" cash budget presented in Table 6.1, the entrepreneur will need to have negotiated the borrowing capacity of $228,000 ($159,000 + $69,000 in January and February) in addition to the initial $50,000 cash infusion. In this example, the entrepreneur can demonstrate to the lender that the $228,000 loan will be repaid in a reasonable time.

A cash budget is an entrepreneur's most powerful tool in demonstrating to lenders that their loans will be safely secured because net profits will generate the cash required to repay them.

Bloom Energy

Bloom Energy, which sells servers that convert fuel into electricity without combustion, was conceived of by founder and current CEO K. R. Sridhar in 2001. His desire was to develop a clean approach to enabling customers to leave the traditional energy grid. This vision meshed well with the desire of thousands of individuals to become clean energy consumers, work toward reducing their carbon footprints, and, in the process, eliminate their current dependency on existing suppliers of electricity. Since Bloom Energy's founding, the company has executed on its vision, enabling office buildings, data centers, universities, and retail stores to utilize the company's technologies to power their facilities. As a result of the deployment and adoption of the company's disruptive technologies, Bloom Energy attained a market valuation of $3 billion in 2018.

Sources:

1. "Bloom Energy: Cleaner Energy," *CNBC*, June 7, 2016 (updated April 30, 2018), https://www.cnbc.com/2016/06/06/bloom-energy-2016-disruptor-50.html.
2. Bloom Energy website, https://bloomenergy.com/.

The cash flow analysis is an excellent tool to use when you approach your bank about a "line of credit" or a working capital loan. These loans give you access to cash to meet your financial obligations. Note, however, that this type of financing must be negotiated *prior* to when the money is needed. Establishing a "line of credit" demonstrates to the lender that you understand the financial needs of your business and are taking proactive steps to avoid a "cash crunch."

Avoiding a Cash Crisis

Cash management is based on developing and aggressively implementing business policies that are designed to protect the firm's cash availability. It is achieved by concentrating on the three primary causes of potential cash flow problems: the poor management of accounts receivable, inventories, and accounts payable. The entrepreneur needs to focus on collecting accounts receivable in a time frame that is consistent with the credit terms offered customers. Inventories need to be monitored to avoid unsalable, unusable, and obsolete inventories. Last, accounts payable need to be monitored to maintain the credit worthiness of the business and to stretch the payment time by negotiating longer payment terms.

Accounts Receivable

In today's economy, the majority of businesses, especially in business-to-business industries, sell on credit. Most industries have what might be termed "normal credit terms and conditions." As an example, the product or service may be sold on "net 30 day" terms, which simply means that the buyer agrees to pay for the purchase 30 days after accepting delivery. As you might expect, most new firms will employ the account receivable norms of their industry when making sales. After these credit terms have been offered to and accepted by a customer, it is essential that the entrepreneur understand that extending them is, in reality, a loan. For this reason, it is vital that sales are made, and credit extended, to customers who

TABLE 6.1 ■ Sample Cash Budget—"Most Likely" Scenario						
	January	February	March	April	May	June
Cash Receipts						
Sales	$200,000	$220,000	$230,000	$240,000	$250,000	$250,000
Credit Sales	$180,000	$198,000	$207,000	$216,000	$225,000	$225,000
Collections of Credit Sales						
70% – 1st Month		$126,000	$138,600	$144,900	$151,200	$157,500
20% – 2nd Month			$36,000	$39,600	$41,400	$43,200
10% –3rd Month				$18,000	$19,800	$20,700
Cash Sales	*$20,000*	*$22,000*	*$23,000*	*$24,000*	*$25,000*	*$25,000*
Total Cash Receipts	**$20,000**	**$148,000**	**$197,600**	**$226,500**	**$237,400**	**$246,400**
Cash Distributions						
Purchases	$100,000	$100,000	$110,000	$110,000	$120,000	$12,000
Rent	$10,000	$10,000	$10,000	$10,000	$10,000	$10,000
Utilities	$4,000	$4,000	$4,300	$4,300	$4,400	$4,400
Wages and Salaries	$50,000	$50,000	$50,000	$50,000	$50,000	$50,000
Overhead Expenses	$10,000	$10,000	$10,000	$10,000	$10,000	$10,000
Interest Expenses	$5,000	$5,000	$5,000	$5,000	$5,000	$5,000
Total Cash Disbursement	**$179,000**	**$179,000**	**$189,300**	**$189,300**	**$199,400**	**$199,400**
End of Month Balance						
Cash (Beginning of Month)	$50,000	$50,000	$50,000	$58,300	$95,500	$133,500
+ Cash Receipts	$20,000	$148,000	$197,600	$226,500	$237,400	$246,400
– Cash Disbursement	$179,000	$179,000	$189,300	$189,300	$199,400	$199,400
Cash (End of Month)	*–$109,000*	*$19,000*	*$58,300*	*$95,500*	*$133,500*	*$180,500*
Borrowing	$159,000	$69,000				
Cash (End of Month after Borrowing)	**$50,000**	**$50,000**	**$58,300**	**$95,500**	**$133,500**	**$180,500**

will pay what they owe on time. A serious potential problem exists for a new venture if the entrepreneur is unaware of the general character of the firm's potential customers.

Unscrupulous customers often take advantage of a new business by making purchases for which they have no intention of paying. The entrepreneur can often become excited about the great start to his or her business based on these initially large sales only to discover that customer payments fail to arrive when they are due. New businesses are extremely vulnerable to fraud when they do not know which customers are honest and creditable. With limited financial resources, a new business can normally least afford the often-crippling damage to its cash flow caused by customers who do not pay or who do not pay on time. Because credit sales may be the norm in the industry, an entrepreneur must develop and aggressively implement a credit policy that protects the firm's vital cash flow. A credit policy that is too lenient will attract slow-paying customers. The impact of these customers' payment behaviors is both a cash budget that is soon a worthless analytical tool and, potentially, a serious cash crisis for the new venture.

Credit Policies

The credit policy for any business must be reasonable and workable. Whenever possible, the entrepreneur should take the time and absorb the expense of screening every customer whose purchase is significant. The goal of a presale screening is to avoid the possibly devastating negative impact on the firm's cash flow that accepting nonpaying or late-paying customers could have, customers that a presale screening would identify as deadbeats, or worse, as frauds. Those customers who have been identified as "slow payers" might be required to pay for all or a portion of the purchase in cash. This presales screening policy will allow the new venture to differentiate the customers that have a positive track record for paying for their purchases from those that are bad credit risks.

Screening Credit Applicants

The presale screening can be implemented by having a detailed credit application form. The credit application form collects an adequate amount of information, which allows the entrepreneur to conduct a credit check. Typically, credit applications ask for the following verifiable information:

- Name
- Address
- Telephone number
- Email address
- Tax identification number of the firm or the individual's social security number
- Form of ownership of the potential customer if it is a business
- Credit references from other suppliers, including contact names, addresses, emails, and phone numbers

It is critical to your firm's reputation that this sensitive information be retained in a confidential manner and used by only trusted staff or third-party agencies in the determination of an applicant's honesty and credit reliability. Expending money and effort in the screening of potential customers reaps the reward of having many fewer accounts-receivable losses.

Evaluating Credit Worthiness

There are a number of organizations that can help in the process. The National Association of Credit Management is a nonprofit organization that promotes standards for the business-to-business credit profession. Also, many companies offer credit reporting services such as Dun & Bradstreet, TRW, Equifax, VERITAS Credit Corp, Experian, and Know X. Fees vary, but in comparison with the potential losses incurred because of "deadbeats" and "scammers," the costs are normally an excellent value.

Components of a Sales Contract

The next step in avoiding bad debt losses and protecting cash flow is the establishment of a well-written and clearly understood credit policy. The terms and conditions of the credit policy, which itself becomes an integral component of the firm's sales contract, should be written in plain language, so they can be explained to every customer. The components of the sales contract that relate to a firm's credit policy include answers to the following questions:

- When will invoices be sent to customers for their purchases? How long after the purchase date will that be?

- When does the payment "clock" begin? Is it the day the product is delivered or the service rendered, or is it the day a customer receives the invoice for the purchase?

- Based on these terms, when is payment due?

- When will a late payment fee be charged? How much? (*Be sure that the interest on the late payment fee does not violate federal or state credit laws.*)

- If legal actions must be taken to collect the accounts receivable, who is responsible to pay court costs and legal fees?

It is always valuable to have your firm's attorney check over your sales contract to insure that it is legal and enforceable.

Invoice Statement

To ensure that your business is not itself a cause of slow account receivable payments, send customers their invoices promptly. Customers will not pay for a product until they receive an invoice and verify its accuracy. It is important that the entrepreneur establish a process that encourages prompt payment of invoices:

- Ensure that the invoices are clearly written, accurate, and delivered in a timely fashion.

- Confirm that invoices clearly describe the goods and services purchased and include relevant account numbers that make verifying the customer's purchases easy.

- Ensure that the invoice price agrees with the price quoted at the time of the purchase. *(Check the purchase order or sales contract.)*

- Highlight the specific terms and conditions of the sales contract on all invoices as a form of reinforcing the agreed-upon sales contract.

- Include the name of a contact person in your business, along with her or his contact information, including phone number, fax number, and email, to facilitate communications if the customer has any questions regarding the invoice.

Finally, it is always important to consider customer feedback and modify invoice statements to address the major complaints raised by customers. Here are the most often received customer complaints regarding sales invoices:

Difficult or confusing to understand . . .

Arrived late and not clearly linked to the purchases made . . .

Addressed to the wrong person and not the individual responsible for making payments . . .

Even with all the positive steps taken to make the invoices of the businesses easy to understand, some customers will fail to pay for their purchases by the agreed-to time. When an account becomes overdue, it is incumbent on the entrepreneur to take action immediately. The longer an account receivable is overdue, the lower is the probability that it will be collected. The first step is to send the customer a second notice that the payment is due, immediately. If this strongly written letter does not get results, the follow-up is a telephone call in which the entrepreneur attempts to speak directly with the purchaser. This is not a social call. The entrepreneur must ask specifically when the invoice will be paid. In a few cases, customers will claim that they do not have the money to pay, or they will admit to being simply unwilling to pay for what they purchased. In these situations, the entrepreneur needs to take aggressive actions.

Steps to Collect Late Payments

A firm's response to nonpaying clients must be strong but measured. Here are some steps to take after all normal follow-up procedures have failed or the client indicates that he or she will not pay:

- Have the firm's attorney send a letter to the delinquent customer explaining the legal consequences of failing to pay what is owed.

- Turn the delinquent account over to a collection agency.

- Hire an attorney who specializes in recovering debts from delinquent payers.

Although attorneys and collection agents charge a relatively high fee to collect outstanding accounts, and often the collection expense is greater than the amount invoiced, the message sent by these actions is clear, and other customers who are slow to pay will learn that the entrepreneur is serious about collecting what is owed. If a firm's attempts to collect late payments fail, it is in danger of becoming an easy target for customers who have a reputation for avoiding payment until the very last minute, or at all.

CASH FLOW MANAGEMENT: INVENTORIES

For manufacturers, wholesalers, and retailers, inventories are a major part of the firm's current assets. Creating or purchasing inventories also necessitates cash outflow. When the inventories of a business become obsolete or difficult to convert into cash, the value of the inventories comes into question. Unsold inventories fail to generate cash. Indeed, they yield a zero rate of return and, until sold, tie up cash that is needed in the business. At some point, the entrepreneur must address the reality that a portion of the firm's inventory is obsolete and very likely unsalable. Then, the often-painful decision is to "bite the bullet" and sell the questionable inventories for what they are actually worth (or less) and take the possible financial loss. This decision is painful because the entrepreneur was the person who purchased or manufactured the inventory and so must admit to making an error in judgment. For this reason, some owners refuse to admit that their inventories are overvalued.

Tracking the use and sale of inventories allows the entrepreneur to address problems as they develop. Slow-selling finished goods, for example, can be priced to sell. Whatever cash is received from such sales can be returned in order to finance the firm's current operations. One trap that should be avoided is the tendency to overbuy inventory because the entrepreneur is offered a "deep discount" for buying in volume. Although these inventory purchases seem like a great deal, in reality, the business might not be able either to use that amount of inventory in its production or to sell that amount of product, resulting in possibly worthless inventories. The result is not a bargain but an increase in nonsalable inventories, which have now become a "cash trap."

In today's world of sophisticated logistics, many entrepreneurs purchase inventory in increasingly smaller quantities, which reduces both their holding costs and the risk of inventory obsolesces. Under these conditions, the entrepreneur can quickly reorder inventories that are needed in production or for sales in the market.

CASH FLOW MANAGEMENT: ACCOUNTS PAYABLE

The timing of paying a firm's accounts payable is the third critical factor in cash management. Managing these accounts begins when the initial orders for goods are placed. In many cases, the terms of payment are more important than the price of the goods and services. Competition will normally hold prices within a relatively tight range, but payment terms may vary. The entrepreneur can benefit from purchasing from qualified suppliers who will extend the time by which the firm must pay for goods purchased. In some cases, suppliers may be willing to provide a new venture with extended payment terms in the hope that, when the new venture becomes successful, it will continue to buy exclusively from them. In many instances, the payment term concessions result in a long-term business relationship in which both parties benefit.

Important to the reputation of a new venture is to pay every invoice when it is due. This means that the new venture must be extremely careful regarding the quantity of inventories it purchases. The firm's sales forecast must be accurate. As a means of reducing its risk of failing to meet its financial responsibilities, a new start-up business with limited financial capital must concentrate on producing excellent sales forecasts and an accurate forecast of when accounts receivables will be collected. Efficient cash management is supported through the establishment of a payment calendar. The payment calendar displays the days during the month when invoices are due to be paid and the amount of these payments. The payment calendar serves to keep the paperwork organized. The simplest technique is to create a physical file folder with a division for each day of the month. Invoices are placed in the folder according to the date when each invoice must be paid.

In many transactions, the seller will offer a discount on an invoice if it is paid ahead of schedule. Even what may seem to be a small discount for early payment can become a significant savings. When a supplier has a "2/10, net 60" credit term, the invoice says that the suppliers will allow you to take a 2% discount off the entire invoice if it is paid in 10 days of its receipt. If the discount is not taken, the entire amount is due in 60 days. When the firm has a positive cash flow situation, it is almost always worth earning the 2% savings. **Table 6.2** highlights the annual interest rate associated with taking advantage of a suppliers discount for early payment.

The invoice payment process should always include verifying that the firm actually received the merchandise being invoiced, that the merchandise was in good condition, and that the invoiced amount is compatible with the agreed price. These simple techniques will ensure that your firm receives value and fair dealing from suppliers. As mentioned, you should always pay on time or earlier and avoid missing a payment. You don't want your firm to create ill will among suppliers or to earn a reputation for being a "slow-pay" customer. An entrepreneur should act with the utmost credibility in relations with all clients, customers, and suppliers. Reputation is a vital aspect to creating an image of trust for the new venture.

The entrepreneur will find it advantageous to schedule controllable cash disbursements, so they do not come due at the same time. Wages and salaries are examples of cash disbursements that can be paid on a schedule that reduces cash conflicts. Monitoring the three big components that directly influence a firm's cash flow can result in the establishment and implementation of policies that allow for the most effective management of the firm's cash.

TABLE 6.2 ■ Benefits From Making Early Payments	
Cash Discount Terms	**Annual Percentage of Early Payment**
2/10, net 30	37.25%
3/10, net 40	37.63%
3/10, net 30	56.44%

AVOIDING THE CASH CRUNCH

Most new ventures can take steps to avoid a negative cash flow position. The key is to develop an objective evaluation of the firm's financial policies while searching for sources of inefficiencies in the firm's operations. The biggest opportunity for improvement is normally found in the firm's excessive overhead expenses. Overhead expenses can easily grow to become a burden on cash flows.

Steps to Avoid a "Cash Crunch"

Here are some steps a new venture can take to avoid a "cash crunch":

- **When practical, lease any "big ticket" assets instead of purchasing them.** Entrepreneurs can save their limited cash through leasing buildings or offices, cars, machinery, computers, and other equipment. *It is the use of those assets, which create value, not their ownership.*

- Avoid nonessential outlays that may make the entrepreneur "look" successful but that make no meaningful contribution to the firm's effectiveness or efficiency.

- Negotiate fixed loan payments that coincide with the firm's cash flow situation.

- When possible, buy used or reconditioned equipment.

- Limit loans and payment advances to employees.

- Initiate an internal security and control system to address the possibility of employee theft.

- Develop a system to prevent check fraud.

- Annually reevaluate your business expenses in an attempt to determine if they are contributing to the performances of the business.

Cash flow analysis allows the entrepreneur the opportunity to identify policies and circumstances that may be detrimental to the success of a new business venture. It is impossible to overstate the importance of establishing and maintaining strict control over a firm's cash flow. The failure to pay the firm's financial obligations when they are due places the firm in jeopardy of being forced into bankruptcy by unpaid creditors.

Investing Excess Cash

For firms with a positive cash flow situation, investing the surplus cash can be beneficial. These investments need to be liquid and extremely safe. Banks and other financial institutions normally offer entrepreneurs one or more of the following types of accounts: money market accounts, zero balance accounts, and sweep accounts. A money market account is an interest-bearing account that allows the firm to write checks to meet its obligations. A money market account is a checking account that pays interest on the firm's balance. The surplus cash adds to the firm's account balance. A zero balance account is another form of checking account that technically never has any funds in it but is tied to a firm's master account. The entrepreneur makes deposits into the master account but writes checks from the zero balance account. The bank then transfers the needed funds from the master account to cover the checks written on the zero balance account. In this way, the entrepreneur can earn interest on the positive cash balance in the master account. A sweep account is designed to allow the entrepreneur to earn interest on funds not currently needed in the business. A firm's bank *sweeps* all funds above a predetermined amount into what is, in effect, a savings account.

When the firm has accumulated what might be a safe cash buffer against anticipated financial outflows, it normally invests surplus cash in other forms of safe and liquid investments. These investments are normally as risk free as possible. Most entrepreneurs will begin by purchasing government notes or bonds. **Surplus cash should never be at rest.** Although the interest earned on these investments may seem small, it continues to contribute to the creation of a firm's positive cash balance.

CONCLUSION

Chapters 5 and **6** have served to provide you with the very basics needed to prepare the essential financial statements and analyses that both investors and lenders expect to see when evaluating your business plan. It is critical to your creditability that any financial analysis you conduct is as accurate as possible and supportive of your business model. Investors and lenders will always evaluate your cash flow model to determine if your business will be able to meet its month-by-month financial obligations.

ENTREPRENEURIAL EXERCISES

Entrepreneurial Exercise 6.1

Part I

Based on the forecast you have made regarding inventory turnover and sales, product delivery time, credit terms from your suppliers, and sales credit terms for your industry, please develop a cash flow cycle for your proposed business venture. Be as accurate as possible with your time estimates. Focus on a single item of inventory.

Order Inventory	Receive Inventory	Pay for Inventory	Sell Inventory	Deliver to Customer	Send Invoice to Customer	Receive Payment
Day 1	Day	Day	Day	Day	Day	Day

Part II

How many days did it take to sell, or "turnover," the item in inventory (i.e., *sell inventory* day minus *receive inventory* day)?

How long was your cash gone (i.e., *receive payment* day minus *pay for inventory* day)?

Entrepreneurial Exercise 6.2

Using **Table 6.1** as an example, please create a "most likely" month-by-month cash budget for the first 12 months of your business operations. Carefully incorporate your sales forecast and all anticipated expenses.

Entrepreneurial Exercise 6.3

Based on your unique proposed business venture, please write a detailed credit policy for your firm. Please include any statements that you believe will clarify the financial responsibility of the purchasers.

Entrepreneurial Exercise 6.4

Construct a credit application for your business that is sufficient to check the credit worthiness of an applicant without excessively imposing on that applicant's privacy.

7

THE FOUNDER AND THE NEW VENTURE TEAM

The essential thing is not knowledge, but character

Joseph LeConte

If your actions create a legacy that inspires others to dream more, learn more, do more and become more, then you are an excellent leader.

Dolly Parton

Professional investors value the new venture's founder and the entrepreneurial team on equal footing with the venture's products and services. The investors must have confidence that the entrepreneur and the team can make this business a success. There is an old adage among horseracing aficionados: "To pick a winner in any race, look at the jockey as much as the horse." For this reason, investors conduct exceptional "due diligence" on the lead entrepreneur and the entrepreneurial team, asking questions about the leadership capability of the entrepreneur and her or his ability to form, support, and grow the entrepreneurial team. The investor's due diligence often uncovers a founder who is exceptionally qualified in terms of technical expertise but has never held a leadership position or worked in a significant managerial position. This finding can have a negative impact on people's willingness to invest.

A founder has both advantages and disadvantages when beginning a business venture with what is clearly a "blank slate." A new CEO of an established business inherits the existing organizational structure, its strategies, and the firm's human resources. The existent organizational structure and strategies have normally evolved over time, yet they may not be efficient, relevant, or effective for remaining competitive in the marketplace. Changes in organizational structure are often difficult to modify without creating substantial organizational disruption and resistance. Just as the already established organizational structures and strategies may no longer be relevant, the established firm's human resources may be out of touch with current industry developments and lacking in needed skills. After all, staff members were acquired to accomplish performance objectives that may no longer be those of the highest priority under the current competitive circumstances. Eventually, new CEOs of established firms will face internal resistance when changes are made to either a firm's structures and strategies or to its human resource expectations.

FOUNDER'S RESPONSIBILITY

The founder of a new business venture has the responsibility to construct an organizational structure with the closest operational fit to the firm's strategies. Structure follows strategy. The primary role of the firm's strategy is to be more effective and efficient in the organization of resources in order to achieve the firm's objectives. The founder's challenge is to identify and acquire the most competent individuals who are capable of implementing the founder's strategic vision. These individuals should be equally committed to the accomplishment of performance objectives that are linked to initial success and to the firm's continuing growth and profitability.

For a new business venture, the founder must recognize his or her responsibilities on these critical tasks; the founder must be capable of translating the firm's strategic vision into organizational realities that guide the actions of every team member. These organizational realities must include the most effective and efficient structure, strategies, business model, and leadership practices, all integrated together to support the most productive entrepreneurial team.

In order to achieve success, an entrepreneur must expend equal amounts of effort in creating a winning business model and in developing strong leadership qualities. The title of owner may make a person the manager, but only the team members' acceptance and respect allows the owner to become a leader. For the vast majority of entrepreneurs, leadership skills and behaviors are learned. Once learned, these leadership skills must become a consistent component of all of the entrepreneur's behaviors. Studies of entrepreneurs have indicated that business owners who personally set up their ventures as founders exhibited greater emotional stability than owners who inherited their companies from families—perhaps because founders have a guiding vision in mind and know what successful outcomes within their ventures look like.[1] Also, most founders have a genuine passion for the product or service that is the basis of their new business. Yet the ultimate success of the business is equally dependent upon the entrepreneur's leadership skills and her or his capability of building and maintaining a positive organizational culture that is supportive of the business model. To lead and motivate people effectively, then, you must develop an understanding of human motivation, personality traits, forms of intelligence, and values.

THE FOUNDER AS LEADER

For those of you who have had a previous course in management or leadership, much of this chapter will be a review of previously mastered concepts. The intent of this chapter is to provide a focused insight into the critical skills of the founder or entrepreneur as a leader. Without leadership skills, an entrepreneur puts a firm's long-term success at risk. This chapter is not a definitive explanation of all of the components of leadership, and significant additional study of the topic will be to your benefit.

Founders often believe that having a personal passion to succeed and superior intelligence translates into being "gifted" with leadership skills. Intelligence *is* very often a key component in the initial development of the firm's product or service, as well as in the analysis of the competitive landscape and the establishment of marketing and financial strategies. However, intelligence alone does not fully address the complex and interactive nature of leadership. A founder must further be willing to, as objectively as possible, assess his or her individual personality traits, values, beliefs, and character, as well as those of key team members. The internal forces that shape the characteristics and views of the management team have the greatest impact on the founder's leadership potential. Personality, values, beliefs, and character combine to shape how any individual responds to competitive challenges and ethical situations, and to other individuals who work in the organization or in firm's with whom the organization does business. These traits also affect how others will evaluate the entrepreneur as a leader and, in turn, respond to leadership efforts. The founders of any business are always "under the microscope" and being evaluated by those with whom they interact.

Many entrepreneurs are ill prepared for the scrutiny that they will receive. Their behaviors as the firm's founder will always be evaluated and judged by everyone with whom they come in contact. For this reason, they must master the skills and practices of leadership. Entrepreneurs must recognize that leading a business is not a simple process. Setting performance goals is valuable but will not stand alone. Leading the firm's team members is an active, not a passive, process. Leading is also a firm-wide as well as an individual process. Leadership requires the entrepreneur to link the firm's success to the achievement of each team member's personal goals. The value of this approach is that team members who are high performers believe that they will continue to be high performers, and that they will be recognized for their performance. Proven success breeds team members who are willing to pursue new performance challenges aggressively. Winners behave with confidence and, in doing so, continue to be winners. The entrepreneur who actively supports the positive efforts of the firm's team members becomes the ultimate winner.

Leadership involves shaping the team members and the work situation for the benefit all. Aggressive leaders are what might be termed "hands on." Leadership is far from a theory; it needs to be practiced daily in every successful firm. High performance and ethical behaviors must not go unrecognized. The entrepreneur continually searches for exceptional performance and immediately rewards those involved through public recognition. Performance and behaviors that are rewarded are reinforced and repeated. Leaders never miss an opportunity to reinforce positive behaviors and reward performances that meet or exceed expectations. Entrepreneurial leadership never ends.

It becomes essential that the members of the entrepreneurial team and the entrepreneur understand correctly what might be termed the "core" of each person and how that person might be capable of fitting into the entrepreneurial team. A new business venture cannot afford to have an entrepreneurial team member whose personality, values, beliefs, and actions prove to be detrimental to the firm. Character traits that conflict with those of the founder and with those of the other members of the entrepreneurial team can result in serious and potentially damaging problems. Of course, you do not want the whole entrepreneurial team cut from the same cloth; diversity of strengths, experiences, and perspectives is useful in a team. However, if one team member has a fatal character flaw, does not possess the core values of the entrepreneurial team, or does not agree with the others about where the company is going, that person could have a very harmful influence. Each time a critical employee fails to perform, the new venture has the potential to suffer substantially. In the early stage of a business, failure to select compatible team members can cripple the entire organization. Intelligence, personality, values, and beliefs are not vague concepts but the base components of each of us.

In leading the entrepreneurial team, the entrepreneur must make every effort to understand how each team member is unique. The better each person is understood, the more effective the leader can be in both selecting the members of the entrepreneurial team and motivating each team member. These fundamental differences in each of us define who we are. The primary sources of individual differences are intelligence, personality, values or beliefs, and character (see Figure 7.1).

Intelligence

Intelligence is the ability to perform mental activities that are associated with thinking, reasoning, and problem solving. Entrepreneurs and team members will most likely have a variety of intellectual abilities. A common misconception is that all intelligence is the same. In reality, there are multiple recognized dimensions of intellectual ability.

The most common form of intelligence is memory. Individuals with exceptional memory skills can be very impressive when a task requires recalling specific facts or figures. Other forms of intelligence include reasoning ability (logical-mathematical intelligence), visualization ability (visual-spatial intelligence), and interpersonal ability (emotional intelligence).

Creative individuals often demonstrate many of these skills. Math wizards typically have a highly developed aptitude for numbers. Other individuals might score high in spatial visualization, perceptual speed, or verbal comprehension. These abilities exist in each of us to some degree while a few individuals may be exceptionally gifted in one or more of these forms of intelligence. A successful entrepreneur benefits from discovering the unique intellectual abilities of each of the team members. Assigning work activities based on the unique abilities of each team member can result in exceptional overall performance. Some individuals have what is termed *social or cultural intelligence*. These individuals can assess very quickly the behaviors, needs, and desired outcomes of each member of a group with which they interact. It is suggested that this ability allows them to behave "correctly," communicate effectively, and make appropriate decisions. These individuals possess a knack for relating well with others.

Personality Traits

Personality is the sum total of the ways in which individuals react to and interact with others. Much of an individual's personality is determined through heredity. Other components of our personality are a product of our environment. Each of us is a product of our genetic makeup and our unique history. By definition, however, personality is extremely difficult to alter, as personality traits are "the relatively enduring patterns of thoughts, feelings and behaviors that reflect the tendency to respond in certain ways under certain circumstances."[2] To a very large degree, our personalities impact the ways we chose to interact with our environment. In very simple terms, the more that you interact with others the more accurate those individuals will become at identifying the components of your personality and at accurately describing and predicting your behaviors.

Over the past decades, psychologists have identified essential personality traits that include the following:

Agreeableness—behaviors that display the ability to get along with others.

Conscientiousness—the extent to which a person works to achieve goals in a careful, disciplined fashion and takes obligations seriously.

Extraversion—behaviors associated with seeking out the stimulation of other people as opposed to enjoying solitude.

Emotional Stability (Neuroticism)—the extent of vulnerability to negative emotions such as anxiety or sadness, e.g., whether one is easily excitable vs. calm, insecure vs. secure, reactive vs. proactive, as well as the nature of one's mood swings.

ENTREPRENEURIAL SPOTLIGHT
VITALIK BUTERIN—ETHEREUM

Vitalik Buterin immigrated to Canada from Russia with his parents when he was 6. Now, at 24, he is a writer and, most famously, the programmer responsible for the founding of Ethereum and cofounder of *Bitcoin Magazine*. Buterin was deemed "gifted" in mathematics at an early age, and, while he was still in high school, he learned about blockchain technology from his father. Since that time, he has dedicated his energies to exploring and sharing his knowledge of cryptocurrencies and of the functionality of the blockchain algorithm.

In 2011, he became a cofounder of *Bitcoin Magazine*, and he contributed to that periodical and published in a variety of other journals that were committed to the study of cryptocurrency and blockchain technology. In 2013, he cofounded

Ethereum, which is a "'decentralized mining network and software development platform rolled into one' that facilitates the creation of new cryptocurrencies and programs that share a single block chain (a cryptographic transaction ledger)." The webpage describes Ethereum as a "decentralized platform that runs smart contracts." The apps run on a custom-built blockchain that enables developers to create markets, store registries of debts or promises, move funds in accordance with instructions given long in the past (like a will or a futures contract) and many other things that have not been invented yet, all without a middleman or counterparty risk." In effect, Ethereum provides the platform for the creation of secure cryptocurrencies that are, as of yet, largely unregulated by most governments.

Sources:

1. "Vitalik Buterin," Website for the Blockchain Workshop, December 15–16, 2016, Nairobi, Kenya, http://blockchainworkshops.org/kenya/speaker/vitalik-buterin/.

2. Front page of the Ethereum website, accessed June 2018, www.ethereum.org.

3. "Vitalik Buterin," *Wikipedia*, last edited June 27, 2018, www.en.wikipedia.org/Vitalik_Buterin.

Openness—the enjoyment of new things and ideas, which reflects an individual's range of interests and level of rigidity in terms of beliefs and habits.

Locus of Control—the degree to which people believe that their behaviors affect events and outcomes. An internal locus of control reflects the belief that personal efforts, actions, and abilities affect outcomes; an external locus of control reflects the belief that outcomes are affected by external factors such as luck, fate, or chance.

Self-assuredness—the belief an individual has about his or her capacity to perform a specific task or achieve an outcome.

Self-monitoring—an individual's capability of adjusting behavior to fit situations or achieve goals.

Self-esteem—the extent to which people believe they are worthwhile and have value.

Risk Propensity—the degree to which an individual is willing to take chances and make risky decisions.

Authoritarianism—the extent to which an individual believes that power and status differences are appropriate within hierarchical social systems, such as an organization.

Machiavellianism—individual behaviors that are directed at gaining power, achieving one's self-interest, and controlling the behaviors of others, even to the extent of dishonesty.

Narcissism—the quality of having a grandiose sense of self-importance and entitlement, as well as excessive self-admiration.

What is essential is to have an assessment of yourself that is as honest and objective as possible. Ask yourself which of these personality traits are important to the success of your proposed new business venture. We recommend that you expand each definition and read in depth the specific characteristics of each trait. The next step would be to evaluate your proposed business and ask yourself if there is a solid positive match between your personality traits and those normally associated with successful leaders of similar businesses.

There is no obligation for an entrepreneur to have or demonstrate a "correct" combination of these personality traits. What is important is that the entrepreneur conducts a serious and thoughtful personal assessment for the purpose of establishing a clear profile of her or his own personality. The founder's behaviors toward others are overwhelmingly affected by this personality profile. Additionally, knowing ourselves will contribute to our ability to understand others and assist in identifying the personality traits preferred in members of the entrepreneurial team.

Because personality is very difficult to change, entrepreneurs need to evaluate potential team members according to the personality traits they actually exhibit, asking whether people with these traits can make a contribution to the business at this particular time. The entrepreneur must lead the business based on the characteristics of the team members and not according to what he or she wants everyone to be like. This requires an entrepreneur to evaluate both the intelligence and personality of team members consistently and to adjust his or her leadership style in response to that evaluation, in order to be most effective. Leaders must learn that it is their responsibility to adjust to these critical personal characteristics if they hope to achieve maximum organizational performance. Entrepreneurs may wish, on occasion, to employ an individual who has "negative" personality traits, but they should not believe that these personality traits can be easily, if ever, modified.

Values

Values are an individual's basic convictions regarding the conduct and outcomes that person considers to be preferable. Consequently, values have both content and intensity attributes. In other words, they are comprised of *what* is valued and of *how much* it is valued by a specific individual. For most individuals, values are well established and fairly inflexible by early adulthood. Individuals have both terminal and instrumental values. Terminal values represent desirable end-states, those things the individual would like to achieve in his or her lifetime. Instrumental values are the preferable behaviors that contribute to the achievement of the desired end-state outcomes. Values are the foundation upon which an individual determines actions and outcomes to be right or wrong. Values typically underlie our attitudes and perceptions, and they serve to guide our decisions and our behaviors. The founder should clearly state all of his or her values. The entrepreneurial team will function better when each member knows and accepts the values of the entrepreneur. Entrepreneurs will discover that sharing their values with potential team members will result in allowing candidates who are uncomfortable with those values to reject an offer of employment. Clashes of values can result in serious performance problems, and any steps that can be taken prior to employment to avoid these clashes are valuable.

From the very outset of the new business, the founder needs to both explain and demonstrate how these values will be an essential component of the firm's organizational culture. As you can imagine, it would be very difficult to work with an entrepreneurial team member whose values were not compatible with your own. Interpersonal conflict is likely to arise when value systems are incompatible. A new business venture cannot afford added conflicts that are deeply rooted and difficult to resolve. As an example, the founder may value honesty in all business dealings whereas a team member is committed to take whatever actions are deemed necessary to make a sale, which might include being less than totally honest with a customer. The team member might believe that the end (making the sale) will justify the means (not being honest). A founder who hires a team member who thinks the terminal value of winning is more important than the instrumental value of behaving with honesty, then, might encounter multiple Machiavellian behaviors from this individual and might be letting the firm in for legal difficulties.

Character

As stated before, the entrepreneurial self-assessment should include questions about intelligence, personality, values, and character. But what is the difference between

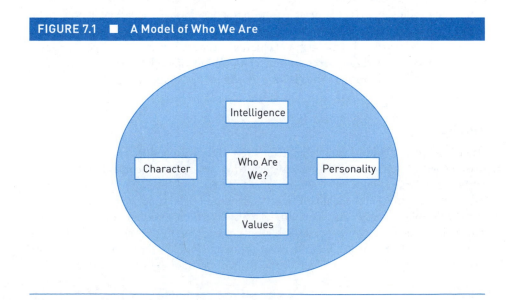

FIGURE 7.1   ■   A Model of Who We Are

personality and character? Personality refers to a range of enduring and distinctive traits, as we have seen. But character refers to a set of distinguishing values and moral characteristics, one that defines how we treat others and ourselves. "The problem in forming judgments about a person's suitability for important roles in our lives . . . is that we all have an uncanny predilection for observing attractive *personality* traits and manufacturing out of them the presence of positive *character* traits (that is, if someone is outgoing, confident, and fun, we're more likely to think they're honest, moral, and kind)."[3] So although assessments of both personality and character are based on observed behaviors, character takes longer to evaluation. Still, it is a judgment made by an external observer. When an outside observer describes a person as being "of good character," it reflects that individual's judgment regarding the observed actions of the person in question.

Typically, good character includes recognizable behavior traits:

Honesty

Trustworthiness

Responsibility

Fairness in All Dealings

Compassion

Respect for Others and Self

Any entrepreneur who has a positive image within the community and with the customer base, as well the reputation of being a person of good personal character, has an extremely valuable competitive advantage in business. An entrepreneur surrounded by team members of good character is likely to reap the rewards of creating a business respected by customers. Customers generally demonstrate a preference for doing business with a firm that reflects the positive character of the founder and staff.

LEADERSHIP IN ACTION

The founder of a new venture is very often a person of deep technical skills and knowledge. These traits often extend to a passion for changing the world and to being highly motivated to achieve success. However, new ventures succeed based on the efforts of the entire entrepreneurial team. Entrepreneurs need to master the skills of leadership. The growth potential of the business venture depends, to a large degree, on the entrepreneur's ability to serve as the firm's leader. Leaders understand their entrepreneurial team members in detail. Leaders continually strive to provide every team member with a work environment enabling employee self-actualization. Gifted leaders create win-win organizational situations and understand that each team member must be committed to the success and growth of the new venture. Self-directed and motivated team members should recognize how they will benefit personally from the firm's achievements and success. Leaders need to identify and understand the needs, skills, and abilities of each key person, and to harness these to create a thriving venture. Under these conditions, the entrepreneur, the firm, and the team members all have an opportunity to become successful.

Power to Influence Behaviors

The firm's organizational structure establishes a management hierarchy. The founder is a manager. As stated previously, being a manager does not make anyone a leader. Managers bring about order and structure. Managers plan, organize, and control to enhance the firm's success. Leadership, on the other hand, involves influencing individuals to perform toward the achievement of the organization's goals and objective. The key word is *influencing*. Leaders have mastered the skills and practices that have proven to be effective at influencing others to perform. To achieve the full potential of a new venture, the founder must become an effective leader, skilled in influencing team members to contribute at their highest level of effort.

Entrepreneurial leadership is not theoretical but operational. The potential to develop and exercise leadership should never be overlooked or undervalued. Planning for leadership, like organizational strategy formulation, is valuable, but implementation is absolutely critical. The founder must be willing to commit to becoming an effective leader and to mastering the skills of implementing leadership. Entrepreneurial leadership can be learned. Leaders benefit by developing the following fundamental skills and behaviors:

1. **Create a vision statement:** The founder must articulate the vision for the new venture to every member of the entrepreneurial team. The vision statement needs to excite and inspire the team members and be understood by them in order for it to direct the actions of the team. Entrepreneurs need to be transformational leaders to infuse the team with high performance expectations. Excellent performance allows each team member to earn the respect of the others.

2. **Demonstrate leadership qualities:** The leader must display personal risk and demonstrate self-sacrifice when working to achieve the firm's mission, objective, and goals. If the entrepreneur wants to gain the trust and respect of team members, it is critical for them to view the entrepreneur as being fully invested in the business venture. As the leader, you are always observed and evaluated by every team member, and your actions are critical to winning your team's confidence. What you do is more powerful than what you say.

3. **Create an atmosphere for growth and change:** The entrepreneur must demonstrate sensitivity to the needs of each team member. The founder needs to be attuned to both the team members' performance-oriented skills and abilities and their personal needs and feelings. Leaders reward performance and continue to expand each team member's opportunity to grow within the business.

4. **Create trust:** Entrepreneurs need to behave in a way that enhances trust among all members of the leadership team. With the knowledge of each team member's skills, abilities, and personal needs, the entrepreneur can shape the firm's work environment to allow all team members to demonstrate

their intelligence and problem-solving abilities—to show themselves to be trustworthy. Leaders create an organizational environment in which team members can earn continuing recognition for exceptional performance and achieve results through decisions and actions that benefit the firm.

Leadership is present when the business's products and services meet the needs of its targeted customers and are delivered by an organizational team committed to earning customer satisfaction. The team members must demonstrate that they have internalized the entrepreneur's vision and values. Team members under good leadership become self-motivated and display high levels of energy in the effective delivery of the firm's products or services. Team members who perceive the founder as an individual who respects them and who can relate to their professional needs will most likely be viewed in a positive way by other employees and by customers. These behaviors reinforce the leader's need to truly understand the members of the entrepreneurial team.

TEAM MEMBER SUCCESS = ORGANIZATIONAL SUCCESS

The key is to link the achievement of the firm's goals and objectives to opportunities for team members to achieve their own personal and professional goals. Obviously, if the founder does not know what team members really want, she or he might offer inappropriate performance rewards. This situation normally results in an unmotivated team that thinks the founder either does not understand members' needs or simply does not care. An example of a common "disconnect" between entrepreneurs and staff is the offer of promotion as a reward for performance. The entrepreneur assumes that everyone wants

Houzz

As a result of frustration when remodeling their home, Adi Tatarko and Alon Cohen launched Houzz in 2009 to enable others to communicate their personal visions for their homes to architects, carpenters, interior designers, and others. This radically disruptive company, which began its official operations in 2010, is composed of five interconnected components. These are products, photographs, links for finding professional service providers, and community users' advice forums. The company has developed into an online products and services platform for home remodeling and design, and Houzz works with the American Institute of Architects (AIA) to increase public awareness of the impact and value of professional interior design. Starting with $2 million in seed capital in 2010, Houzz has grown into a global presence with a market valuation of over $4 billion in 2017.

Sources:

1. Erin Griffith, "Houzz Worth $4 Billion in New Funding Round," *Fortune*, June 9, 2017, http://fortune.com/2017/06/08/houzz-worth-4-billion-in-new-funding-round/.
2. "About Houzz," Houzz website, accessed June 2018, https://www.houzz.com/.

to be promoted into management when, often, this is simply not true. Many highly skilled and competent employees have no interest in becoming a member of management. They enjoy the respect they currently earn for their professional knowledge and technical achievements.

Understanding the values and aspirations of each team member allows the entrepreneur the opportunity to deepen his or her leadership credentials. Entrepreneurs will need to display what is termed "transformational" leadership behaviors. In addition to communicating the entrepreneur's vision, the leaders establish ways that every team member can be recognized for the achievement of exceptional performance. The leader communicates high performance expectations and never misses an opportunity to recognize each team member who achieves or exceeds these performance expectations. Leaders also serve as performance coaches who encourage and support the development of the team's problem-solving skills.

A powerful leadership tool is establishing a connection between a team member's terminal values and the firm's objectives. When a business offers an employee the opportunity to achieve one of his or her terminal values, outcomes will be very positive, as that employee will be highly motivated to excel. In contrast, a business that does not provide a linkage between organizational outcomes and an individual's terminal values cannot expect the individual to view that business as a good fit in the long term. For these reasons, the entrepreneur needs to determine the value system of applicants in order to determine if they will benefit from working in the business.

The entrepreneur who recognizes that the future of the business is linked to the professional and personal growth of its team members will logically invest time and energy in building high-performance personnel. An unfortunate reality is that some entrepreneurs try to make every decision and only want team members to implement those decisions. These behaviors result in growth and venture success that is limited by the knowledge and skills of the entrepreneur. When the knowledge and experience limits of the founder are reached, problems may remain unsolved. Worse, they may spread, growing and infecting other organizational components and systematically reducing the firm's ability to compete. An entrepreneur who is unwilling to learn to lead effectively will never achieve the full potential of her or his business. When team members discover that their roles will be limited to "carrying out" the directives of the boss, they will inevitably leave in search of greater personal opportunities. Innovative and potentially highly valuable products or services may never reach the market if poor leadership stifles the creativity of team members. Founders need to embrace employee empowerment through delegation and through assisting team members in developing confidence in their decision-making skills. As the team members are encouraged to make more decisions, the entrepreneur can focus on the unique and challenging dilemmas and opportunities that emerge in the course of doing business.

This section of the chapter provides the entrepreneur with a short, cursory overview of the four components of every individual. These components—intelligence, personality, values, and character—are unique to every person. When hiring, then, the entrepreneur must develop an accurate profile of the type of individual needed for each position on the team and then find an applicant who suits. Consequently, the entrepreneur must establish whether the applicant has the type of intelligence needed to perform the task; the personality traits that will support successful performance;

the character to maintain positive relationships; and, finally, values that are compatible with those of the business and the entrepreneur. Finding answers to these fundamental questions requires a detailed questioning and an in-depth evaluation of the final applicants. When a business makes a general statement that its people are its most valuable resource, there should be abundant evidence that every effort was made to acquire team members who are an excellent fit with the firm and who possess the capability to be the firm's greatest asset.

Creating and Maintaining a High-Performance Organizational Culture

The entrepreneur in the establishment of a new business venture has an opportunity to shape its culture. The culture of a business is a system of shared meanings, which are held by both the entrepreneur and the team members. These shared meanings distinguish the business from other businesses. These shared meanings produce a set of unique characteristics that become what is recognized, both internally and externally, as the culture of the organization. Positive values, which support high performance, are recognized to be a major factor in the success of any business. Positive cultural values would include, but not be limited to, the following:

- A focus on the achievement of results or outcomes that meet, or exceed, the performance expectations of the mission statement and the business's objectives

- The encouragement of employees to take personal responsibility for meeting the needs and expectations of the firm's customers

- An emphasis on every employee paying attention to the details of his or her job in order to serve the needs of customers and enhance performance

- The effort to collaborate with team members and work together in a supportive fashion (Individual competitive behaviors are subordinated to the enhanced outcomes that group efforts produce.)

Apple, Inc., guided by founder Steve Jobs, is a high-profile example of how an entrepreneur and founding team can generate value in the marketplace through the cultural impact created by superior product and service offerings. Steve Jobs died in late 2011, but his legacy lives on in the Apple brand, which has had a profound impact on modern technology. Jobs and his founding team revolutionized the computing world in the late 1970s by serving the personal computer market in a way that completely changed how consumers interact with machines, media, and one another. Later, the Apple team developed digital devices such as the iPod, iPad, Nano, and iPhone, all of which exhibit technological advances and aesthetics that are iconic and that changed the way people live, work, and socialize.

If entrepreneurs fail to take actions to create and support a positive organizational culture, they will find themselves dealing with the organizational culture that evolves *without* leadership. The organizational culture expresses the core values that exist among the team members. Thus, by carefully selecting quality team members and instilling and reinforcing in them positive performance expectations, the entrepreneur can establish a strong culture with positive core values that are widely, if not universally, shared. A firm's positive organizational culture has the capability of creating a powerful competitive advantage in its operational dealings with customers.

Establishing Performance Expectations

The founder must never assume that team members understand, accept, and internalize the firm's performance expectations. Entrepreneurs lead their firm through the establishment of realistic value-creating performance expectations that are consistently reinforced. Leaders must clearly define the performance expectations of each position in the firm. Performance expectations link every employee to the entrepreneur, and to one another. The firm's performance expectations are tangible measures of outcomes, and telling each new employee of your confidence in her or his ability to meet or exceed these expectations can be motivational. High expectations very often result in high performance. That said, performance expectations must be reasonable and achievable. If team members have trust in the entrepreneur and believe that an expectation is realistic and attainable, they will make every effort to meet it.

The establishment of a positive organizational culture always begins with an entrepreneur who articulates a vision for how the business must operate, both internally and externally. The founder's vision is paramount. Next, the founder hires and retains only team members who are willing to accept the founder's values. The founder leads this process through creating and implementing an employee socialization process that immerses the team members in the firm's core values. All training of new employees supports work and interpersonal behaviors that reflect these core values. The founder must serve as a role model. Only in this way can the founder encourage each team member to internalize the firm's critical core values.

What are some of the most essential core values a founder might wish to establish and reinforce? That is, in some ways, the same question as the one regarding what behaviors attract and retain customers and team members. Here are some of these values:

- Trust and respect

- Honesty in all dealings

- Ethical behaviors

- Organizational cooperation in resolving customer's problems

- Positive conflict resolution

- Finding self-fulfillment and self-motivation from the achievement of high performance outcomes

Entrepreneurs need to recognize that an organization does not automatically create a high-performance organizational culture. In reality, it takes a great deal of continued reinforcement of the behaviors that are desired. This means aggressive positive leadership to master the human resources function.

TEAM MEMBER SELECTION

The worst employee hired is inevitably the weakest link in any new venture's performance. The more challenging the task and the higher the performance expectations, the more critical the process of team member selection becomes. What could be more challenging for a new venture than survival in a highly competitive business environment? The failure rate statistics clarify the ugly reality that the odds are against the survival of most new businesses. Consequently, it is essential to screen carefully every team member in whose hands a new venture will be placing its future. The first step in the selection process is to know precisely what type of person you wish to hire. The entrepreneurial team members must

- Have the proven skills and abilities to perform the technical components of the task for which they are being screened (in a start-up situation, the selected team members must be technically competent, as few start-ups can afford a "learn-on-the-job" hiring strategy);

- Possess personal values that are compatible with firm's desired organizational culture; and

- Have the potential to grow in their jobs as the organization itself is successful and the requirements of positions expand (each team member will need to be capable of rapidly adjusting to the changes brought about by a dynamic and competitive market).

With growth and change comes the need for team members to find self-motivation in the job and accept greater authority. The founder will not be able to make all of the operational decisions. Empowering team members must be encouraged so that individuals "step up" and demonstrate their competency in solving problems and making decisions.

Finding, screening, and selecting the venture's team members are critical steps to early success. Most successful entrepreneurs have personally created the new venture on their own or with the assistance of a few trusted friends. The founder alone may have undertaken the analytical assessment of the product and that of the market niche. Now, in order to reach the full potential of the new venture, the founder must attract and hire team members that are willing to accept and capable of implementing the founder's vision for the business.

A few lucky entrepreneurs know potential team members. These potential employees have known "track records" for technical competencies, as well as personal values that are compatible with those of the founder. These known individuals can become the "core" of the new venture's workforce.

Entrepreneurs who do not have a pool of qualified team members will need to start from "scratch" in attracting and interviewing possible candidates. Attracting quality team members is the first and often most difficult task. In the case of a new start-up business, the entrepreneur will need to convince highly skilled and talented individuals to leave their current employers to join an unproven entrepreneurial business. What will motivate people to leave dependable work positions, where they are recognized for their talents, skills, and performance, to join a new and unproven business? Also, in their current positions, potential team members are normally well compensated for their proven performance, and these salaries may be difficult for the new firm to match. What is one to do?

First, the entrepreneur must recognize that the new business needs these individuals more than they need to take a risk with a new business. One path forward is for the entrepreneur to create an inspirational message that has the power to overcome some of the barriers an experienced professional might face when joining a new venture. The components of such a message might include some of the following points:

- The new business will allow team members to achieve their full potential. Large organizations often "cubbyhole" employees because they are so productive in specific tasks or jobs, whereas the new venture will provide a wider range of opportunities.

- The new business will offer a positive work environment and a supportive culture designed to create an emotionally superior work experience.

- The new business will allow team members a higher level of decision-making responsibility. In many large organizations, the existing organizational structure does not encourage, or allow, nonmanagerial employees to make any decisions, and it only lets managers make decisions under an extremely narrow and restrictive set of circumstances.

- The new business has the potential to achieve exceptional profitability and, consequently, generate the ability to pay superior wages, salaries, and benefits to the initial team members.

In some cases, the founder may be willing to allow the early-stage critical team members the opportunity to purchase an equity position in the business when the business has proven to be competitive and profitable. The entrepreneur needs to recognize that the "financial hook" of future higher income or of an attractive equity position must be substantial to attract individuals whose talents are essential to the long-term success of the business. Unless these talented individuals are fundamentally risk takers, they will be difficult to attract. Why would they leave a known and secure paycheck for an unknown and insecure financial future? The entrepreneur will need to make a compelling argument that the new start-up has opportunities well beyond those offered by the organization where they are currently employed.

One popular view of corporate culture is on the side of the entrepreneur wanting to attract professionals away from established companies—start-ups are seen as innovative, interesting, and hot places to work. In popular culture, movies such as *Office Space* and television shows such as *The Office* openly ridicule the corporate culture of staid, established businesses, while the start-up companies like Facebook and Google are often portrayed as somehow more hip, lean, and rapidly evolving. Software as a service (SaaS) and media-based start-ups, in particular, have generated an image of youth, vigor, and values centered on individual contributions within organizations. An entrepreneur of a start-up having a vibrant and evolving culture might be able to benefit from these views to attract expert staff away from a staid corporate environment.

Job Specifications and Descriptions

Screening potential team members begins with well-defined job specifications and a comprehensive job description for each position. The entrepreneur must be able to write the detailed requirements for each position and describe the performance expectations. These tools are absolutely necessary to identify the best-qualified applicant. These objective standards allow for every candidate to be evaluated fairly. Position specifications will normally include some of the following components:

- Specific technical or managerial skills and abilities
- A particular knowledge set, often documented by a record of experience and education
- Problem-solving skills relevant to the position
- Interpersonal skills consistent with the firm's culture
- Personal values relative to work
- Ethical behavioral requirements
- Cognitive skills and abilities

Every position would require these components to be rated differently. Weighting the importance of each component allows for the specific position to reflect which skills, abilities, knowledge, and behaviors are critical for success. The unique job specification for each position can then be used to develop the specific job descriptions, which, in turn, are communicated to potential candidates. The job specifications and description comprise the new venture's critical selection criteria. Applicants who do not meet these two basic screening criteria can be quickly rejected. Those who meet the criteria, based on their professional résumés, should submit a more detailed job or position application. Based on this detailed application, the entrepreneur can take proactive steps to verify that the applicant's claims are honest and correct. As an example, did the applicant actually attend the schools listed on the application? Did she complete that degree? The same is true for the verification of the applicant's employment and work history. Did he work for that company in that position for that length of time?

In some cases, it might be possible to speak with persons in the industry who are willing to discuss the applicant's work skills and personal behaviors. This opportunity to discover details about the applicant is not the norm. Most firms will only verify the dates of employment and the applicant's salary or wage rate. Yet it never hurts to search for an objective individual to comment on the applicant's skill and work behaviors. Social media websites have recently provided a new view into prospective employee's personal lives. Many feel that looking into an applicant's public profiles is an invasion of privacy, yet companies now are more often relying on social networks to identify morally undesirable traits in applicants. It is highly recommended that potential applicants take steps to ensure the privacy of photos, online posts, or blogs (especially those related to work); any activities that could be construed as having a negative impact on job performance should not be documented online.

Screening Applicants

These initial screening procedures assist the entrepreneur in selecting the smaller group of applicants who will be invited for an interview. It is valuable to ask those applying for some positions to take performance tests that serve to verify the their skills. In a few limited cases, psychological tests are used to determine personality traits that the entrepreneur believes are correlated with effective job performance. The entrepreneur will normally benefit from inviting a few key team members to assist in the interview process. The reality is that three or four persons asking questions and listening to answers will most likely result in obtaining a deeper insight into the applicant. Interviewers can ask questions based on the issues they believe will illuminate the applicant's fitness to both perform the technical tasks of the job and interact with other team members and the firm's customers. After all interviews are completed, the interviewers can independently rank the applicants and provide specific comments about each applicant's potential to contribute to the firm. These independent rankings and comments allow for a more effective and objective evaluation of each applicant. The group interview method normally brings the entrepreneur greater detail and some unique perspectives about the applicants. The discussion amongst members of the interview team provides the entrepreneur with information that would not have been obtained through a one-on-one interview.

The next step in the selection process involves limiting the number of applicants based on all the information obtained to date. The final selection process involves procedures that may include drug testing, law enforcement checks for previous felony arrests and convictions, and a thorough background check. Applicants are normally required to submit references on their applications. These references are the starting point of the entrepreneur's background check. One valuable technique is to ask each reference contacted to also provide a second set of persons who know the applicant. These secondary references often provide a more accurate evaluation of the applicant. Most applicants only provide references that they are confident will provide a positive evaluation.

Whatever the amount of time and money you invest in the selection process, it will fade in comparison with the cost of the damages resulting from "a bad hire" in a new and vulnerable start-up venture. Many persons feel that intrusive background checks are not ethical. However, applicants have voluntarily applied for a position and should expect that their backgrounds will be a factor in the selection process. Unfortunately, some applicants are not completely honest about their previous achievements and behaviors. The result is that entrepreneurs must be diligent about whom they select to staff their business.

Addressing Poor Performance

Not all employees will be successful in the new venture. When employees are not achieving performance goals, the issue must be addressed immediately. The initial step would include a face-to-face discussion of the problem. What specific performance target or expectation is the employee failing to meet? What are the behaviors that fail to support which of the established values of the business? Perhaps additional training will allow the employee to improve performance. Unfortunately, in some cases, employees are unable to improve their skills or modify their behaviors, and you will need to fire these people. No employee selection process is perfect. In some cases, the individual was not as good a "fit" with the business as anticipated. In other cases, the person changes, displaying attitudes and behaviors toward fellow team members or customers that become inappropriate and detrimental to the organization's work culture.

You are absolutely the one to address these human resources problems. The other employees expect you to act as a leader. Poor performance or inappropriate behaviors impact the work environment of the team and undermine any reward system in place. Your team members often experience these problems, sometime every day, and they expect you to take action.

Sometimes, poor performance or behavior can be addressed by better ways of reinforcing expectations. In general, encouraging high performance focuses on three interrelated expectations and relationships:

- Team member efforts will be sufficient to achieve the entrepreneur's desired level of performance.

- Team members believe that the attainment of the requested performance will result in both personal recognition and the receipt of desired rewards.

- Rewards are valued by the team members and actually satisfy personal goals or needs.

These three factors are interrelated because failure at any stage causes the process to fail. An entrepreneur cannot set performance expectations at levels that the team members believe are unrealistically high. A team member's reaction to unrealistic expectations is to become frustrated, unmotivated, and fearful of being terminated. In the second situation, if the team members believe that the entrepreneur is unwilling to reward them for the successful achievement of a requested performance outcome, they quickly view their relationship with the founder as one sided. In this situation, performance is very likely to decline. The third component requires that the entrepreneur really understand every team member's personal goals. Too often, an entrepreneur offers only one type of reward for performance. If the reward offered does not meet the team member's personal goals, that team member does not value the reward and may fail to perform at a high level again.

CREATING AN ETHICAL ENVIRONMENT

Entrepreneurs are expected to work hard, be innovative, take risks, and create a business that can deliver goods or services effectively, efficiently, and profitably. Earning a profit is expected by everyone. However, ethical behavior is not only *expected* but must be *demanded*. Society's demand for ethical behavior and honesty is at an all-time high. The failings of a few have unfortunately given all businesses and business leaders a "black eye," as instances of dishonesty and lack of ethical behavior become public. US firms operating in China, for example, have been accused of collusion with the more negative factions within the Communist regime. Negative press generated from activities such as dumping toxic chemicals into the environment, distributing toys with lead paints (a known toxin), violating worker's rights, and otherwise jeopardizing human health are among the negative images that American businesses working at home and abroad must contend with in the marketplace. The poor judgments of a few can affect the way the world sees a company, and for a long time. These issues, and others, have historically plagued developing economies—in the United States and Great Britain, the rise of the Industrial Age marked an era of severe human rights violations that took generations to resolve, in part. Even today in the United States, the National Labor Relations Board issues complaints about corporate violations of labor laws, for example. But we emphasize that most businesses and entrepreneurs are extremely careful to act both ethically and within the law.

Code of Personal Conduct

The most positive response to this negative publicity is for business leaders to reevaluate their responsibilities, both to society in general and to *all* relevant stakeholders. Business ethics involve the creation and consistent implementation of a code of conduct based on moral values and behavioral standards that serve to guide organizational decision makers. An entrepreneur must make a commitment to enforce these values and standards. If the values and standards are not made specifically clear, the "gray areas" of decision making can result in unethical behaviors. The situational "gray areas" need to be addressed by

Always Question Before Acting

Ethical behaviors are not theoretical. Ethical behaviors can be reinforced by involving team members in answering together a series of questions that include the following:

Does this decision or action meet our personal standards for interacting with others?

Would I want everyone to behave in this fashion?

How will these behaviors make me feel about myself?

Does this decision or action support my personal belief system?

Would these actions infringe or impinge on the dignity of others?

Are these actions fair and just?

What are the anticipated consequences of these actions?

How would I feel if these actions were made public?

How would people that I respect view my decision or action?

the entrepreneur. The entrepreneur must describe what actions should always be taken. Honest team members, who know and understand the firm's ethical standards and how these apply to workplace situations, normally behave ethically.

The entrepreneur needs to invest time and effort to ensure that the firm's ethical standards are enforced in a way that creates and protects the firm's positive reputation. Entrepreneurs should view setting and enforcing high ethical standards as the norm, never the exception. A new business venture needs to make every effort to hire team members who have high ethical standards. Additionally, the entrepreneur must support team member's positive ethical behaviors. Ethical behaviors are not accidental.

Ethical decision or actions will become much clearer when the entrepreneur and the team members evaluate potential decisions or behaviors based on their answers to these questions.

The entrepreneur can further shape an ethical organizational environment by the following:

Whenever an ethically challenging situation arises, the entrepreneur serves as a highly visible role model who takes appropriate actions and makes the team members aware of the nature of the situation, why the decision was made or the action taken, and the implications of the ethical decision or action.

It is also important to provide training for the team members, training that reinforces the message that ethical behavior produces long-term positive results.

Finally, the entrepreneur should continue to communicate the firm's expectations regarding ethical behaviors. Recognize and reward team members for adhering to the firm's ethical standards, and punish those who do not.

Ethical behavior is so essential to earning and retaining customers. Entrepreneurs' behaviors are based on their personal values. These values must be integrated into the firm's code of ethics. Screening potential team members based on their demonstrated adherence to high ethical standards can give the entrepreneur confidence that the business will respond properly to a potentially ethically challenging situation.

CONCLUSION

Entrepreneurs understand that the ability to create a business venture with the capability to achieve maximum potential requires

A willingness to become an active, committed entrepreneur who will make every effort to master the skills and behaviors of leaders;

The creation of a high-performance organizational culture supportive of both organizational and individual success;

The selection of an entrepreneurial team that best "fits" the current and future needs of the business venture;

The establishment of high performance expectations for each team member;

Leadership based on a deep understanding of the concepts of personality, intelligence, character, and values and on how each of these components affects every team member's current and potential contribution to the firm; and, finally;

The creation of an ethical environment for the organization—without exception, all decisions and actions must meet the firm's code of ethics.

ENTREPRENEURIAL EXERCISES

Entrepreneurial Exercise 7.1

Part I

Based on your readings in the chapter and on your personal experience, please list what you believe are the most critical components of leadership. Next, rate your criteria on a scale of 1 through 5, with 5 being absolutely critical and 1 being the least important.

Criteria	Rating 1–5
1.	
2.	
3.	
4.	
5.	

Part II

Please use the same criteria you listed in Part I to rate yourself as a leader. Please provide examples to support your self-rating.

5 (Extremely High) to 1 (Adequate)

Criteria Ranking	Your Self-Rating	Example to Support Your Rating
1.		
2.		
3.		
4.		
5.		

Entrepreneurial Exercise 7.2

Based on your self-ratings from the previous exercise, please detail how you plan to improve on those leadership skills that you rated as less than 4.

Criteria	Plans for Improvement
1.	
2.	
3.	
4.	
5.	

Entrepreneurial Exercise 7.3

Part I

Based on your personal experience and your readings, what do you believe are the most powerful motivational factors that entrepreneurs must create to achieve maximum individual performance? What results or outcomes flow from each motivational factor?

Motivational Factors ⟶	Results When Present
1.	1.
2.	2.
3.	3.
4.	4.
5.	5.

Part II

Please write a summary of your beliefs about motivation and the achievement of positive outcomes. Include any examples of motivational techniques that you have experienced and describe their positive affects.

Entrepreneurial Exercise 7.4

Using your proposed new business venture as a model, describe what you are planning to do to create an internal organizational "culture" that will support a high-performance organization. Please be as specific as possible.

My firm's high-performance organizational culture will be achieved through

1.

2.

3.

4.

5.

Entrepreneurial Exercise 7.5

Based on the chapter and your personal experience, please describe the steps you plan to take when hiring your entrepreneurial team members.

Hiring steps (in sequence):

1.

2.

3.

4.

5.

6.

7.

8.

Entrepreneurial Exercise 7.6

The best way to understand the importance of intelligence, personality, character, and values is to use yourself as a model. Please describe each of these critical components.

Part I

As objectively as possible, please describe and evaluate your intelligence.

Part II

As objectively as possible, please describe and evaluate your personality.

Part III

As objective as possible, describe and evaluate your values.

Part IV

Please combine the elements of your intelligence, personality, character, and values into a composite that describes which aspects of entrepreneurship you will probably find easy and which you will find challenging. Based on your summary, how will these components impact the success of your proposed new business venture? (Please be as specific as possible.)

Part V

Building on your responses to the first four parts, outline at least two personal elements of intelligence, personality, character, or values that might inhibit you from leading your new business venture toward achieving its maximum potential. What are your plans to overcome these barriers?

Entrepreneurial Exercise 7.7

Every entrepreneur must recognize that positive ethical outcomes do not occur accidently. Please list the components of your proposed business venture's "code of ethics." Please be as specific as you believe is needed to ensure that team members understand your ethical standards and what their behaviors must be.

FORMS OF OWNERSHIP

If historical experience could teach us anything, it would be that private property is inextricably linked with civilization.

Ludwig von Mises

Just as man can't exist without his body, so no rights can exist without the right to translate one's rights into reality, to think, to work and keep the results, which means: the right of property.

Ayn Rand

CHAPTER LEARNING OBJECTIVES

Upon completion of this chapter you will be able to

List the different intellectual properties

Discuss the value of protecting intellectual property

Explain the different types of ownership

Compare the benefits of sole proprietorship and partnerships

Debate which type of ownership is best

Describe why ventures must obtain licenses and permits

Identify potential legal obstacles to business ventures

Τhis chapter does not replace the need to obtain legal counsel in addressing issues such as the protection of intellectual property, the writing of a founder's agreement, selecting an appropriate form of ownership, or obtaining a functional understanding of contract law. Every entrepreneur, large or small, operates in a society governed by laws and regulations. Ignoring the laws and regulations that govern your decisions and actions is always a threat to the business, and often to you.

PROTECTING INTELLECTUAL PROPERTY

A business venture that has at its foundation new or unique knowledge must take every effort to protect what is termed its *intellectual property*. Intellectual property can take any one of the following forms: patents, trademarks, copyrights, or trade secrets. Patents, trademarks, and copyrights are the legal instruments that provide protection for the firm's inventions, trademarks, names, and identities, as well as for any other original works. The entrepreneur who fails to protect these intellectual properties as assets may lose property rights forever. In this area of law, the entrepreneur must normally find experienced legal counsel to act swiftly and aggressively to ensure that these critical intellectual property rights are secured and, if necessary, defended.

The Patent Process

A patent is a grant from the federal government's Patent and Trademark Office (USPTO) to an inventor of a product giving the applicant the exclusive right to exclude others from making, using, or selling the invention in this country for a period of 20 years (for a utility patent) or 14 years (for a design patent) from the date of the patent application. In effect, the patent provides the inventor with a virtual monopoly over the manufacture, use, and sales of the product. The intent of the patent process is to reward inventors for the generation of new knowledge as well as to encourage and stimulate creativity and innovation.

There are two main obstacles to obtaining a patent, and these are detailed in Title 35 of the United States Code §102. Section A prevents a patent if there is any evidence that the invention is already known (called having *prior art*) before the applicant's date of invention. Section B denies patentability if the invention was patented or described in print in the United States or a foreign country or was in public use or on sale in the United States more than one year prior to the date of the application for a U.S. patent. The entrepreneur needs to apply for a patent, then, within one year of her or his initial invention. After submitting the patent application to the USPTO, the inventor can label the product as "patent pending." The reason prompt application for a patent is necessary it that the inventor loses potential protection if the invention has been publicized in print anywhere in the world or if it has been used or offered for sale in this country prior to the date of the patent application. "Patent pending" status is critical, as it provides the inventor protection until the actual patent is issued. It currently takes approximately four years for patent review prior to one being issued. This lengthy time lag between the patent filing and its issuance can be very frustrating, but going through the process is necessary in order to protect "knowledge goods" that might become profitable machines, manufactured products, business methods, cosmetic design features, or software programs, for example.

The two major types of patents are utility patents and design patents. Utility patents cover equipment, machinery or parts of machinery, processes, or software. Design patents are generally related to the physical appearance of an article. In recent years, the patent office has issued patents for business methods as well. A patentable business method, like any other thing seeking a patent, must be new, useful, and nonobvious. In other words, the business method needs be an innovative process that produces a useful, concrete, and tangible result. The patent office has attempted to remain current through the willingness to respond to new business methods and processes.

The patent process can be very intimidating. For this reason, most entrepreneurs employ a patent attorney to guide them through the process. The patent process involves a number of steps:

Step 1: Establishing the novelty of an invention. Completing this step requires meeting the following criteria:

- Others cannot have used the invention in the United States prior to the patent application.

- The invention has not already been patented by anyone else in the United States or described in a printed publication.

- The invention has not been in public use or offered for sale in the United States.

These criteria assist the inventor in determining whether to go further with the patent process, which can be extremely time consuming, especially if the inventor is not familiar with U.S. Patent Office procedures. The patent office examines the novelty of an idea by conducting a detailed search of the scientific and popular literature and the previously issued U.S. patents in the area. Any publication of this idea more than one year before the application seriously jeopardizes an inventor's chance of receiving an issued patent.

Step 2: Documenting the proposed invention. To protect the patent's claim in situations where others have a similar or identical invention, the applicant must provide verification of when the invention was discovered. Inventors need to retain detailed descriptions and drawings and proof of these facts and dates. To be acceptable, all documents need to be supported by the testimony of other individuals who have first-hand knowledge of the development of the invention. The inventor benefits from having well-documented records of the invention process that can be witnessed by a knowledgeable person. Drawings are always valuable if dated and witnessed. The laboratory notebook is crucial in research settings and provides critical documentation related to novelty.

Another option is for the inventor to file what is termed a *disclosure document* with the U.S. Patent Office before applying for a patent. A letter describing the invention, including drawings, can be sent via registered mail to the USPTO. The patent office will send the inventor a registration number. Once a registration number is issued, the patent office agrees to retain the disclosure document for two years. This disclosure document is of great value when the patent examiner is determining the conception date of the invention.

Step 3: Determining if the invention is actually original. The inventor establishes this via a patent search to differentiate the new invention from existing prior art that may be related to the patent application. An entrepreneur can attempt to conduct this search on his or her own, but the search is normally very difficult. To avoid making costly errors, the inventor frequently has the staff of a patent attorney conduct the search—a very valuable idea. Legal professionals who conduct patent searches on a regular basis know where and how to conduct a patent search and can more accurately determine the originality of the invention in a timely fashion. A patent search requires knowledge of the search process and a level of expertise not normally held by an inventor or the entrepreneur who capitalizes on the idea.

Step 4: Evaluating the search results. Based on what the entrepreneur or inventor discovers in Step 3, she or he must decide whether the search results justify submitting a patent application. Seldom do the results indicate that nothing has been patented that would conflict with the proposed invention receiving a patent. However, there may be technical niches where an invention could be evaluated as new or original. At this point, the inventor must determine if filing for a patent is a viable and feasible option. There may be patented devices that are similar, but the patent reviewer could determine that the entrepreneur's new invention is different enough to be granted a patent.

Step 5: Submitting the patent application. Once the inventor decides to pursue a patent, the formal application process has begun. The patent application requires the inventor to describe the invention in detail. It becomes essential that the inventor submit all of the documentation discussed in Step 2. A patent application includes the following components:

- An oath or declaration that clearly states that the filer is the true inventor.

- A detailed description of the invention, called the specifications, and a definition of the invention, called the claim, which identifies the patentable new features of the invention.

- If applicable, a set of detailed drawings of the invention. The drawings should be as accurate as possible and show all of the invention's parts. Nothing can be added later, so it is imperative that the drawings submitted be complete and very accurate.

- A "small entity declaration," stating that the inventor is not a large corporation. This declaration allows the inventor to pay a lower application fee.

- The filing fee, which must be submitted with the application.

The most important parts of the patent application are the claims made because these are the components that define the parameters of the patent rights and determine the level of protection the invention receives against possible patent infringements. The scope of the patent is also critical. If the scope is too narrow, the patent may not be defendable in a use beyond what the inventor submits.

Step 6: Prosecuting the patent application. When the U.S. Patent Office verifies that the patent filing is complete and correct, the inventor receives a serial number and a filing date. The patent examiner then investigates whether prior patents have been issued. If the investigation determines that a prior patent has been issued, the inventor is advised that a patent will not be issued. The inventor can challenge this ruling by responding with an amendment that presents an argument outlining why the patent office should issue the patent. If the patent application is rejected again, the inventor can appeal to the Board of Patent Appeals for a fresh review of the invention. This panel is comprised of three chief examiners; it reviews all submissions related to the patent application and the decision of the patent examiners. The panel decides whether to uphold or to overturn the original examiner's decision.

Step 7: Defending the patent. The U.S. Patent Office grants the inventor the right to the benefits of a patent but does not defend the inventor against patent infringement. Enforcement of a patent rests solely with the owner of the patent. The patent office neither polices possible infringement nor provides technical or legal support if an infringement case goes to court. In many situations, the potential infringer is a major organization with a large legal staff able to challenge the patent ownership of the inventor aggressively. Defending the entrepreneur's patent rights can quickly become very expensive.

Trademarks and Service Marks

A trademark provides protection for a specific word, symbol, name, logo, or slogan that is employed by a firm to identify itself to the public. Service marks act the same way for firms that provide services. The protection provided to the owner is identical, so in this section the authors will simply use the term trademark. A successful trademark serves as a firm's signature in the marketplace. Many of the most successful trademarks are recognized globally. Possibly one of the best examples would be Coca-Cola. The Coca-Cola trademark is easily recognized anywhere you find the product.

Start-up companies can create and file a trademark with the U.S. Patent and Trademark Office under what is termed the "intent-to-use" provision that protects the trademark if the product is brought to market in fewer than 4 years. If a firm finds that its trademark is effective in the marketplace, the trademark can be renewed every 10 years. Clearly, the trademark must be original. A firm can create a valid trademark by taking the following steps:

- Select a distinctive word, symbol, graphic design, phrase, or other image that serves to identify your product or service distinctly. The trademark should link the potential customer psychologically to the business, product, or service.

- Existing firms with unique and valuable trademarks will take extremely aggressive legal action against anyone whom they feel infringes on their trademark; therefore, a firm must research existing trademarks to avoid expensive litigation in the future. Consequently, having a qualified attorney conduct a trademark search is money well spent.

- Register the trademark with the U.S. Patent and Trademark Office. This step serves to provide the firm with greater protection against future trademark infringement.

- Common advice is to use your trademark as an adjective followed by a noun (e.g., the Trampoline® rebound tumbler) and not as a noun or a verb (e.g., to Google the concept). Doing so helps you avoid having your trademark declared generic, which would mean a loss of protection. As you can see, there is a fine line between establishing a well-known trademark and having that trademark become generic. When was the last time you jumped on a rebound tumbler? To be most effective, the trademark should stand out from the context of surrounding words.

- Make others aware that the trademark is that of your business. Once a trademark is registered with the U.S. Patent and Trademark office, the firm should use it consistently with the ® symbol to communicate to all that the trademark is registered. (The symbol ™ is also often used, although this just indicates that the owner is claiming rights to the trademark, not that it is nationally registered.)

When we look at most highly successful firms, we can easily identify their trademarks. This recognition by potential customers represents the power of an effective trademark.

Copyrights

A copyright is an exclusive right that protects the creator of original works of authorship. Copyrights protect the creators of written works, art, music, and movies. Registration with the U.S. Copyright Office provides protection against the illegal copying, theft, or plagiarism of a creator's work. Copyright protection is relatively easy to obtain and not costly. The types of material that a firm can copyright include computer software, promotional material, sound recordings, presentations, business plans, and photographs. Copyrighting such works gives the creator the exclusive rights to reproduce, revise, distribute, display, or sell the material.

Trade Secrets

An important part of a firm's intellectual property would include any valuable knowledge that is retained as a trade secret. These trade secrets are normally protected by employee contracts that include both nondisclosure and noncompetition agreements. The nondisclosure document should be used by the firm in any detailed discussions with individuals outside the firm. If people sign such a document, they are held liable if they use the firm's proprietary knowledge or share it with others. The protection of trade secrets falls under both federal and state statutes but is enforced only by legal actions taken by the firm that believes it has been infringed upon. The firm is expected to take aggressive actions to protect its trade secrets. These actions include having a wide variety of individuals sign nondisclosure agreements, including board members, consultants and advisors, employees, suppliers, and anyone else who has access to the firm's proprietary knowledge that it wishes to protect.

Noncompetition agreements (sometimes called *non-compete agreements*) usually apply when employees who have knowledge of the firm's trade secrets leave to work for other firms or to start a new business venture. Any use or disclosure of the trade secrets can be legally acted upon by the firm whose trade secrets are revealed or stolen. In a globally competitive environment, protecting trade secrets has become a growing problem. Unfortunately, entrepreneurs cannot normally anticipate success in their attempts to protect their trade secrets outside of the United States.

PROTECTING INTELLECTUAL PROPERTY RIGHTS

Patents, trademarks, copyrighted material, and trade secrets are all forms of intellectual property that must be protected actively and aggressively. It is the responsibility of the owner of the intellectual property to protect these rights or secrets. Aggressively pursuing legal action against infringers is the only way an entrepreneur can protect the firm's ownership of intellectual property. In some cases, a letter from the entrepreneur can gain compliance from the infringer; other cases will require an infringement lawsuit. As you can imagine, these lawsuits can be extremely expensive and time consuming. If the infringer is a large corporation with legal resources, its attorneys will likely drag out the litigation, costing the entrepreneur significant amounts of money to enforce intellectual properties rights. In contrast, litigation against small firms is more likely to be successful, but the infringer might not have the financial resources to pay any compensation.

In many cases, entrepreneurs may choose to seek the resolution of intellectual property rights infringement through alternative dispute resolution techniques such as mediation, arbitration, or even the minitrial. Mediation employs a neutral third party to hear both sides of the argument and recommend a solution. The mediator's recommendation is not binding. In arbitration, the process is similar, but the arbitrator's decision is binding on all parties. The third option is a minitrial that brings both parties and their attorneys together before a private judge for a one-day hearing. The minitrial is much less costly than a full court case.

Founders' Agreement

Especially when two or more entrepreneurs start a business together, it is valuable to delineate each founder's rights and responsibilities. Does one own a patent? Is equity shared equally? The founders' agreement places in writing answers to these and similar questions, and it can minimize the potential for future conflicts. Here are some of the issues a founders' agreement can address:

1. How will each founder's equity in the business be based on his or her contribution to the business? These contributions can be difficult to evaluate. They could be assets such as cash or patents, but other contributions could be what might be termed *sweat equity*, *market knowledge*, or *industry connections*. Agreement on each founder's percentage of ownership is often the most difficult issue to be resolved.

2. How will income earned by the business be distributed? Some founders may wish to have all revenues reinvested in the business for an extended time in order to finance the firm's growth from within. Other founders might want the net income to be distributed as dividends.

3. What happens to the equity of a founder who leaves the firm? A buyback clause requires any founder to sell her or his ownership stake in the business to the remaining founders in the event of death, incapacitation, or retirement from the business.

4. How will the firm's shares be valued in order to facilitate the buyback clause provision?

As you can see, the founders' agreement serves to reduce potential sources of conflict that can arise as the business becomes successful.

SELECTING AN APPROPRIATE FORM OF OWNERSHIP

Once the new business venture has taken actions to protect its intellectual properties and create a founders' agreement, the next step is the selection of a legal form of organization. There is no one best form of business organization. Entrepreneurs need to assess their specific situations before making their choice. Each form of ownership has positive and negative factors that need to be analyzed. The simplest form of ownership is a sole proprietorship.

ENTREPRENEURIAL SPOTLIGHT
FINN BRICE—CHUCKLEFISH, LLC

Finn Brice is an independent video-game developer and the founder of Chucklefish Games, a firm based in London, England. The firm's successful video games such as Starbound and Spellbound are recognized worldwide by gamers.

As Brice describes it, Spellbound is a "wizard-school sim" role-playing game (RPG) inspired by the likes of Harry Potter and other RPGs such as Harvest Moon and Shadow Valley. He goes on to say that the game "revolves around your path through school, the relationships you build, and your mastery of the several schools of magic at your disposal."

Chucklefish was founded in 2011. The firm has both developed its own games (e.g., Starbound, Stardrew Valley, and Spellbound) and worked with other developers to publish games such as Risk of Rain and Pocket Rumble. Chucklefish's proactive collaborations have benefited the artists behind some of the best video games. Thus, Finn Brice has proven to be more than a highly creative video-game developer; he is a shaper of a market segment.

Finn Brice is an example of an entrepreneur in a nontraditional industry that relies heavily on the protection of artistic creations.

Sources:

1. "Finn Brice: Profile," *Forbes*, accessed July 2018, https://www.forbes.com/profile/finn-brice/.

2. "Chucklefish 'Massive Fans' of Switch, Open to Bringing Upcoming Project Spellbound to the System," Nintendo Everything [blog], accessed July 2017, https://nintendoeverything.com/chucklefish-massive-fans-of-switch-open-to-bringing-upcoming-project-spellbound-to-the-system/

Sole Proprietorship

A sole proprietorship is an unincorporated business owned by its founder. This form of business ownership is considered the easiest and simplest. In the United States, it is also the most popular. Sole proprietorships can be what some term *income replacement* businesses; these are usually going to be smaller as they are designed to provide for the income needs of the founder and family.

Advantages include the following:

1. Sole proprietorships are extremely easy to create. A simple business license may be all that is required if the business is operating under the owner's name. Start-up costs can be very low if they involve only the payment of any business fees or licenses and the acquisition of the firm's trade name, if necessary.

2. This form of legal structure is easy to discontinue. If the entrepreneur decides to end the business, the sole proprietorship can be closed quickly, even though it might still have outstanding liabilities or debts.

3. An entrepreneur has full and complete decision-making authority. Consequently, the entrepreneur can move quickly in response changing market conditions.

4. The entrepreneur retains all profits after paying personal income taxes, as the business itself is not taxed separately. Consequently, the entrepreneur has a strong motivation to maximize profits.

There are an equal number of disadvantages to being an entrepreneur in a sole proprietorship:

1. The most commonly mentioned disadvantage of sole proprietorships is that owners can be subjected to personal liability. If the business fails and the liabilities are greater than the cash available to meet them, the entrepreneur's personal assets can be attached and sold to meet the uncovered debt. The laws of most states declare that some personal assets (such as the family home and car) cannot be attached and sold.

2. The firm has limited access to financial capital beyond that of the entrepreneur. This disadvantage can seriously limit growth when the owner's collateral is inadequate and banks are reluctant to provide loans. In many cases, the only source of growth capital is the firm's net profit. The firm's assets are normally invested in its working capital and in accounts receivable and therefore not available to fund a growth opportunity.

3. The entrepreneur has personal limitations in knowledge, skills, and capabilities. As an example, the founder may be exceptionally skilled in manufacturing the firm's product but not possess any meaningful capabilities in marketing or finance. The lack of scope in knowledge, skills, and capabilities is a major cause of new venture failure. When the entrepreneur has significant deficits in managerial or technical skills, some

critical problems can go unrecognized until they are too large to cope with, resulting in business failure.

4. The business ends if the entrepreneur dies or becomes disabled. Lack of continuity is a serious threat. Unless there is a preexisting plan to transfer the business to another person, the business often simply stops.

5. The entrepreneur may have difficulty in attracting and retaining long-term employees. Sole proprietorships frequently offer only limited opportunities to employees, making them less attractive places to work. Employees who believe that the business limits their personal growth opportunities often begin to search for employment in larger firms, so the business suffers from disruptive turnovers in staff.

These disadvantages of sole proprietorship are why firms with proven growth potential might select a different form of ownership, one allowing them to attract additional capital and a stable workforce.

Udacity

Founded in 2011 as an outgrowth of free computer science courses offered at Stanford University, Udacity has grown into a truly disruptive force in online, technology-directed education. Through the leadership of its cofounder Sebastian Thrun, who invested $200,000 of his own funds to start the company, Udacity identified a clearly unmet customer need and married it with emerging learning platforms to create a vibrant, growing company. Other cofounders include David Stavens and Mike Sokolsky, and Udacity also received funding from Charles River Ventures. The company's name came from its founders' desire to be "audacious for you, the student"—hence Udacity. The company capitalized on its corporate vision by developing a core focus and competency to provide working professionals with the knowledge to advance in their technical careers. The company's business model includes the use of a low-cost educational and training platform offering "nanodegrees" in everything from artificial intelligence to data analysis. In 2017, Udacity enrolled "nearly a million-and-a-half new students residing in virtually every country on the planet." As a result of Thrun's vision and attention to execution, the company had reached a market valuation of $1 billion by 2015.

Sources:

1. Ed Surge, "Can Google's Thrun Create the First Real Online College Degree?" *Fast Company*, January 23, 2012, https://www.fastcompany.com/2679192/can-googles-thrun-create-the-first-real-online-college-degree.
2. Robert A. Rhoads, *MOOCs, High Technology, and Higher Learning* (Baltimore, MD: Johns Hopkins University Press, 2015), 45.
3. Christopher Watkins, "Udacity 2017: The Year in Review," *Udacity* [blog], December 20, 2017, https://blog.udacity.com/2017/12/year-in-review-2017.html.
4. "About Us," Udacity website, accessed July 2018, https://www.udacity.com/.
5. Alex Konrad, "Udacity Reaches $1 Billion Valuation for its Online 'Nanodegrees' with New $105 Million Raise," *Forbes*, November 11, 2015, https://www.forbes.com/sites/alexkonrad/2015/11/11/udacity-reaches-1-billion-valuation-for-its-online-nanodegrees-with-new-105-million-raise/#32805975785c.

Partnership

Another once popular form of ownership is the partnership. In its most basic form, a partnership is an association of two or more persons who co-own a business for the purpose of making a profit. In recent years, legal and taxation issues have rendered the partnership less popular. These issues will be discussed in the section on the disadvantages of a partnership. Not all partners are necessarily equal owners of the business. The legal documents related to the partnership will delineate the specific ownership rights of each partner. If all parties share in the ownership and management of the business, each would be termed a *general partner*. Each general partner has unlimited personal liability and is expected to exercise an active role in the management of the business.

Some partnerships will have one or more general partners and other limited partners. In a limited partnership, only the general partners have unlimited personal liability; the liability of limited partners is restricted to their investment in the business. Also, limited partners cannot take an active role in the management of the business. If limited partners do actively manage the business, they lose their limited personal liability protection. Among limited partners, there are both silent and dormant partners. Silent partners are generally known to be associated with the business. Dormant partners are not known by others to be associated with the business. As both a silent partner and a dormant partner are limited partners, neither manages the business. Other types of partnerships involve secret partners and honorary partners. A secret partner takes an active part in the management of the business but is unknown to the public. Because of the secret partner's active role in the management of the business, he or she will be considered a general partner in the eyes of the law. In contrast, honorary partners may lend their names and reputations to a business even though they neither own a stake in the business nor play an active role in its management. An honorary partner is normally compensated for the use of her or his name in publicizing the business.

Partnership Agreement

Although the laws of most states do not require a partnership agreement or "articles of partnership," these are valuable documents to create. If partners lack a written partnership agreement, the courts will apply the Uniform Partnership Act to resolve any legal disputes. The Uniform Partnership Act defines a partnership as "an association of two or more persons to carry on as co-owners of a business for profit."[1]

The three key elements of any partnership are

1. a common ownership interest in a business,
2. a sharing of the profits and losses of the business, and
3. the right to participate in the management of the business.

Under the Uniform Partnership Act, each partner has the right to

1. Share in the active management and operation of the business,
2. Share in any profits from the operation of the business,

3. Receive a formal accounting of the business affairs of the partnership,

4. Have access to the books and records of the partnership,

5. Receive compensation for expenses incurred in the interest of the partnership, and

6. Receive interest payments on loans made to the partnership.

Additionally, the Uniform Partnership Act sets forth what might be termed the general obligations of the partners. Each partner is obligated to

1. Share in any losses incurred by the business,

2. Submit to majority vote or arbitration any unresolvable differences between or among partners,

3. Work for the partnership without compensation, and

4. Provide all partners with complete information about all business affairs, and a formal accounting of the business activities.

A partnership agreement is a formal legal document that spells out, in writing, the specific status and responsibilities of each partner and all of the terms of the partnership. Every partnership agreement needs to include a well-delineated method for conflict resolution. Spelling out the operational details in advance of starting the business is always valuable. A partnership agreement can include any legal terms or conditions that the partners wish to include.

The following are some of the most common elements of a partnership agreement:

1. Name of the partnership

2. Purpose of the business (what the business intends to do)

3. Domicile of the business (the address of the principle location of the business)

4. Duration of the business venture (the length of time the partnership will operate, either on a continuing basis or for a defined period)

5. The names and addresses of all partners

6. The specific contributions of each partner to the business, whether these contributions are tangible or intangible in nature

7. How all profits and losses will be distributed to the partners

8. The salaries or drawing rights against profits that each partner is entitled to receive

9. Procedures for the inclusion of new partners

10. How the absence or disability of a partner will affect the continuity of the partnership

11. Procedures for selling a partnership interest and any limitations placed on the partners

12. How to modify the partnership agreement

13. How assets will be distributed if the partnership dissolves

A partnership agreement is never intended to be a "cookie-cutter" document. The partners need to discuss, in detail, the components of the document and address all issues that, if not defined, could later become serious impediments to the success of the business.

Advantages of a Partnership

The following are the advantages of a partnership form of business ownership:

1. *Easy to create.* A partnership is both easy and inexpensive to establish. Like a sole proprietorship, the partnership needs to obtain the required business licenses and file a few necessary forms. If the business plans to operate under a trade name, the owners must file a Certificate for Conducting Business as Partners.

2. *Complementary skill set.* Many successful partnerships represent a blending of complementary skills that improves the probability of success of the business venture.

3. *Larger pool of financial capital.* The personal wealth of partners directly and indirectly impacts the financial strength of the business. In a direct fashion, the business has additional start-up capital. Indirectly, the combined financial strength forms a greater base for borrowing needed capital.

4. *Ability to attract limited partners.* Because of the personal liability of general partners, some investors might be willing to become limited partners. Perhaps investors have confidence in the managerial skills and capabilities of the general partners and are excited about the opportunity to invest in a business with the potential to become highly profitable.

5. *Taxation benefits.* Profits distributed to the partners are taxed at their personal rates. The partnership itself does not pay federal income taxes.

6. *Quick response time.* After partners agree, they can make changes, responding quickly to market developments.

7. *Flexible profit distribution.* Profits can be distributed in any way agreed upon in the partnership agreement.

8. *Limited red tape.* The partnership is subjected to very little government regulation.

Disadvantages of a Partnership

The disadvantages of a partnership are slightly more difficult to explain. Here are some of them:

1. *Unlimited personal liability.* At least one of the partners must accept unlimited personal liability for partnership obligations. This legal reality should cause entrepreneurs to think about the potential consequences of the business failing and significant debts remaining, even if this circumstance is unlikely.

2. *Lack of continuity.* Although more stable than sole proprietorships, partnerships can end quickly if one of the partners dies or becomes incapacitated. The partnership agreement may include a provision stating that partnership interests are nontransferable through inheritance, for example. Also, it is common for a partner not to wish to continue with someone other than the original partner. In these situations, the partnership is, by law, dissolved.

3. *Problems with selling a partnership interest.* Associated with the issue of lack of continuity is the problem of disposing of a partnership interest without dissolving the partnership. In many cases, the partnership agreement will describe, in detail, the procedure for the sale of a partner's interest. Most partnership agreements specify that the partner wishing to sell can do so only to the remaining partners. This provision blocks the sale of a partner's interest to an "outsider" that might not be acceptable to the remaining partners. In this situation, the remaining partners need to purchase the selling partner's interest in the business. Two distinctive issues then arise: how to value the interest of the partner and whether the remaining partners are able to fund the buyout. To avoid the first problem, the partnership agreement needs to include the precise process by which the value of a partner's interest will be calculated. These calculation methods are critically important to establishing a fair value for the partner's interest in the business. If the remaining partners cannot find or borrow the amount needed, they may need to accept a "new" partner or dissolve their partnership. When a general partner dies, becomes incompetent, or withdraws from the business, the partnership automatically dissolves, although a new partnership can be established.

4. *Limited resources.* The partnership must always face the reality that it may be unable to raise additional financial capital without searching for and enlisting more limited or full partners.

5. *The law of agency.* Partners are bound by the law of agency, meaning that a decision made by one partner in the name of the partnership legally binds all partners. This disadvantage has resulted in a large number of business failures and lost investments.

6. *Conflict.* Sometimes, partners disagree and personalities clash. Over time, people often change and conflicts can arise. The law of agency can magnify these conflicts if one partner assumes the mantle of being the "best qualified" to make the most critical decisions and does so without consulting the other partners—and makes a mistake. No partnership agreement can always control someone with a superiority complex.

These disadvantages put a great deal of stress on the partnership. What is clear is the need for a detailed partnership agreement that does its best to address the issues facing any partnership.

Dissolution and Termination of a Partnership

Dissolution of a partnership occurs when a general partner ceases to be associated with the business. On the other hand, termination of a partnership is the final act of winding up the business. In a termination, the intent of the partners is to cease operations.

Dissolution ends the partnership as a business whereas termination winds up its affairs for good. Dissolution occurs when any one of the following events occurs:

1. A partnership founded for a specific time period or a specific activity reaches the end of either

2. A general partner desires to cease the operations of the business, which can happen at any time

3. One or more of the partners expels a partner under the provisions of the partnership agreement

4. A general partner dies, suffers from insanity, retires, or otherwise withdraws, unless the partnership agreement provides for a method of continuation

5. The bankruptcy of the partnership or of any general partner

6. Continuing losses resulting in the partnership's inability to meet its debts

7. Improper or illegal behaviors of a general partner that reflect negatively on the business

8. The formation of a new partnership to operate the business

In this last circumstance, the old partnership is dissolved and replaced by a new partnership in a smooth transition.

The Limited Partnership and the Master Limited Partnership

A limited partnership is a simple modification of a general partnership and is comprised of at least one general partner and at least one limited partner. The general partner is treated exactly as that individual would be treated in a general partnership. The limited partner is treated as if she or he were simply an investor in the business. Limited partnerships are normally required to operate under the Revised Limited Partnership Act. The general partner is required to file a Certificate of Limited Partnership in the state in which the business plans to operate.

A master limited partnership is similar to a limited partnership except the shares in the master limited partnership are traded on stock exchanges. In reality, businesses operating under this form of ownership act like corporations.

"C" Corporation

Under law, a corporation is an "artificial being, invisible, intangible, and existing only in contemplation of law."[2] The creation of the corporate form of business ownership was essential for the growth of the capitalistic system. The corporation, as a separate legal entity, can engage in business, make contracts, sue and be sued, and pay taxes. The advantages of the corporate form of ownership include the limited liability of its stockholders. This legal protection of an investor's personal assets is a major attraction to potential investors in a business. An investor's financial risk is limited to his or her investment in the business. Additional financial capital can be secured through the sale of stock in the firm. Limited only by the number of shares authorized in its corporate charter, the firm can finance its growth as opportunities arise. The corporate charter can be revised to expand the number of authorized shares if and when it might need to do so. Investors can sell their shares to others, and this transferability of ownership makes shareholders' investments highly flexible and fluid. The shareholders are not "locked in" to the business. Their capital can be recovered through the sale of their stock. One of the characteristics of the corporate form of ownership is the potential for the business to continue indefinitely. This legal provision creates confidence in both investors and customers. Last, the management of the business can gain valuable knowledge, skills, and expertise through the creation of a board of directors. Board members can provide the organization's leadership with insight on critical issues based on their knowledge and experience.

The corporate form of ownership has a few significant drawbacks as well. For an entrepreneur starting a new business, the incorporation process can be both complicated and costly. Although it is possible to incorporate without an attorney, that option can be more costly in the long run. An attorney who has experience in advising entrepreneurs and incorporating start-up businesses can guide the entrepreneur through the incorporation process in a cost-effective fashion. Once incorporated, the business will discover that it faces a variety of time-consuming and costly regulatory reporting requirements. These generate no increase in sales or profits but do increase the firm's cost of doing business. A business operating under the corporate form of ownership also faces the obligation of paying taxes on its profits because, as stated, it is regarded as a separate legal entity. The result is that income is taxed twice: first, as corporate income tax and, second, as income received by the firm's shareholders. The distribution of corporate income to its shareholders comes normally in the form of dividends. The shareholders then are required to pay personal income taxes on their dividends. This double taxation is a distinct disadvantage that is not likely to change. In most cases, the initial entrepreneur will not be able to retain 51% of the firm as the corporation issues stock to raise the needed growth capital. Some critics suggest that this reality will tend to diminish the founder's incentive to continue to put forth an exceptionally high level of energy and effort.

"S" Corporation

In 1954, to address some of the disadvantages of "C" corporations (which are taxed separately from their owners under subchapter C of the Internal Revenue Code), the Internal Revenue Service introduced the concept of what is now termed an "S" corporation (in which profits are passed on to the shareholders and taxed based on personal returns under subchapter S). This distinction is made only by the Internal Revenue Service, and in legal terms, an "S" corporation does not differ from a "C" corporation. To qualify, an "S" corporation must meet the following criteria:

1. The business must be a domestic corporation.

2. It cannot have a nonresident alien as a stockholder.

3. The firm can issue both voting and nonvoting common stock, but with that exception, all shares must have the same rights.

4. The number of shareholders cannot exceed 100, and shareholders are limited to individuals, estates, certain trusts, employee stock ownership plans (ESOPs), and pension plans.

5. Less than 25% of the corporation's gross annual revenues during three successive tax years must be from passive sources.

The entrepreneur wishing to be treated as an "S" corporation must file with the Internal Revenue Service within the first two and a half months of the corporation's first taxable year. Entrepreneurs who select an "S" corporation form of ownership retain all the advantages of a "C" corporation while avoiding being taxed at the corporate rate. Profits can be passed directly to shareholders who pay income taxes at their individual tax rates. This avoidance of "double taxation" is a significant factor in the growing popularity of the "S" corporation form of ownership. Like all forms of ownership, this one is affected by modifications in the U.S. tax rates. It is always important to consider the actions of Congress, especially those related to tax policy, regardless of the form of ownership you choose. And ask your firm's accountant how your firm, and you, will be affected by proposed changes.

Limited Liability Company (LLC)

One of the most popular forms of ownership for new start-up has become the Limited Liability Company, or the LLC. The LLC has most of the benefits of the "S" corporation without some of its restrictions. While retaining the attractive features of the "S" corporation (avoidance of double taxation) and the "C" corporation (limited liability for owners), the LLC provides increased flexibility. There are no restrictions on the number of shareholders called members or on the level of participation of members.

An LLC is formed by an entrepreneur filing two key documents with the appropriate LLC office (usually the secretary of state's office for the state in which the company will be based). These documents are the LLC's articles of organization and its operating agreement. The LLC's articles of organization include its name and address, its method of management, the name and address of each organizer, and the proposed duration of the LLC. Unlike a corporation, an LLC does not have perpetual life and is generally limited to 30 years. The second key document in establishing an LLC is the operating agreement. This agreement sets forth the provisions that govern the way that the LLC will conduct business. This document will normally describe the member's capital contributions to the LLC, the conditions of admission and withdrawal for members, the distribution of the profits of the LLC, and how the LLC will be managed. In order to maintain its favorable tax treatment, the LLC needs its operating agreement to include provisions more closely in line with those of a partnership. The Uniform Limited Liability Act should also be studied to insure that all requirements are met. As with most legal issues, the entrepreneur should consult an attorney who is experienced with the creation of LLC's to avoid potential problems.

Is There a "Best" Form of Ownership?

One of the most frequently asked questions is whether there is "one best" form of ownership. The answer depends on your specific situation. You can prepare for a visit with your attorney prior to making the organizational ownership decision by answering the following questions:

1. What is the amount of financial capital needed to sustain the business until it reaches profitability, and where do I plan to obtain this financial capital?

2. What does my financial model show as the net profit for each of the first five years?

3. Which of my skills are relevant to the operation of the proposed business venture? Which skills relevant to managing and operating the proposed business do members of the founding team lack?

4. What is a realistic assumption about the growth rate and ultimate size of this business over the next five years? Am I qualified to lead, manage, and grow the business to reach its potential?

5. How much control do I wish to exercise over the decision making at all levels and for all functions in the organization? How much of the profits am I willing to share with others based on their ideas and contributions to the business?

6. Are tax considerations important to me? Are there other sources of income that I wish to shelter legally from tax liabilities?

7. In case the business fails, to what extent am I willing to be personally responsible and liable for its debts?

8. Is it important that the business continue operations in the event of my incapacity or death?

9. Do I want to retain complete financial control of the business and reap all of the financial rewards?

10. What are the legal and bureaucratic regulations that I am willing to cope with?

Every founding entrepreneur needs to respond to these questions before deciding on the form of ownership that will best meet his or her needs.

BUSINESS LICENSES AND PERMITS

Whatever form of ownership an owner chooses, a business will need to obtain all of the relevant licenses and permits needed to operate. The specific licenses and permits needed are determined by city, county, and state regulations. The process is normally simple to comply with.

Additionally, the IRS requires that the business obtain a federal tax identification number to be used in filing a business tax return. This requirement does not apply to a sole proprietorship. The sole proprietor would simply use her or his social security number.

Operating permits are required for businesses that are located in communities that have enacted restrictions on certain aspects of a business within their jurisdiction. Examples are regulations that limit the size of signage in particular areas or the total number of occupants allowed in restaurants, movie theaters, and many other entertainment venues. For most communities, the regulations are easily obtainable online, and the entrepreneur can determine if a permit will be required.

If a business plans to operate under a fictitious name (i.e., any name different from its legal, registered name), the entrepreneur must typically file a fictitious business name permit with the state's attorney general. For example, Carol Avery, the sole proprietor of a shop specializing in bird cages, would be taxed under her own name so she might file so she could be "doing business as" Avery's Aviaries. In this way, the state ensures that the name of the business is unique. This permit is used to open a bank account in the name of the business as well as to enable the entrepreneur to conduct business under that name, including signing contracts and taking legal actions.

CONTRACTS

All businesses find themselves involved in a series of what might be called *contract issues*. A firm makes contracts with others on a wide range of things. A shareholders' agreement is a contract, for example. When there are shareholders in your business, you, as entrepreneur, are legally required to act responsibly in the operation of the business. Indeed, all the firm's officers and directors have a fiduciary responsibility to shareholders not only to exercise reasonable care in the operation of the business but also to demonstrate that they have acted in good faith and taken prudent action on behalf of the business and the stockholders.

As entrepreneurs begin to staff new business ventures, they enter into many legal contracts. The employee contract is one of the most important. An employment agreement is a complex contractual document and needs to be specific regarding such things as job responsibilities, salary, benefits, special agreements (e.g., nondisclosure or patent ownership agreements), and other promises (e.g., guarantees of stock options or profit sharing). An employee contract with a clear and specific job description can prevent future conflicts between the founders and employees. As mentioned, the employment contract will also outline financial issues such as salary payment schedules, amount of pay, and all information related to stock options, benefits, and bonuses. The specific components of the employees' benefits should include information about the retirement program and what share each party contributes, as well as when the employee becomes eligible to receive the benefits. Typically, there is a "vesting period" before the employee is entitled to the employer's contribution to the employee's retirement fund. If the contract promises stock options, it should include information on when these can be exercised, at what price, and for what specific number of shares. The employee contract should also explain any profit-sharing plans, if the employee is eligible, detailing how and under what circumstances the employee can share in the profits of the business.

The clarification of all these issues in the employment agreement will reduce the sources of potential conflict with employees. In some cases, a new business will choose to enter into a contract with an independent service provider. These independent contractors are not entitled to employee benefits and can be less expensive. An independent contractor is also different from an employee in that, though the contracted task can be defined by the employer, the hiring firm cannot direct or control the action of the independent contractor. The entrepreneur needs to have appropriate documentation that clearly creates a legal contract for independent contractors, a contract that will be enforceable in court.

As the contracting of work and the hiring of staff are such important functions, a business needs to clarify its human resources policies in an employee manual. Like most legal documents, this employee manual should be reviewed carefully by an attorney. In this way, the entrepreneur has greater assurance that the firm's human resources policies are fully compatible with national and state laws. Once the employee manual or handbook has been written and approved by the firm's attorney, the entrepreneur avoids legal problems by ensuring that all managers and employees follow strictly and consistently the human resources policies it sets forth.

At the very least, the employee manual or handbook should have policies that state the firm's rejection of any form of employee discrimination in employment or promotion, as well as its disallowance of employee harassment or workplace violence. Positive policies should demonstrate a commitment to employees with disabilities, workplace safety, equity in compensation, and fair employee disciplinary procedures. Having and operating a company based on correct employee policies significantly reduces the potential of a lawsuit by employees over the firm's violations of federal and state labor laws. Such lawsuits can be costly and usually result in the entrepreneur losing focus on the objectives of the firm.

Sales Contracts

Doing business also requires that the entrepreneur have appropriate contracts to cover both purchasing supplies and resources and selling its goods and services. Typically, when purchasing goods and services for the business, the entrepreneur signs a contract with the seller. It is critical that the buyer reads, in detail, the seller's contract. As the buyer, the entrepreneur must clearly define terms and conditions regarding quality, delivery date and place, and terms of payment, as well as those terms specific to the business. A contract between the supplier and the firm can normally be negotiated, resulting in terms and conditions that are beneficial to both parties.

The sale of the firm's goods is covered by the Uniform Commercial Code (UCC). The UCC is a broad set of laws that covers sales of goods, negotiable instruments (e.g., promissory notes), bank-customer relations, letters of credit, bulk sales, documents of title, investment securities, secured transactions, leases of goods, and funds transfers. Entrepreneurs need to become aware of the provisions of the UCC that have a direct or indirect effect on the way their businesses are conducted. The firm's attorney can assist the entrepreneur in creating contracts that both support the firm's ongoing operations and are legal and enforceable in court.

SELECTING AN ATTORNEY

There is no "one best" attorney. In most cases, attorneys, like doctors, focus on a specialty such as new venture formation, intellectual property law, or contract law. During the life of a business, an entrepreneur may require the services of a variety of attorneys depending on the specific situation. It is time to select an attorney when the entrepreneur is developing a business plan and is confident that research demonstrates that a market exists for the proposed firm's products or services. This research should prove that the firm's business model seems viable. At this stage, ask businesspeople in your proposed industry for recommendations. Recognize that yours is a "start-up" business, and ask about attorneys with experience in new venture formation. Another valuable source is the state bar association, which will provide an entrepreneur with the names of attorneys with experience in new venture formation. Now, there are online databases that rank lawyers based on their successes in various areas of practice; some even provide peer reviews or assessments based on their demonstrated ethics since graduating law school. Call multiple attorneys and verify their level of experience as well as their fees. Visit with a number of potential attorneys to determine how compatible you find each.

It is important that the entrepreneur feels "comfortable" with her or his attorney. Communication is key in this business relationship, and the attorney's ability to communicate clearly how the law will potentially impact the operations of the firm is of utmost importance. Determine if the attorney has a proven record of accomplishment in the numerous areas of the law of relevance to your firm. Last, can the firm afford the fee structure of the attorney? Some of the most qualified and experienced attorneys earn professional fees that might be beyond what an entrepreneur can afford in a start-up situation.

CONCLUSION

Like it or not, a business requires dealing with a number of legal issues. The entrepreneur must use the legal system to protect its tangible and intangible assets. Patents, trademarks, copyrights, and trade secrets can be protected under our legal system. The entrepreneur needs to begin with a founder's agreement to clarify the most critical business issues.

A firm's form of ownership must also be decided. Selecting the most effective form of ownership, however, depends on the entrepreneur's specific situation, and every effort must be taken to understand the advantages and disadvantages of each. For the entrepreneur, life involves a series of contracts that control behaviors and guide the actions and decisions of employees, shareholders, contractors, business partners, and suppliers. A failure to address the sources of potential legal issues can result in costly distractions and even business failure. A qualified attorney can serve to protect the entrepreneur and the assets of the new venture.

ENTREPRENEURIAL EXERCISES

Entrepreneurial Exercise 8.1

If your proposed business venture has a product that might be patentable, an original trademark concept, or material that can be copyrighted, please describe your plans for achieving a patent, trademark, or copyright.

Patent

Trademark

Copyright

Entrepreneurial Exercise 8.2

Please write a founder's agreement for your proposed new business. Include all of the relevant details.

Entrepreneurial Exercise 8.3

After reading the material in Chapter 8 regarding the advantages and disadvantages of various forms of business ownership, which form of ownership do you think will best fit the needs of your proposed business?

Form of ownership chosen:

What are the features of the form of ownership that most influenced your choice?

What concerns do you have about the form of ownership you chose?

Entrepreneurial Exercise 8.4

Based on your proposed business, what are the "areas" of contract law for which you must develop contracts (in cooperation with your attorney)? Please be as specific as possible.

THE BUSINESS PLAN

You can't overestimate the need to plan and prepare. In most of the mistakes I've made, there has been this common theme of inadequate planning beforehand. You really can't over-prepare in business!

Chris Corrigan

A clear vision, backed by definite plans, gives you a tremendous feeling of confidence and personal power.

Brian Tracy

One very interesting anomaly is the difference between the number of entrepreneurs who say they support planning and the number of entrepreneurs who have actually created a business plan. Most will use the excuse that they never took the time to put the ideas in their head down on paper. Entrepreneurs experienced in the development of business plans normally will explain that the first tangible value in developing such a plan is that it forces the entrepreneur to reexamine continually every element of the plan and how each segment interacts with and reinforces the others. It may be safe to say that the greatest benefit is the planning process itself. Entrepreneurs who create plans for their proposed new business ventures discover details about their customers, markets, competitors, and even themselves, which can drastically increase the probability of the new ventures' success.

THE VALUE OF WRITING A BUSINESS PLAN

A business plan is a written document that describes a firm's objectives and the strategies for achieving them. You can determine the critical components of a business plan by answering these questions:

- What exactly does the business intend to accomplish, what products or services will it offer, and specifically how will these products or services and the firm's business model create customer value?

- What are the founder's vision statement and mission for the business venture?

- What, in detail, is firm's business model?

- What specific market niche does the business intend to serve? What does the entrepreneur know about this market niche? How do all of the applicable demographics concerning the market niche relate to the firm's business model?

- What are the targeted customer buying characteristics? What do we know about the psychological and economic factors that influence their buying behavior?

- Who are the competitors currently serving the targeted market niche, what is their market share, and what are the sources of their competitive advantages?

- What firms are likely to be future competitors in this market niche, and what possible competitive advantages might they have?

- What are the sources of your business model's competitive advantage?

- What is your firm's anticipated start-up cost?

- What are your firm's projected financial plan and its plan to manage cash flow?

- What are the specifics of the firm's marketing strategies and tactics?

- Based on the firm's business model, the characteristics of the market niche, the targeted customers' buying behaviors, your competitors' strategies and tactics, and your firm's resources, what are your proposed business strategies and tactics?

- Based on all the preceding answers, what are the details of your request for funding from an investor?

Any investor, indeed anyone who reads your business plan, needs to feel comfortable with your business model and with the logic of your plan's presentation. The business plan needs to be specific enough to demonstrate to the reader the market feasibility and financial viability of the new venture. A successful business plan attempts to answer every question an investor might have about the proposed business. Details and specifics always trump assumptions. Anticipate the reader's questions and answer these questions in a logical method employing facts and figures based on your detailed research.

The Nature of the Business Plan

The nature of the business plan depends on the following:

The level of sophistication and complexity of the firm's product or service. The more sophisticated and complex your product or service, the longer it will take to explain in terms that can be understood by the reader. Never assume that the reader understands the technical terminology used by experts. If investors do not understand your product or service clearly after reading the first page or so of your business plan, they seldom read further.

The complexity of the market niche. The greater the complexity of the market niche, the more details your business plan should present. The investor does not want to read a general description of the market niche. Vague and nonspecific market niche descriptions communicate a lack of adequate research.

The current and potential competition in the market niche. The number and strength of current and potential competitors will dictate how deep this section must be. If the market niche is comprised of large and aggressive competitors, the business plan must focus on how this new business venture will achieve a sustainable market position.

The number and magnitude of barriers to entering the market niche. The plan must focus on how these barriers will be overcome with the resources at the disposal of the new business.

ROAD MAP TO SUCCESS

Each of these important criteria will influence the length of the business plan. Simple business plans can be as short as 20 to 25 pages, whereas complex markets, products or services, customer demographics, and competitive and economic conditions may require a plan that is 75 to 100 pages long. The key question is always the same: "Does the plan answer all of the questions of the reader?" The business plan is the entrepreneur's road map to success. If the reader is unable to follow the map presented, the entrepreneur faces rejection. Few entrepreneurs have the opportunity to make an initial face-to-face presentation of their business plan. Investors and lenders read the business plan and then, if they find potential value in the proposed new venture, invite the entrepreneur to present ideas and answer questions. Poorly written or incomplete business plans are simply discarded. The business plan almost always precedes the entrepreneur and, one hopes, establishes creditability.

The business plan is also a powerful internal document. It lets the entrepreneur describe to team members why this new venture has the potential to become a successful business.

Additionally, the entrepreneur can clearly express the values to which the business will adhere, a vision of what the business can achieve, and an inspiring mission statement for the business. The entire entrepreneurial team can read the business plan to comprehend what the entrepreneur believes this business can become and what each member's role will be in achieving that success. To some extent, the business plan is a multipurpose document, allowing team members to relate to the values of the new venture and to determine how the business will conduct itself in a competitive marketplace. Ethics and social values are not "wispy ideals" but solid behavioral expectations. Other firms, such as suppliers or lenders, can assess the firm's viability and values by reading the business plan, and become more confident in working with the start-up.

It is important to reinforce why an incomplete, poorly written, or confusing business plan is worthless or, indeed, damaging. Professional investors are trained to read a business plan with a critical eye. They know that although every entrepreneur believes that her or his new venture will become a success, many start-ups fail. In reality, very few business plans will be attractive enough to earn the entrepreneur a face-to-face meeting with the investor. At the earliest stages of beginning a business, you *are* the business model, and the business plan must represent you fully. The business plan must be the vehicle that presents to the reader your values. Your heart and soul must be found in the plan.

CHALLENGES OF THE BUSINESS PLAN

Building on the critical components outlined in the previous section, you are now ready to face the challenges of developing a business plan. One challenge is to design a plan to address the competitive issues that the new business venture will face. The road from start-up to financial success is never smooth. Investors want to read how the entrepreneur plans to cope with any roadblocks to success. Consequently, the business plan should, at least,

- Spell out the linkage between the specific factors upon which the targeted customers make their buying decisions and the unique value-creating components of the entrepreneur's product or service, as well as

- Clarify the firm's strategies and techniques for addressing competitors' current market advantages, the existing barriers to market entry, and the anticipated defensive strategies and tactics of the competition.

Another recognized problem an entrepreneur faces when creating a business plan is the difficulty of integrating the functional components of the proposed business to present a unified picture. The solution is to conduct detailed research and analysis that guides the decision process for each of the firm's proposed functional components and then integrate these findings into a unified business model that demonstrates a high probability of guiding a venture toward becoming a viable and financially solid business.

STRUCTURE OF THE BUSINESS PLAN

The business plan should emphasize the unique competitive advantages of the proposed venture and how the business creates value for its targeted customers, and it should be written in a standard format that is consistent with what investors and lenders read daily.

ENTREPRENEURIAL SPOTLIGHT
SIDDARTH SATISH—GAUSS SURGICAL

Siddarth Satish founded Gauss Surgical in 2011, and he led the company from its initial invention of a mobile platform for the real-time monitoring of surgical blood loss through six United States and European Union regulatory approvals and into its commercialization phase. Satish is a young man with an exceptional record of accomplishment; he is the inventor of 25 issued or pending patents.

Gauss Surgical has attracted venture capital successfully to support its production of a technologically based product to assist physicians in accurately measuring the loss of blood during a surgical procedure. Prior to this invention, the operating-room team would make an "educated guess" about blood loss. Doing so was a problem, as Satish says, "Humans aren't very good at visual estimation, so it's a number that they come up with as a way of making sense of the decisions that they've made." Another earlier and cumbersome method of measuring blood loss was to have the nurses weigh the blood-soaked sponges, which is also inaccurate. Thus, surgeons would always err on the side of giving the patient additional blood through transfusion. Research has concluded, though, that from 20% to 60% of these blood transfusions are not needed, which results in a $10 billion unnecessary expense annually. Gauss Surgical's patented device leverages mobile technology to achieve the effective and efficient real-time monitoring of surgical blood loss. The new procedure employs an off-the-shelf iPad's camera function with a portfolio of products known as the Triton™ system to more accurately measure the patient's blood loss. The system sends the images captured in the surgical suite to the "cloud" where highly sophisticated computer algorithms estimate the hemoglobin content and overall blood loss.

Sources:

1. "Gauss Surgical," TMC Innovation website, assessed July 2018, http://www.tmc.edu/innovation/companies/gauss-surgical/.

2. "Gauss Surgical Announces $12.6 Million Series B Financing," *PRWeb: Online Visibility from Vocus*, March 30, 2016, http://www.prweb.com/releases/prweb13303441.htm.

The content needs to be original, but the format is normally standardized. The following is a recommended business plan format:

I. Executive Summary

The executive summary needs to get the reader's attention while also conveying factual information and the most relevant points of the plan. It should contain these elements:

— The name, address, email address, website URL, and phone number of the business

— The names, addresses, email addresses, and phone numbers of the founders and all key members of the entrepreneurial team

— A brief description of the proposed business venture with a clear focus on its unique business model

— A detailed description of the products and services to be sold, along with a very brief discussion of the intellectual property supporting these

— Distinct discussions of all market niches and targeted customers for the business

— A brief discussion of the critical dimensions of the market niches

— A brief discussion of the known characteristics of the targeted customers, including buying behaviors

— A brief discussion of the business-level strategies best suited to your unique business model that you are confident will result in superior performance

— A brief description of the founders and of the key managerial and technical talent within the current or anticipated entrepreneurial team

— A brief statement of the financial request along with when the money will be needed, how it will be spent, and what tangible outcomes or milestones will be achieved, as well when those milestones will be achieved

— Charts and tables that highlight the firm's financial forecast based on receiving the investment or loan

II. Vision and Mission

The vision statement expresses the ideals that drive the entrepreneur while the mission statement demonstrates how the venture will go about executing the purpose of the new business. The vision and mission statements should include the values that will guide both the operation of the business and its relationships with customers, creditors, suppliers, government agencies, and the firm's stakeholders.

A detailed discussion of the firm's business model should also be included in this section. This discussion should answer the following questions:

— Why and how the business model is unique?

— How does this business model deliver superior value to the firm's targeted customers?

— What are the specific sources of the firm's competitive advantage?

— How sustainable is the firm's competitive advantage in the face of competition and competitor innovation?

— If the firm's products are based on patented technology, what level of protection is guaranteed?

— Has the product or service name been trademarked?

III. Company History

Some new ventures are not exactly brand new but the result of years of work and trial and error by the entrepreneur. It is valuable to describe the process that was undertaken along with the bumps along the way. What did the entrepreneur learn in these failures? Investors will appreciate how past events shaped the current business model, and this history will help them better understand your business plan.

— When was the company founded?

— Are the original founders the same? If not, where are the original founders? Have they retained any financial interest in the current business? If so, what?

— What are the company's operational and financial achievements to date?

IV. Industry Profile

This section of your business plan and the next (V. Market Analysis) should help the reader identify the specific industry or market niche in which your business plans to compete. Present details about the industry or market niche to insure that the reader understands the market and recognizes that your research is current and accurate. An investor needs to be confident that you know the details of the market niche and that what is presented in the business plan is consistent with the realities of the situation. You need to present and honest and accurate picture and analysis of the target market for which your business model is designed:

— What is the current stage of the industry life cycle?

— What are the current and projected industry growth rates?

— What are the current and projected market niches in the industry for the firm?

— How profitable is each market niche now and how profitable will each be over the next 5 to 10 years?

— What critical forces influence the growth and profitability of each market niche?

— Which current and anticipated fractures influence market-niche growth and drive profitability?

— How large are the major competitors in each niche?

— What level of aggression have competitors displayed in the protection of their market share in each market niche?

V. Market Analysis

— What specific details about the market niche and the targeted customers has your research uncovered?

— What are the targeted customers' buying behaviors?

— What is the nature of the buying cycle?

— Are the goods and services purchased on a regular basis (weekly, monthly, yearly)?

— Are the goods and services purchased seasonally?

— Are the goods considered "durable goods" and only repurchased when they need to be replaced?

— What major external forces influence the targeted customers' ability and willingness to purchase the firm's goods and services? Some examples might include

  ○ Economic factors, such as inflation, recession, unemployment rate, personal income, and disposable income, and

  ○ Social factors, such as age of the targeted customers, unique motivational factors, size of the household, location demographics, and specific societal attitudes and values.

VI. Business Profile

This section of your business plan and the next (VII. Products and Services) give the reader details about your proposed business and its products and services:

— How large is the proposed business relative to market niche competitors?

— What is the projected growth rate of the business in each market niche in which it plans to compete?

— What are the organization's objectives in terms of revenues, costs and profits?

VII. Products and Services

— What products or services will the firm offer? What are the specific features of these products or services, and what customer benefits do these features offer? What product warranties or performance guarantees will the firm provide?

— What intellectual property rights, including patents, copyrights, and trademarks, are possessed by the firm?

— How will products be manufactured? (Give details about production processes, including access to raw materials, parts, unit labor cost, and key suppliers.)

— Do you anticipate offering additional, new, or modified products? (Describe them.)

Pinterest

Established to enable individuals to create, collect, and share ideas online by "pining" representations of these ideas to personal visual bulletin boards, Pinterest was born in late 2009 and had its business launch in March 2010. Cofounders Ben Silbermann and Evan Sharp, along with a few programmer friends, began the business from Silbermann's apartment, working there until the summer of 2011. Within nine months of the launch of the company, Pinterest's corporate website had over 10,000 users. The company expanded its online presence via cell phone applications. Within one year of its mobile phone launch, the company had grown to become one of the top 10 social network services. Pinterest expanded in the United States and internationally in 2017 after having identified a significant but unmet customer need—being able to point a mobile phone at an object to obtain immediate information on that object and on others inspired by it. By the summer of 2017, the company had a market valuation of $12.3 billion.

Sources:

1. See the company's website: https://www.pinterest.com/.
2. Ki Mae Heussner, "Pinterest Founder: Early Adoption Works Differently Now," *Adweek*, March 13, 2012, https://www.adweek.com/digital/pinterest-founder-early-adoption-works-differently-now-138926/.
3. Casey Newton, "Pinterest Introduces Lens, a Shazam for Objects in the Real World," *The Verge*, February 8, 2017, https://www.theverge.com/2017/2/8/14549798/pinterest-lens-visual-discovery-shazam.
4. Katie Benner, "Pinterest Raises Valuation to $12.3 Billion with New Funding," *New York Times*, June 6, 2017, https://www.nytimes.com/2017/06/06/technology/pinterest-raises-valuation-to-12-3-billion-with-new-funding.html.

VIII. Competitor Analysis

Now that you have described your proposed business and its products and services in some detail, it is time to assess competitors and describe what marketing tactics you will use to compete. That is what this section and the next (IX Marketing Strategies) are all about:

— Who are the firm's existing competitors? (Give specific details about these competitors.)

— What are the critical success factors of the industry you plan to enter, and how does your firm rank in comparison to others according to these criteria? (Provide a competitive profile matrix.)

— What are the unique strengths and weakness of each current competitor?

— Who are your potential competitors in the firm's targeted market niche?

— What strengths might these potential competitors bring to the market?

— When do you anticipate these potential competitors to enter the market?

— What would be the potential impact on your business if any of these potential competitors chose to enter the market niche?

IX. Marketing Strategies

— What marketing strategies do you anticipate or have you developed?
  ○   Product strategies? (Include all details.)
  ○   Place strategies? (Include all details.)
  ○   Pricing strategies? (Include all details.)
  ○   Promotional strategies? (Include all details.)

— In what unique ways will the business achieve optimal benefit from the integration of the specific components of the firm's marketing strategies?

X. Financial Analysis

This section answers one main question: How do you know that your business will be financially viable? It should include these items:

— Financial statement (most likely a pro forma statement)

— Balance sheet

— Income statement (profit and loss statement)

— Cash budget (cash flow analysis)

— Breakeven analysis

— Details of all start-up expenses

— Ratio analysis providing comparisons with industry standards

XI. Entrepreneurial Team

This section and the next (XII Organizational Structure) give details about the management and organization of your proposed business:

— Who are the founders, and what special skills and knowledge do they bring to the enterprise? (Include a brief biographical sketch for each founder and a detailed discussion of the specific areas of expertise that impact the potential success of the new venture.)

— Who are the key managers and employees, what roles will they play in the new venture, and what specific skill and abilities do they possess?

XII. Organizational Structure

— What form of ownership has been chosen and why? (Discuss the benefits to the new venture.)

— How will the enterprise be organized? (Provide a description of its organizational structure and organizational charts.)

— Which decision-making responsibilities will be assigned to each founder and key manager? (Provide a brief description.)

— What compensation packages for founders and key personnel do you project?

XIII. Strategies and Tactics

This section outlines the actions a business will take to achieve success. These strategies and tactics should be developed based on the analysis of the industry profile (Section IV), the market analysis (Section V), the business profile (Section VI), the description of the firm's products and services (Section VII), and the analysis of competitors (Section VIII). Here are some questions to help you generate this section:

— What essential functional strategies will be employed, and what is the firm's overall business strategy? (Discuss both in detail.)

— What specific market tactics will be needed in order to implement the firm's business strategies effectively?

— How will the firm's performance be tracked and measured?

XIV. Investment or Loan Proposal

In this section, you detail your "ask." What is it that you want, and why should you get it?

— How much money is being requested?

— How do you propose to use these funds, and what anticipated financial benefits to the investors do you expect as a consequence of receiving this money?

— How and when will the investors be able to "cash out" or the lender be repaid?

— What are the details for implementing and scheduling the actions proposed?

XV. Appendices and Other Supporting Documents

In this section, you present detailed material that your reader might want to consult but that is too long or complex to insert directly into the main part of your plan without disrupting its persuasive effect. Here are some things that traditionally go in this section:

— Market research

— Financial statements

— Organizational charts

— CVs and résumés

— Any other critical documents

PRESENTING THE BUSINESS PLAN

When an entrepreneur gets the opportunity to speak to a potential investor or lender about a business venture, rehearsing for that presentation is critical. Recognize that the presentation should not exceed 30 minutes. The following are a few of the most critical components to be considered in preparing for and making the presentation:

- Do not read the business plan! Discuss the elements of the proposed business venture that have the greatest impact on its success.

- Express clearly how the investor will benefit from financial involvement.

- Avoid using overly technical terms that might be beyond the investor's knowledge base. But, if the investor asks technical questions, be prepared to "drill down" into the technical specifics.

- Be both positive and enthusiastic about the nature of the business venture and its potential for success and profitability.

- Ensure that the investor understands the logic behind the business, how the targeted customers benefit from the proposed products or services, and how the business's products or services will provide superior customer value in comparison with those of competitors.

- Use PowerPoint slides or other visuals to support the presentation.

- Close by reinforcing the nature of the business and how the investor will benefit.

- Leave time for questions and answers.

After the presentation, it is appropriate to follow up with the investor, but be professional. Being modestly proactive demonstrates continued interest and should include thanking the investor for the opportunity to make the presentation.

ENTREPRENEURIAL EXERCISES

Entrepreneurial Exercise 12.1

Business Plan Evaluation Scale

In 1993, Bruce J. Blechman published a valuable article in *Entrepreneur* entitled "Go for the Gold." This entrepreneurial exercise is adapted from that work. When potential investors evaluate your business plan, they are attempting to assess the degree of risk that they will assume. Will they lose some or all of their investment if failure occurs? Correspondingly, they are attempting to assess the potential rewards that would flow to them from a successful new venture. The following are the twelve (12) factors that most professional investors are attempting to evaluate from your business plan.

This self-assessment exercise should be completed by both you and a number of fairly objective individuals who have had the opportunity to read your business plan in depth.

Please rate your business plan on the following twelve (12) statements, with 1 being the lowest score and 10 being the highest possible score.

This business plan clearly describes a marketable idea.

1	2	3	4	5	6	7	8	9	10
Hypothetical customers who exist only on paper.									Firm purchase orders in hand from customers.

Logic of the question: Investors want to see proof that customers want to purchase the firm's product or service and are willing to make that purchase at a price that is sufficient to earn a reasonable profit. The greater the tangible evidence that can be demonstrated, the higher your score.

The business plan demonstrates good profit potential in a short period of time.

1	2	3	4	5	6	7	8	9	10
Annual rate of return of 10% or less.									Annual rate of return of 50% or more.

Logic of the question: Because a new business venture is considered to have an above average level of risk, there needs to be an above average financial return. Many authorities believe that the minimum return on equity should be 25%. The higher the rate of return that the business plan indicates as possible, and the faster the business produces these returns, the higher your score.

The business plan targets a clearly defined market niche whose size and purchasing power are sufficient to product a profit.

1	2	3	4	5	6	7	8	9	10
A small, specialty market with little or no growth potential.									A large market with high growth potential.

Logic of the question: Investors look for business ventures whose target markets are clearly defined and possess high growth potential. Investors will normally avoid a business that attempts to be "everything to everybody."

The business plan explains clearly the "competitive edge" of my product or service or its unique value-creation properties over those of its competitors.

1	2	3	4	5	6	7	8	9	10
The "me-too" products or services are no better than those of competitors.									The products or services have unique properties that produce results superior to those produced by the products or services of competitors.

Logic of the question: Investors recognize that a new business venture's success is generally dependent on products or services that are truly unique and superior and that create recognizable value for the customer—beyond the value created by competitors' offerings. Investors look for clear evidence of this "competitive advantage."

The business plan clearly demonstrates the ability of the business to control both the delivery and the quality of the product or service.

1	2	3	4	5	6	7	8	9	10
Totally dependent on outside contractors for the production, sales, distribution, and servicing of the product or service.									Completely "in-house" contractors and control of all resources in the production, sales, distribution, and servicing of the product or service.

Logic of the question: Dependence on outside contractors and sales representatives is a potential weakness—especially when the quality of delivery, installation, and service is a key factor.

The business plan demonstrates that managers and employees have the skills and experience to make the new business venture a success.

1	2	3	4	5	6	7	8	9	10
Managers have never operated this type of business, and staff need to be trained									All managers and staff have experience in a business of this type.

Logic of the question: Investors are often known to say that they do not invest in businesses; they invest in people. Skilled, experienced managers and employees can make a business work even when resources are stretched thin and conditions are tough.

The business plan is not overly technical and complex.

1	2	3	4	5	6	7	8	9	10
My product or service is extremely complex and potential customers must be educated about its benefits.									My product or service and its benefits can be understood by potential customers.

Logic of the question: Investors can be wary of products or services that are extremely technically complex and difficult for the customer to understand. The business plan must be able to make what is complex easy to understand. Customers seldom purchase a product or service that they do not understand or know how to operate.

The business plan clearly reflects the entrepreneur's personal investment in the new business venture.

1	2	3	4	5	6	7	8	9	10
Entrepreneur has only "sweat equity" in the business but refuses to risk any other personal assets.									Entrepreneur has almost fully invested all personal assets in the business.

Logic of the question: If the entrepreneur does not believe in the new venture enough to invest a significant amount of her or his personal wealth, it will be difficult to find investors who have confidence in the business. Money in the game is normally viewed as a positive motivator.

The business plan clearly describes how the firm's product or service creates long-term customer value and benefits.

1	2	3	4	5	6	7	8	9	10
The product or service does not create value, and may be harmful.									The product or service creates positive value for the customers.

Logic of the question: Investors avoid any product or service that might fail to create value or, even worse, that might prove to be harmful.

The business plan lays out a clear, well-conceived, workable strategy for getting the business up and running.

1	2	3	4	5	6	7	8	9	10
No real strategy exists. The strategies are not written.									A well-designed, clearly formulated business strategy exists in writing.

Logic of the question: Nothing scares off investors faster than an entrepreneur who is either unable or unwilling to describe, in detail, a clearly defined, workable business strategy for the proposed new business venture. Without a strategy, the entrepreneur does not have a "road map" to follow for the achievement of goals.

The business plan contains realistic financial projections covering most likely, pessimistic, and optimistic scenarios.

1	2	3	4	5	6	7	8	9	10
No realistic financial projections, only financial guesses.									Complete financial projections based on clearly identified reasonable assumptions.

Logic of the question: Investors want to be confident in the entrepreneur's financial projections. Investors search for realistic assumptions underlying the numbers.

The business plan clearly communicates the entrepreneur's vision of the business and why the business will be successful. These messages must be clear and motivational.

1	2	3	4	5	6	7	8	9	10
The business plan lacks any presentation of the entrepreneur's vision for the business.									The business plan is well written, professional, and clearly presents the entrepreneur's vision for the business.

Logic of the question: The entrepreneur is responsible for "selling" to investors the value and viability of this business. The business plan is the vehicle to communicate with investors; be sure that it tells the entrepreneur's "best story."

Scoring

Please add your score on each of the twelve key factors.

1.	4.	7.	10.
2.	5.	8.	11.
3.	6.	9.	12.

Total points _____

Points Earned	Implications of Your Score
108 to 120	Exceptional score. Very good chance of getting funding.
96 to 107	Plan needs some polishing, but you may attract some funding.
72 to 95	It may be difficult to obtain funding.
71 or below	Funding is not likely. The business plan needs significant improvements.

Source: Adapted from Bruce J. Blechman, "Go for the Gold," *Entrepreneur* (April 1993): 20–22.

EQUITY CAPITAL

Our combination of great research universities, a pro-risk business culture, deep pools of innovation-seeking equity capital and reliable business and contract law is unprecedented and unparalleled in the world.

Marc Andreessen

Sweat equity is the most valuable equity there is.

Mark Cuban

I think this is also a great time to invest in private equity, helping companies grow from the ground up.

Jim Rogers

CHAPTER LEARNING OBJECTIVES

Upon completion of this chapter you will be able to

- List sources of equity financing
- Discuss which source of equity capital is appropriate for different ventures
- Define the role of angel investors
- Explain the role of venture capital firms in equity financing
- Describe the most common forms of equity instruments
- Evaluate which factors impact a company's ability to raise capital

EQUITY CAPITAL

Equity capital is the basis of entrepreneurship. Equity investors are risk takers. Entrepreneurship is dependent on individuals and venture financing organizations that are willing to risk their financial capital intelligently by investing in new businesses. Without experienced risk takers, only entrepreneurs who have their own financial resources would ever bring a new business to market.

The biggest test of an entrepreneur's ability is to access and utilize financial resources that the entrepreneur neither possesses nor controls. The ability to attract and manage these scarce resources effectively to launch and grow the enterprise is the singular distinguishing characteristic of the successful entrepreneur. Entrepreneurs learn to become resourceful and skilled in the art of converting ownership in game-changing ideas into financial support for building the new venture. This process of converting participating investor ownership in the new business into financial resources generating returns that are substantially above prevailing market rates is what equity capital is all about.

In this chapter, we will explore the various sources of equity financing, the different stages of raising equity capital, the various types of equity capital available to the entrepreneur, the factors influencing the success of raising equity capital, and the various issues the founding entrepreneur should consider as he or she utilizes equity capital to finance the new company.

SOURCES OF EQUITY FINANCING

Equity financing is defined as the sale of a portion of the ownership of a new venture to an investor through the purchase of a percentage ownership in the venture. These percentages of partial ownership are commonly referred to as "shares" or membership percentages in the company (in the case of limited liability corporations, or LLCs, for example). As opposed to the entrepreneur who has multiple objectives and reasons for creating and growing the company, the professional investor has one primary reason for securing equity in the company—to generate a substantial return on the financial investment placed into the company. How large the expected return may be will depend upon the nature of the business, the length of time necessary to harvest the investment, and the risk of the investment in the venture, among many other competitive factors. To accomplish this goal of harvesting the investment with increased value, the investor must be provided an exit strategy through a liquidity event. The most common ways to accomplish this goal are through the acquisition of investor ownership by new investors, sometimes referred to as recapitalization; the merger of the company with another company; the sale of the company; or the public listing of the company on one of the public stock exchanges. This listing is most commonly accomplished through an initial public offering (IPO) of the company's securities (discussed further in Chapter 14), but it can also be accomplished through the reverse merger of the private company into a publicly traded company. The use of equity capital to grow a company therefore necessitates that the entrepreneur have a well-defined strategic plan to grow and harvest the company.

Equity Capital for Small Businesses

New ventures that will become what are considered family-owned businesses could lack the potential for dramatically expanded growth; nevertheless, financial capital will still be needed. In these situations, investment most often comes in the following ways or from the following sources:

- *Self-financing.* The entrepreneur will be expected to have a substantial amount of her or his personal assets invested in the business. Other potential investors considering the new venture will expect to see that the entrepreneur is "all in," as the saying goes. That normally means that the entrepreneur has a mortgaged home, maxed-out credit cards, and a substantial personal debt, having borrowed all the money he or she possibly can to invest in the business. Remember, it is expected that entrepreneurs are themselves risk takers. Potential outside investors are normally reluctant to invest unless the entrepreneur, who has the greatest amount to gain, demonstrates his or her full commitment to the business venture.

- *Bootstrapping.* Entrepreneurs will normally employ what is termed *bootstrapping* the start-up, which involves conserving the firm's limited resources by finding others who are willing to provide material assistance at little or no cost. As an example, the entrepreneur could find a friend or associate willing to provide technical advice or the use of facilities and equipment when building the product prototype. The goal of bootstrapping is the preservation of the firm's limited financial capital. In the early phase of growth, "cash is king." Although this approach to capital management and equity retention by owners provides a viable avenue for early-phase growth, many entrepreneurs find that they quickly outstrip their capacity to obtain operating capital from close associates and will need to turn to outside sources of investment capital to sustain the growth of the enterprise.

- *Personal Savings.* Personal savings is the first place the entrepreneur is expected to look for start-up expenses. The more that entrepreneurs employ their personal financial resources, the less of their ownership they will need to sell to someone else, and the more confident investors will be that the founders are committed to the enterprise's growth and success.

- *Friends and Family.* The next step in funding a smaller start-up business is normally obtaining financial capital from family and friends. They are investing in the entrepreneur or entrepreneurial team above the return on the future enhanced enterprise value. Many know of your desire to start a business; they know how you have worked and studied in preparation to launch your business. They know you as a person. They trust you. They respect your knowledge, dedication, tenacity, and character. Because of this positive personal knowledge, friends and family are a very likely source of financial investment. The entrepreneur must be careful, however, never to misrepresent (either intentionally or unintentionally) to their friends and family the risks associated with a new business venture. The reality is that most investors of this sort are not what we would call sophisticated investors. They most likely have not been involved in investing in a start-up business. It is imperative to explain to family and friends the risk associated with investing in a start-up business.

Inherent dangers lurk when your family and friends invest in your business, however, no matter how carefully you explain the risks. Unrealistic expectations or misunderstood risks have destroyed many friendships and have ruined many family reunions. To avoid such problems, entrepreneurs must present the investment opportunity honestly and as clearly as possible, detailing the nature of all currently understood risks. Here is some guidance to help you avoid alienating investors who are also friends or family members:

1. *Consider the impact of the investment on everyone involved.* Will the investment or loans work a hardship on anyone? Are relatives and friends putting up money because they want to or because they feel obligated to? Can all parties afford the loss if the business folds?

2. *Keep the arrangement strictly business.* The parties should treat all loans and investments in a businesslike manner, no matter how close the friendship or family relationship. Professionalism avoids problems down the line. If the transaction is a loan exceeding $10,000, it must carry a rate of interest at least as high as the market rate; otherwise the IRS may consider the loan a gift and penalize the lender.

3. *Set the details up front.* Before any money changes hands, both parties must agree on the details of the deal. How much money is involved? Is it a loan, an investment, or a hybrid financial instrument such as a convertible note, which carries elements of both an investment and a loan? How will the investor cash out? How will the loan be paid off? What happens if the business fails? Is there a personal pledge by the entrepreneur to repay the note?

If the entrepreneur self-finances the start-up, he or she bears the risk of the initial investment and raises funds through pooling resources (personal securitization) and pledging assets. Sometimes, additional founders also contribute and bear this initial risk. In this scenario, the founders are taking the highest risk by betting their own resources on the success of the venture and the capabilities of the entrepreneurial management team. The advantage of bootstrapping and using founder financing is the preservation of ownership in the company. The disadvantage of self-financing is the size of the personal investment that the entrepreneur might need to make in the venture. For many companies, significant additional resources will soon be required to grow the company.

Close associates, the entrepreneur's personal or professional friends, and family members generally provide the next wave of financial resources, beyond those provided by the founding company's entrepreneur. Usually but not always, these individuals are not professional investors, as will be the case in latter rounds of equity financing. These close associates and friends are investing in the concept of the venture, in its promise of return, and specifically in the entrepreneur. The funds raised from these investors range from several hundred dollars to as much as several hundred thousand dollars. They are used to support the development of the company, the creation of its initial products or services, and the initial operations of the business. The challenge for the entrepreneur is to try to separate personal relationships from business decisions. The entrepreneur will most likely have frequent social interactions with these investors outside of the business. Managing these relationships can be difficult, especially if the venture does not meet the expectations of the investors. For this reason, the entrepreneur should weigh carefully the risks of accepting initial financing from this potential pool of investors. Another challenge faced by the entrepreneur is in structuring the investment for this round of financing. The tendency for inexperienced entrepreneurs is to value the company more highly than it is worth. This sets unreasonable expectations for the value of the investments purchased and may adversely affect the entrepreneur's ability to structure latter rounds of equity financing.

On close inspection, we find that most new ventures (as high as 75% of all new business creations) are initially capitalized using the financial resources of the founding entrepreneurs. These companies generally begin with an average start-up capitalization of around $10,000. As mentioned, entrepreneurs decide to provide initial funds for their ventures for two main reasons. First, doing so preserves their ownership equity. Second, it demonstrates to future investors and lenders (i.e., other sources of equity capital) a clear and dedicated commitment of the entrepreneurs to the creation and growth of the business. This initial pool of funds may be used by the entrepreneur to complete the development of the company's product or service and generate initial sales for the enterprise. Further, the initial funds may be used to recruit and hire additional key personnel to augment the entrepreneur's skills and capabilities. Even with the founder's seed capital and other early-stage private investments, the company is not guaranteed success, but without both sources of initial financing, the venture cannot grow.

Angel Investors

After dipping into their own pockets and convincing friends and relatives to invest in their business ventures, many entrepreneurs still need more seed capital. Frequently, the next stop on the road to business financing is private investors. These private investors—called *angels*—are playing an increasingly important role in financing business start-ups. Originally used to describe investors who put up high-risk, early-stage seed capital for Broadway shows, the term *angels* now refers to private investors who will back an emerging entrepreneurial company with their own money.

Angel investors are private investors or groups or syndicates of private investors. These investors are high-net-worth individuals (HNWIs), as defined by some segments of the financial services industry and state and federal statutes. As investors, many angels specialize in financing the early-growth phase of companies. Their investments tend to be geographically centered, meaning that they invest in companies that are within a short drive from where they live. These investors generally fall into one of two broad categories. Some are called "strategic angel investors." These individuals invest in types of businesses in which they have personal and professional experience. Further, a strategic angel investor often participates actively in the venture, assisting the entrepreneur not only with financial resources (equity) but also with professional experience and networks, helping the company to grow and develop new products and services. Other angel investors are generally referred to as "financial angel investors." These individuals, unlike strategic angel investors, generally do not take on an active role in the operations of the business but view their equity investment from a financial standpoint. Either strategic or financial angel investors could play an active role in the operations of the entrepreneur's business, however. If active, they may serve on the board of directors, in advisory roles, or as executives within the company. Many angel investors participate in equity financing thorough pooling their financial resources and creating syndicates or angel firms, clubs, associations, family agencies, or angel networks. Depending upon the type of the company (e.g., whether it is a partnership or an S corporation) and stage of the company's development, these angel groups could be useful investors.

This source of equity financing (generally offering $50,000 to $2,000,000) contributes significantly to the pool of investment capital available for small entrepreneurial companies. It has historically provided many times the volume of investment capital dollars to small companies than that provided by venture capital firms. According to Huang and Wu, "Recent estimates suggest that annual US angel investment activity may total as much as $24 billion each year."[1] As opposed to friends, family and associates, and other sources of investment capital (e.g., venture capital, public markets, private equity firms) that are readily identifiable, although not always easy to access, angel investors are neither easy to locate or access. Because they are private individuals, prospective angel investors may not be readily known to the entrepreneur. They are best accessed through networking with other business owners, professional service providers (bankers, attorneys, and accountants), or local, regional, or state angel or venture forums.

This first stage of external financing generally requires a working business plan, be it a traditionally structured business plan or one based on the "Lean LaunchPad" approach championed by Dr. Steven Blank, which focuses more heavily on early customer discovery as a test for the validity of the business concept and of the business's product or service offerings. In addition, the entrepreneur will need a well thought out financial plan, a thorough description of the use of investment proceeds to build value and to advance the company's development, a working demonstration of the company's new product or service, and, if possible, an analysis of the company's unique and defensible position against existing competitors, one that identifies customer demand through the early stage of the company's sales. (Being able to distinguish a new venture from competitors' businesses provides a compelling value proposition to both prospective customers and investors.) The funds raised during this round of equity financing should be used to recruit and complete a strong management team, refine the business model, and better define the product or service offerings.

Crowdfunding

Modern crowdfunding began in the late 1990s as an alternative to both equity and debt financing. In many cases, crowdfunding does not dilute the ownership of those seeking investment funds. Currently, the two primary forms of crowdfunding used by entrepreneurs are rewards and equity crowdfunding. Rewards crowdfunding allows the business owner to presell a service or product without incurring debt or diluting equity ownership.

In equity crowdfunding, the business owner sells shares of a company in exchange for money pledged. The shares may be nonvoting, so as not to dilute the entrepreneur's control of the company. To execute this financing strategy requires a platform or moderating organization that brings together the entrepreneur and the individuals who might be interested in supporting the entrepreneur's idea or business venture. Often, that crowdfunding platform receives a cut. Yet crowdfunding can be extremely profitable: in 2015, $34.4 billion was raised globally through crowdfunding platforms, according to Massolution.[2]

Crowdfunding is generally used to launch efforts that are strongly customer focused and that have capital-raising goals between $1,000 and $250,000. They may take the form of an "all-or-nothing" proposition, which sees the entrepreneur setting a goal and keeping nothing if that goal is not reached. This approach is similar to the traditional processes of raising capital in which a minimal goal is required to "break escrow" or release investment funds to the entrepreneur. The other form of crowdfunding is the "keep-it-all" type in which the entrepreneur sets a goal for the capital to be raised but keeps the entire amount raised regardless of whether the goal is achieved.

Reward-based crowdfunding has been used successfully to finance civic projects, motion-picture production, and software development, just to name a few examples. A variation of reward-based crowdfunding is the "sale" of software value tokens: an investor receives a token to be used toward the purchase of software products that will be developed using the proceeds of his or her investment. Crowdfunding using debt provides a "marketplace lending" format to make money by providing loans with repayment,

Blue Apron

Beginning in 2012, cofounders Matt Salzberg, Ilia Papas, and Matt Wadiak began sending customers boxes containing the ingredients necessary to prepare meals. From the humble start of packing and shipping their first 30 orders from an industrial kitchen in Long Island City, these entrepreneurs have established a company, the Blue Apron, with centers in Richmond, California, and across the country. The company quickly grew to national prominence through 2016, bringing in between $750 million and $1 billion in revenue that year. This pioneer in meal-kit delivery now offers multicourse dinner-party boxes that serve six and a direct-to-customer wine delivery service. According to the company's website, Blue Apron delivers about 8 million meal kits each month.

At its peak, the company's market valuation was in excess of $2 billion, but since then other companies have entered the meal-kit delivery market. Because Blue Apron now faces strong competitors in a highly competitive market, the company's market valuation post IPO has decreased to $560 million.

Sources:

1. Jing Cao, "Inside Blue Apron's Meal Kit Machine," *Bloomberg*, April 10, 2017, https://www.bloomberg.com/news/articles/2017-04-10/inside-blue-apron-s-meal-kit-machine.

2. "Our Story," Blue Apron website, accessed July 2018, https://www.blueapron.com/.

3. Rich Duprey, "Can Blue Apron Survive After this Latest Meal-Kit Buyout?" *The Motley Fool*, June 4, 2018, https://www.fool.com/investing/2018/06/04/can-blue-apron-survive-after-this-latest-meal-kit.aspx.

loan-servicing fees, and interest repayment on the loan. Litigation-based crowdfunding has provided a means for plaintiffs or defendants to obtain donations or even investors; sometimes donors are offered a reward for funding based upon the expected settlement of a claim that they have financed. Another form of crowdfunding is real estate crowdfunding, which has provided financing for both commercial and residential real estate purchases. A final form of crowdfunding is donation based: individuals with common interests contribute to opportunities that may have social benefits and that require resources beyond those of a single individual.

Though crowdfunding serves as an alternative to more traditional, established sources of investment capital, risks exist relating to the protection of the entrepreneur's intellectual property. Also, an entrepreneur using crowdfunding risks failing to meet her or his fund-raising goals due to a wide variety of circumstances, including donor exhaustion and the public fear of being scammed by the crowdfunding platform or the fundraiser.

Venture Capital

Venture capital firms are professionally managed closed-end funds organized in limited partnership arrangements. These legally chartered and regulated firms manage equity investments for other investors. Sources of funds may come from private equity sources, other professionally managed investment funds (e.g., a fund of funds, or FOF), or institutional sources of capital, including professionally managed public retirement funds and corporate investment funds. Through the partnership arrangement, the professional managers within the fund function in the role of general partners. This business arrangement provides managing partners with the flexibility to operate the business on behalf of the remaining investors or limited partners. Venture capital funds are closed-end funds with a defined fund life of typically 7 to 10 years. The assets of these funds must be converted into liquid assets and the proceeds distributed to the partners in accordance with the terms of the preapproved partnership agreement.

Venture capital firms may organize themselves to finance companies in a variety of ways. Some organize themselves according to the stage of development of the company in which they plan to invest. In this scenario, a venture capital fund may be a seed stage fund (investing during the first round of post founders' investment), an early stage fund (investing in companies that have received their first round of post founders' investment), a growth-oriented or middle stage fund (investing in companies that are seeking capital to expand their business operations or capture market share with new products or services), or a late stage or mezzanine fund (investing in companies that are positioning themselves either to be acquired or to acquire additional assets or businesses or that are preparing to transition from a private company to a publically reporting one through an initial public offering).

In addition, venture capital firms can also be organized according to the particular interests, professional experiences, and competencies of each firm's partners and analysts. Examples include venture capital firms that invest in companies having to do with the life sciences (biotechnology and related businesses), real estate, health care, energy exploration, alternative energy production, or some other business interest. Another approach that has gained interest is investing in businesses that have more than economic benefits to offer. Some venture capital firms have as a precondition that they will only invest in ventures that are socially conscious and ecologically friendly. Finally, among a wide range of other options, venture capital firms can be organized to place investments within specific geographic regions and locations.

Venture capital firms look for investors themselves. They compete for access to future sources of private investment funds through the performance of the funds that they manage. A venture capital firm's fund performance is monitored and measured against the performance of other venture capital funds by the venture capital investment industry. The funds are placed into quartile rankings according to performance, from highest performing to lowest performing funds, for the selected period of review and analysis. The top performing venture capital funds, those in the top two quartiles, generally have an easier time raising subsequent venture capital. However, the lowest performing funds, those in the bottom two quartiles, have increasing difficulty in securing investments for future funds. Venture capital funds operate in a highly competitive, free-market environment, so only the most successful venture capital firms survive. They do so by carefully identifying high-value opportunities, clearly understanding the financial horizons of the investment instruments, and skillfully analyzing the competitive landscape for each investment. They also ensure a defined exit strategy for harvesting each investment.

Venture capital fund managers, who are the general partners of a venture capital firm, make money in two ways. As managers, they are entitled to an annual percentage of the total amount of the fund—to pay for their expenses and the fund's management usually 1% to 3% of the fund's value. Upon successfully exiting a fund they manage (harvesting an investment), they also receive a lump sum payment, called "the carry," which is approximately 20% of the fund's liquidated asset value, after distributing the other 80% or so to the limited partners. In some circumstances, fund managers must repay the limited partners first, giving them back their initial investment before allocating whatever proceeds have been generated by the managing partners of the fund.

ENTREPRENEURIAL SPOTLIGHT
LIAM BERRYMAN—NELUMBO

Liam Berryman is the cofounder of Nelumbo, a business venture based on new technology that creates an advanced heat exchanger—the primary component in any refrigeration system. Nelumbo was formed in 2015 to develop new materials that can increase the efficacy of existing refrigeration equipment. The firm is applying nanotechnology in the heat-transfer process.

The firm's initial product, Ice-Nein™, reduces defrosting times while maintaining the cleaner operation of cooling coils. The product both extends the life of the refrigeration equipment and improves energy efficiency by up to 30%.

If the firm's product achieves widespread market acceptance in this country, the United States could save $11 billion annually in energy costs.

Sources:

1. "Liam Berryman: Profile," *Forbes*, accessed July 2018, https://www.forbes.com/profile/liam-berryman/.
2. Alberto Moñino, "Two Innovative Tech Startups Created by Engineers Like You," *Ennomotive*, May 10, 2017, https://www.ennomotive.com/innovative-tech-startups/.

In recent years, two trends have shaped the availability of equity investments for entrepreneurs and their businesses. First, due to the economic pressures for funds to perform, venture capital firms have become increasingly risk averse, investing at later stages when the risk of failure is perceived to be lower and the risk of equity loss diminished for the fund's investment. This strategy shifts the risk-return ratio and favors investment in older, less risky firms rather than in younger companies that, while riskier, have the potential to yield higher returns. The second trend has been the formation of ever-larger pools of investment in each of the particular funds under the management of venture capital firms. This upward spiral of fund size has diminished how available venture capital funds are to smaller entrepreneurial ventures. To understand this condition in the venture capital market, consider the fund manager who, up until a few short years ago, managed an investment pool of $100 million. Most likely, the fund manager would have spread the money among 10 to 20 companies, investing an average maximum of between $5 and $10 million and an initial investment per company of between $1 and $5 million. This scenario provided smaller fundable companies and smaller growing companies with reasonable access to venture capital. Today, the same fund manager might be managing a fund of between $500 million and several billion dollars. Using the same strategy of investing in 10 to 20 companies, the manager would invest an average of between $25 and $50 million (on the low side) with an estimated average initial investment of between $10 and $25 million. Because of this scenario, many growing entrepreneurial companies will never reach the minimum threshold of being able to return between 5 and 10 times the investment within 7 to 10 years, the rates expected by venture capital funds. This has caused a significant gap in the availability of equity investments between $2 and $15 million from venture capital funds.

Mezzanine Financing or Pre-IPOs

A pre–initial public offering (pre-IPO), which is also known as mezzanine financing, is usually undertaken one to two years before the execution of a planned IPO of the company's securities on the stock exchanges (NYSE, AMEX, NASDAQ, and others). Access to these sources of funds is based on the market conditions for IPOs, the strength of the business sector of the company, and the valuation of the company. These funds are used as a source of bridge financing to help the company meet its financing requirements until it enters the public markets with tradable securities.

This pool of investors has traditionally been passive. Financial investors as well as mutual funds, financial institutions, and the private-capital divisions of larger investment brokerages are often sources of pre-IPOs. Although these investments are generally equity-type investments, in recent years, bridge financing has begun to adopt the use of convertible debentures that provide a hedge for funding sources by offering the option of interest-bearing financial instruments with an equity kicker in the form of warrants for the company's securities and a right senior to that of other shareholders.

Traditional mezzanine financing has also utilized convertible debentures. The term mezzanine financing refers to a type of financial instrument that lies between traditional debt and equity. The rate of interest on the debenture typically lies between 10 and 30 percent, with the rate of interest based upon the company's perceived ability to repay the note (perceived risk of failure of the loan). Mezzanine financing is available to developing companies to support corporate growth and accelerate the sale of products and services. Sources of mezzanine financing include commercial banks and insurance companies. The advantage of mezzanine financing to the entrepreneur is the avoidance of equity dilution through the service of the debt component of the debenture.

TYPES OF EQUITY INSTRUMENTS

The most common forms of equity instruments currently used by entrepreneurs to finance their businesses are

- common stock,
- warrants and options,
- preferred stock, and
- convertible debentures.

Common Stock

Common stock is the simplest form of equity instrument or security currently available to the entrepreneur. Each share of common stock usually carries one vote. Common shares of stock are, in general, not convertible into another class of stock. When dividends are declared by the company's board of directors, common stock shareholders may receive, without limit, dividends. In the event of the liquidation of company assets, common stock shareholders receive asset value after the distribution of assets to all other classes of shareholders.

Warrants and Options

Warrants and options are securities instruments that give their owners the right to purchase a stock security at a fixed price, commonly referred to as the exercise price. Warrants function as short-term options to allow for the purchase of the company's securities. Warrants may be issued alone as investment instruments or in conjunction with the purchase of either common stock or other classes of shares of securities including preferred stock shares. Under this scenario, the warrant may be issued with a debt component attached (such as a convertible debenture instrument). Options, on the other hand, are generally issued to employees and may carry an exercise term as long as 10 years. Generally, these financial instruments are structured to minimize initial tax consequences for the option holder and to incentivize the holder to perform well for the duration of the option term. Many options are granted and vested over a period of time. Should the employee leave the company prior to the completion of the stock option vesting period, in most but not all cases, the unvested stock options are forfeited by the option holder and the remaining vested options are required to be exercised and converted into company stock. Both options and warrants, for accounting purposes, are considered as common stock equivalents.

Employee Stock Ownership Plans

An employee stock ownership plan (ESOP) enables employees to gain an ownership interest in the company in which they are employed. This instrument provides potential benefits to both the employee and the company. The employee obtains stock with little or no upfront cost. ESOPs are viewed by the Internal Revenue Service as payment for work performed by the employee. While the employee remains with the company, the shares are generally held in an ESOP trust. When the employee leaves the company, the ESOP shares are either bought back by the company or voided, depending upon the conditions of the ESOP plan and under which conditions the employee exits the company. In the United States, the ESOP is currently regulated as a qualified retirement plan. Over 11,000 ESPOs currently exist in the United States, including at such companies as Publix Super Markets, Hy Vie, and the New Belgium Brewing Company.

An ESPO, like other tax-qualified compensation plans, cannot discriminate in its operation in favor of any individual or group of individuals within the company. Employees are able to receive a distribution or payment from the plan when leaving the company and can roll the amount into an individual retirement account (IRA). The major potential disadvantage of the ESOP is that it can be risky for the employee. The entire value of an employee's shares is tied to the company employing the individual participating in the ESOP. Consequently, there is a lack of both investment diversification and of control, as, in most cases, the individuals participating in the ESOP do not participate in the senior management of the company. So, should the company fail, their entire set of options (investments and in most cases retirement savings) would be valueless.

From the company's perspective, the advantages of the ESOP include the anticipation of enhanced performance by employees because their interests are aligned with those of the company and a shared ownership among employees. Both of these advantages can lead to reduced employee turnover and better employee work satisfaction. Another benefit to the company is that, currently, ESOPs are the only retirement plans that are allowed to borrow money. This unique feature provides company owners and managers with the ability to use the ESOP as a vehicle to arrange corporate financing and owner succession.

Preferred Stock

Preferred stock as a class of securities comes in many forms depending upon the desired intent of the company issuing the security. The company can fix the privileges of the stockholders owning a particular preferred stock, as well as their voting and conversion rights. The preferred stock instrument can be viewed as a convenient way to adjust the relationship between cash and noncash investors by creating special privileges, such as increased or diminished voting rights, anti-dilution protection, and "super majority" veto rights. As contrasted with common stock, which generally carries one vote per share, preferred stock may be voting or nonvoting, or holders of preferred stock could be allowed to vote under very specially defined conditions. Also, those owning preferred stock usually have a higher claim on a firm's assets and earnings than those owning common stock. Generally, the owners of preferred stock are paid first in the event of the liquidation of the company, and they often receive higher dividends than common stockholders. Further, preferred stock can be structured to grant specified conversion rights in the event the stockholder wants to convert preferred stock to common stock.

To summarize, preferred stock securities generally provide

- Preference for shareholders during asset liquidation;

- Preemptive rights or rights of first refusal to purchase the company's securities prior to outside investors;

- Preference to receive dividends, if granted by the company's board of directors;

- Conversion rights to convert preferred shares into common shares;

- The right to sell shares before other shareholders;

- Anti-dilution protection;

- Negotiated voting rights; and

- Negotiated veto rights.

RAISING EQUITY CAPITAL

With a clear understanding of the sources of equity financing available at the different stages of a company's development and a capital structure that allows for the growth of the company through investment, the founding entrepreneur is now ready to raise equity capital. Still, every successful entrepreneur must be cognoscente of the factors that influence her or his ability to attract investment. These include but are not limited to the following:

- The quality and experience of the management team

- The business model chosen by the company

- The proprietary positioning of the company's products and services

- The revenue model for the company

- The capital requirements of the company

- The strength of the business sector for the company

- The dynamics of the equities market

The importance of choosing an experienced and outstanding management team cannot be overstated. An excellent leadership team with demonstrated success creates confidence in the company and helps reduce the perceived risk for potential funding sources of investing in the venture.

The choice of an appropriate business model is also an important factor in helping the entrepreneur to attract and close equity financing. If that choice demonstrates a clear understanding of which business models and strategies have been used successfully by other businesses in the industry, potential investors will see that the company's leaders understand their competition and can develop appropriate strategies to capitalize effectively on business opportunities.

The proprietary positioning of the company's products and services through the thoughtful and prudent use of intellectual property protection provides a differentiated placement of the company among its competitors and yields unique opportunities for collaboration with and licensing to other companies. This strategy may involve a balanced portfolio of intellectual property assets, including the patents, trademarks, copyrights, trade secrets, and know how. With the proper management of these assets, the company increases its value to investors, mitigates the risk that investors assume, and provides addition opportunities for revenue generation.

The revenue model selected by the company is important because it enables the potential investor to understand how and when the company's revenue stream will grow, which helps the investor to understand the future financial requirements tied to the execution of the company's business plan. Further, it helps the investor to project how valuable the company will be in future years when revenue milestones are met.

The financing requirements of the company significantly influence the decisions of potential investors. They will consider, for example, whether the company's current financial requirements align with its stage of development and whether anticipated financial needs will allow the company to execute its business plan. The investors carefully weigh these considerations as they evaluate the possible success or failure of the venture, the anticipated return on their investment, and the length of time before they can harvest that investment.

The strength of the business sector in which the company has chosen to compete may dramatically influence a potential investor's decision. If the company's business sector is weak and underperforming compared to other business sectors, people may choose to invest in a more rapidly growing or better performing market sector.

The dynamics of the equities market can have either a positive or negative influence on the ability of the entrepreneur to both attract equity investment and close the deal under terms acceptable to the company. In an upturned, rising economy, the liquidity and availability of investments from all sources of equity financing are much stronger than in a slow-growing, stagnant, or downturned economy (recessionary). These external factors do restrict the flow of investment capital to entrepreneurial companies due to the conservation of investment capital by potential funding sources or the increased costs to entrepreneurs of acquiring investment financing. In adverse market conditions, conservation of investment capital takes precedence over the placement or flow of funds to support new venture creation or growth. Unfortunately, this dynamic is completely out of the control of the entrepreneur. Bootstrapping techniques and the effective and frugal use of all available financial resources still afford opportunities for entrepreneurs in difficult economic times.

Navigating the sea of financing options available to the entrepreneur may seem daunting, but entrepreneurship is all about identifying opportunities when others see challenges, marshaling the resources necessary to create products and services of strong value to customers, and creating financial rewards for the entrepreneur, investors, and employees.

The entrepreneur should also consider several factors when using equity financing to fund his or her company. Whenever entrepreneurs use equity financing to grow a company, they risk diluting their ownership. Such restrictions tend to ensure that the management team remains in place during the vesting period. The entrepreneur should always discuss with investors what his or her post-financing equity position will be. That entrepreneurs maintain adequate equity positions is important for their continuing commitment to the growth and success of the firms they establish. Additionally, entrepreneurs must ensure that they have adequate representation in their companies' governance and operations and that they experience a financial "upside" when their companies are successful. Also entrepreneurs may wish to negotiate earn-up agreements, which entitle the entrepreneurs to increase their equity holdings if the company exceeds the performance thresholds agreed upon by all parties. Finally, founders should consider active participation in performance options tied to their employee agreements.

ENTREPRENEURIAL EXERCISES

Entrepreneurial Exercise 10.1

Where do you plan to find the initial financing for your proposed business venture? How much from each source?

Self-financing (cash, securities, credit cards, etc.) $_____

Bootstrapping (approximate value) $_____

Friends, family, and interested associates $_____

Angel investors $_____

Venture capital firms $_____

Total capital anticipated to be raised $_____

How much are you above or below what you project is needed?

$_____

If below, what percentage of your initial capital needs will you need to find elsewhere? From what sources of equity capital?

Entrepreneurial Exercise 10.2

In no more than two paragraphs, write your proposed "pitch" to an interested angel investor.

Entrepreneurial Exercise 10.3

Please detail the steps you would take to identify venture capital firms that would most likely consider investing in a business venture such as yours?

If the venture capita firm were willing to provide your business with 80% of its financial needs for the first year of operations, would you be willing to give the firm 50% of the equity in the firm? Why or why not?

If not, how much equity in your business would you willing sell to an investor and for what price?

DEBT AND ALTERNATIVE FORMS OF INVESTMENT CAPITAL

Nowadays people can be divided into three classes—the haves, the have-nots, and the have-not-paid-for-what-they-haves.

Earl Wilson

The debt is like a crazy aunt we keep down in the basement. All the neighbors know she's there, but nobody wants to talk about her.

H. Ross Perot

Creditors have better memories than debtors.

Benjamin Franklin

(Continued)

Describe the sources of capital available from government agencies

Explain the role of the Small Business Administration (SBA) in venture financing

Explain the role of SBIR and STTR programs in advancing technology-enabled ventures

FUNDAMENTALS OF NON-EQUITY FINANCING

Debt financing and government sources of financial investment provide the entrepreneur with alternatives to equity capital investments. Debt instruments are either significantly less dilutive or non-dilutive to the entrepreneur's ownership than traditional equity investment vehicles. In this chapter, we will explore the types of debt instruments and the various sources of debt financing. We will also examine government programs as sources for investment capital to create and grow new businesses, including the Small Business Innovation Research (SBIR) and Small Business Technology Transfer (STTR) programs, the U.S. Small Business Administration's Express program, and programs targeted to assist minority and Native American business owners.

Debt Financing

By definition, debt-financing instruments require an agreement between the lending individual or institution and the recipient of the funds. The terms and conditions vary, but the general premise of debt instruments requires repayment of the principal amount loaned to the individual or company and an agreement to repay an additional premium for the use of the funds, commonly referred to as interest. Debt instruments do not require transfer of partial ownership of the company, as is the case with equity investments.

Debt financing generally falls into two basic categories of financial instruments. These are known as "unsecured" or "secured" debt. Unsecured debt or loan instruments have the following basic characteristics:

- They provide the lending institution no priority over any common creditor or borrower.

- They are granted as a percentage of the net current assets of the borrower.

- They impose no lien on the assets of the borrower.

Unsecured debt instruments can have different terms or schedules of repayment. Here are the most common forms:

- *Short-term, or closed-end, debt instruments* are for fixed periods of time; that time is generally less than a year but may extend to several years.

- *Revolving or renewable credit (also known as open-end credit)* is used for repeated purchases, although limits are imposed on the line of financial credit extended to the borrower, and, generally, the debt is repaid monthly; an example is a company credit card.

- *Flexible, fixed, or "balloon" (terminal)[1] repayment schedules* are used to repay a term-dependent debt with the principal and/or interest being paid on a flexible schedule, a fixed repayment schedule, or a schedule in which payment in full is due at the end of the term of the financial instrument.

Secured debt or loan instruments require the borrower to provide collateral to back up the loan in the event of the borrower's inability to service or repay the loan. These liens provide the lending organization a priority claim on specific assets isolated behind the loan for the benefit of the lending institution. Here are some of the securities that can be pledged as collateral:

- Personal savings

- Real estate

- Stocks and bonds

- Personal endorsers

- Life insurance

- Accounts receivable (factoring)

- Warehouse receipts (warehousing)

- Assignment of leases or rents

- Inventory

In all the above cases, most lenders will require personal guarantees on the loan instrument secured by the business owner or partnership members.

A number of sources exist for debt financing for entrepreneurial (but not necessarily start-up) businesses. Some of the most common are the following:

- Commercial banks

- Credit unions

- Savings and loan associations

- Friends and family

- Life insurance providers

- Credit card companies

- Mortgage companies

- Personal loan companies
- State and local sources
- The Small Business Association
- Other federal government sources

Commercial Banks

Commercial banks are easy to locate. They are found on nearly every street corner. Regardless of whether they are national, regional, local, or community lenders, commercial banks are very conservative and are generally risk averse when it comes to loaning bank assets for early-stage and start-up business ventures. They do provide debt financing (loans) at fair market interest rates. These rates are generally much lower than the adjusted cost of capital from most equity sources. The credit worthiness of the entrepreneur and the business, along with the presence or absence of a positive personal and professional history with the lending institution, will determine whether the bank will provide the loan and what conditions it might impose on the loan structure. These may include

- the type of collateral required,
- the term of the loan,
- the structure of the loan's repayment, and
- the interest rates charged on the loan.

If the loan is to be made to the entrepreneur's company, a bank will generally require two or three years of historical financial records from the entrepreneur's company to demonstrate the several years of successful business operations. In addition, the bank may require minimum deposits be held by the back during the term of the loan.

Banks, Credit Unions, and Savings and Loan Associations (S&Ls)

Banks provide a variety of financial debt instruments for entrepreneurs and their businesses. These include

- Lines of credit
- Commercial loans
- Investment loans
- Financing for accounts receivable
- Factoring

Credit unions provide debt financing as loans to members in good standing with deposits on hand in the credit union providing the loan. The structure of the loan may vary from borrower to borrower, but in general, these loan arrangements are less complex than those offered by other commercial lending institutions.

Savings and loan associations generally provide loans to individuals who can demonstrate adequate collateral to cover the loan in the event of default on the repayment of the loan. These loans are often collateralized and secured by funds held by the S&L, which the borrower has agreed to leave within the S&L for the term of the loan.

DocuSign

In 15 years, cofounders Tom Gonser, Court Lorenzini, and Eric Ranft have transformed the secure online execution of documents through the creation and deployment of DocuSign's products and services. More than 100 million users and over 250,000 companies in 188 countries and territories around the world have signed and sent documents electronically using the company's e-signature technology. The customer benefits are strong as the company's offerings reduce document transmission time, eliminate the need and cost for paper, and increase the encrypted security of documents all the while creating an electronic audit trail for signed and sent documents. Continuing as an innovator in the electronic documents transmission business space, DocuSign launched in 2017 its service enabling customers to collect both a signature and a payment in a single electronic transmission. The strong customer focus and the security of the company's product offerings have enabled DocuSign to attain a market valuation of over $3 billion by 2015 and $6 billion by April 2018, after its first day of trading on the stock exchange.

Sources:

See "About Us" and the home page of the company website, accessed July 2018, https://www.docusign.com/.

Alex Konrad, "DocuSign Doubles Valuation to $3 billion with $233 Million Raise," *Forbes*, May 12, 2015, https://www.forbes.com/sites/alexkonrad/2015/05/12/docusign-raises-233-million/#c7495437f2f2.

Alex Barinka, "DocuSign Climbs in Trading Debut After $629 Million U.S. IPO," *Bloomberg*, April 26, 2018, https://www.bloomberg.com/news/articles/2018-04-27/docusign-gets-629-million-in-above-range-u-s-tech-offering.

Friends, Family, and Close Associates

When you start a new venture, friends, family, and close associates may be helpful in providing debt financing (loans). To avoid complications with the Internal Revenue Service, you should structure loans of this type as if they were any other sort of loan, requiring that the loan be executed by all parties with a statement of fair market interest to be repaid. If you obtained a loan from friends or close associates, timely repayment of the loan is necessary to avoid turning friends and close associates into enemies. An alternative to obtaining loans from friends and family is to allow them to cosign a promissory note so that the lending institution will be more receptive to loaning you funds for your new venture.

Other Nongovernmental Sources

Life insurance policies may serve as potential sources of debt financing. This source of loans is relatively simple. In most cases, the policy owner borrows most of the cash-surrender value of the policy. This type of loan is attractive also because of its generally low rate of interest repayment.

Factoring companies may provide short-term debt financing based upon your firm's accounts receivable. These loans of short-term capital depend upon the credit worthiness of the accounts receivable. Also, the lender can apply a premium charge in the form of a discount on the value of the accounts receivable to cover the risk of nonpayment.

Using credit cards or the lines of credit extended by credit card companies can be, in many cases, the only alternative for many entrepreneurs starting businesses for the first time. The downside risks are high due to the traditionally high interest rates charged to the borrowers.

Personal loan companies charge the highest rates of interest of all debt-lending sources, with rates as high as 40 to 50 percent per year (as governed by individual state laws and regulations). Laws vary widely state to state regarding the terms and conditions that can be imposed by these lenders on the loans they provide. In spite of these high rates, personal loan companies do offer some benefits: they often specialize in particular industry sectors, for example, and can be more reliable than many other sources of debt capital.

University-based convertible debt provides medium-term debt financing for new ventures utilizing technologies licensed from the university's technology transfer office. These debentures allow for debt repayment of the financial instrument or, in some cases and under prearranged terms, conversion to equity in the venture.

GOVERNMENT SOURCES OF CAPITAL

Various state, regional, and local agencies are sources of debit and alternative financing for entrepreneurs and their businesses. State funding is generally available from the departments of economic development or of commerce or their equivalents. These sources of funds are designed to stimulate entrepreneurial venturing, new business start-ups, and corporate growth, as well as to enhance economic development, often with a geographic or industry-specific focus.

Regional sources of funds, similar to state sources, are generally administered through nongovernmental agencies or public-private partnerships. These funds are designed to promote the economic growth of a multi-county or parish region and stimulate the transfer of technologies from colleges and universities to the private sector. The outcomes expected of these programs are the creation of new companies and more employment opportunities for local residents.

Local funds may be available through community development corporations. These funds are designed to promote the local stimulation of economic development, revitalization, and growth.

The Small Business Administration (SBA)

This federal program provides financial assistance to qualifying businesses in the form of loans. This agency is often a last resort for businesses that otherwise cannot obtain loans from a commercial lender at reasonable interest rates or for companies that cannot obtain

ENTREPRENEURIAL SPOTLIGHT
BEATRICE FISCHEL-BOCK—HUTCH

While in her senior year at George Washington University, Beatrice Fischel-Bock created Hutch (formerly known as ZOOM Interiors and Homee). Hutch, a combination software application and website, allows customers to upload actual photos of rooms in their homes and "virtually" redecorate these rooms. Customers can then choose to purchase the items they have used in the redecoration of their virtual interior spaces. With Hutch, physical inventory issues that brick-and-mortar stores must face when selling do not limit customers—this 3-D interior design places the customer in complete control. The process is simple, beginning with the customer uploading photos of the space he or she wishes to redecorate. Next, the customer applies the 3-D design tool to try out new looks with furnishings, paint, smaller items such as paintings, or whatever appeals. The final step is purchase. Free returns and free shipping on these furnishings ensure that customers maintain a high level of confidence throughout the process, from start to finish, even if they lack experience in interior design. Any error in judgment can be undone. The company's price-matching guarantee policies add to customer comfort with Hutch.

Fortune Magazine described how the firm's proprietary technology allows the customer to upload photos and then select a "style filter." An interior designer then transforms the space with a virtual design and sends the transformed image back to the customer. The customer can then choose the furniture and other design elements. Revenues come from the sale of the furniture and other pieces, purchased at wholesale and sold at retail. The initial business has gone through a number of iterations—initially, Zoom and Homee focused on direct consultations or "chats" with interior designers. Hutch now focuses on the most popular feature of Homee—a picture of the transformed space.

Sources:

"About Us," Hutch website, accessed July 2018, www.hutch.com.

Yitzi Weiner, "Meet the Female Founders of Tech: Beatrice Fischel-Bock, CEO & Co-Founder of Hutch, 2018's *Forbes* 30 Under 30," *Forbes*, November 15, 2017, https://medium.com/thrive-global/meet-the-female-founders-of-tech-beatrice-fischel-bock-ceo-co-founder-of-hutch-2018s-forbes-457633c0d557.

Polina Marinova, "This App Lets You Redesign Your Apartment Using Snapchat-Like Filters, "*Fortune*, February 1, 2017, fortune.com/2017/02/01/hutch-interior-design-app/.

financing without selling essential assets of the company to secure the financial transaction. The SBA programs vary state to state but may include the following:

- Regular business loans with terms of up to 10 years

- Special loans to assist companies with short-term financing, for example, loans to aid local companies or citizens seeking to improve their communities, seasonal line-of-credit guarantees, energy loans, and handicapped assistance loans

- Disaster assistance loans to cover the repair or replacement of damaged or lost property and working capital to pay the financial obligations of small business owners

- Pollution control financing to assist small business owners by guaranteeing their private financing for as long as 25 to 30 years

- Surety bonds for which the SBA guarantees payment or performance bonds issued to contractors

- Microloans that assist with short-term working capital of no more than $50,000

SBIR and STTR Grant Programs

The Small Business Innovation Research Program (SBIR) is administered by the Small Business Administration. This program allocates over $1 billion annually for the development and translation of scientific and engineering innovation. Funds are dispersed to businesses in competitive phases. Phase 0 grants are available for the planning phase of the grant application and are awarded in the amount of $5,000. Phase 1 grants are provided to investigate the feasibility of an innovation. These grants generally provide awards of between $100,000 and $200,000 for the term of the project, usually less than one year in duration. This phase allows the company to demonstrate the proof of principal of the innovation, including developing prototypes, conducting basic market research for the new product, and reporting on the success of the project. Phase 2 grants can provide up to $1 million for operating and project expenses. Currently, there is a two-year deadline to complete this project phase. Activities can center on further testing and validation of the new innovation, pilot production of working prototypes, and further market research. At the completion of Phase 2 of the SBIR, a report is required explaining progress achieved and how the funds were expended. Phase 3 provides no federal funding but involves other help toward the early commercialization of the product or service developed during Phase 1 and 2. The funds provided to the company in Phase 1 and 2 of the SBIR provide direct validation of the scientific and engineering merit of the new product and, through peer-reviewed outside professional review of the proposal, an independent validation of the value and merit of the new innovation evaluated during the project. SBIR funds provide sources of research, development, and operations capital with no equity dilution and no requirement for repayment of funds provided through the SBIR program.

The Small Business Technology Transfer Program (STTR) is similar in many regards to the SBIR program in that it is designed to foster research and development activities in smaller businesses. The major difference between the two programs lies in the purpose of the STTR to foster joint ventures or partnerships between small businesses and nonprofit research institutions and universities. Like the SBIR program, the STTR program is conducted in competitive, peer-reviewed phases with slight variations in the amount and duration of the financial awards to the companies. For fiscal year 2018, a Phase 1 award may not exceed $163,952, and a Phase 2 award may not exceed $1,093,015.[2] Like the SBIR, the STTR requires no repayment to the SBA of the funds provided to the company.

SBA Express

The Small Business Express program was created to provide businesses with a fast (under 36 hours) loan decision for an SBA-backed loan of up to $150,000. The reduction in time and paperwork provides the business owner with a rapid loan approval process.

The SBA Express program only provides government guarantee of 50% of the face value of the loan.

SBA Assistance to Groups Underrepresented in Business

The SBA also provides assistance to economically and socially disadvantaged business owners and to those traditionally underrepresented in the entrepreneurial class, for example, women, veterans, and those living in rural areas. Additional programs are also available for minority-owned businesses. The current definition of a minority-owned business is one in which 51% or more of the business is held by a qualified minority or female owner. Additional SBA programs provide targeted federal assistance to Native American business owners through programs that enhance employment, business growth, and economic development on Native American lands.

ENTREPRENEURIAL EXERCISES

Entrepreneurial Exercise 11.1

What do you plan to tell a banker who is reviewing your business plan that will help overcome his or her reluctance to lend money to a start-up business?

Entrepreneurial Exercise 11.2

Please research the many sources of governmental loans. For which loans would you or your firm qualify? Please be specific regarding the qualifications, the amount of money available, the length of the loan, and the conditions regarding repayment of the loan.

Entrepreneurial Exercise 11.3

Would your proposed business venture qualify for a grant either under the Small Business Innovation Research Program (SBIR) or the Small Business Technology Transfer Program (STTR)?

   If so, please describe the required step to obtaining funding under either of these two government grant programs. If not, please research other agencies that award small grants to businesses or to entrepreneurs developing business plans. Try to find a grant that might be applicable to the location or industry in which you plan to begin a new venture.

STRUCTURING THE DEAL

I have found no greater satisfaction than achieving success through honest dealing and strict adherence to the view that, for you to gain, those you deal with should gain as well.

Alan Greenspan

Start-up financing is not just about raising funds, it is a holistic process that involves proper business planning with thoughtful growth targets, deciding business valuation as per current market standards, planning potential exit options for investors, calculating financial returns for investors, negotiations with investors, evaluating and deciding appropriate term-sheet clauses, and finalizing shareholder's agreements.

Nucleus Partners

CHAPTER LEARNING OBJECTIVES

Upon completion of this chapter you will be able to

Identify potential investor expectations

Describe how investors determine the value of a company

Recall the elements of a successful investment transaction

Discuss investors' decision-making processes

Explain the private placement memorandum (PPM)

Entrepreneurs tend to be "big picture" individuals with a strong focus on bringing innovation to the marketplace and creating value for stakeholders and customers. To accomplish these objectives, entrepreneurs must also be able to drill down, when needed, and develop the skills necessary to structure and negotiate the terms of the financial deals necessary to create and grow the company. In this chapter, we will examine the different philosophies and objectives of strategic and financial investors, the simple financial models used to value a company, and the importance of due diligence during the negotiation of any financial deals. We will also present a sample term sheet outlining the terms by which investors will finance a fictitious company, NUCO. This example will enable you to view how financial deals are structured.

MANAGING INVESTOR EXPECTATIONS

Different investors view every deal with somewhat different expectations. It is important to understand the shared and different expectations among the various types of prospective investors. All investors expect to receive a financial return greater than that which they could have achieved through secure, government-backed financial instruments, and all their expectations of financial returns are based upon the perceived, and real, risk of the deal. Angel investors generally will tolerate the highest risk when investing in de novo, growth, or early-stage companies. They seek reasonably short time horizons to exit and have moderate to strong financial return expectations. Crowdsourcing investors have the same risk profiles and return expectations as angel investors. In both cases, their personal assets are tied to the investments they make. Venture capital and private equity investors could invest at any stage of the investment cycle, from seed funding to mezzanine financing. In general, they tend to invest in companies that are beyond the seed round of financing. Unlike either angel or crowdfunding investors, venture capital and private equity investors usually manage funds raised from individuals and organizations other than themselves. They require time-dependent terms of investment and strong financial returns, and they want risk adjusted to the returns on their investments. Mezzanine financing may come from a variety of sources. In general, this money is provided by professionally managed investment funds. These investments are usually short term and have a debt component or a convertible option at either the completion of the public offering of securities or the transfer of ownership through the sale of the business. Public shareholders have other reasons for investment: they generally hope to sell their shares at a substantial gain after these shares appreciate, they might want to secure regular dividends, and they could hope to convert warrants tied to tradable securities into shares of public stock. The relationship between any one of these various investors and the company seeking funds, when properly structured and managed, can lead to a truly synergistic financial arrangement for both parties.

VALUING THE START-UP COMPANY

A variety of techniques are commonly used to aid investors in determining the value of a company and hence the pricing of the securities or debt to be offered to the company. From a practical standpoint, most entrepreneurial start-up companies, especially those in the early phases of business operations, will have extreme difficulty in predicting with any degree of certainty or accuracy, their expenses, revenues, and financial requirements beyond their first or second year of operations. These early-phase business ventures, which constitute the overwhelming majority of new businesses, may best be valued against existing companies in the same business sector that are of comparable age and stage of corporate development.

In addition, current prevailing economic and market conditions significantly influence the value of pre-revenue enterprises as risky early-stage investments. As most of these investments are made by private individuals or groups of private individuals, the availability of investable liquid assets waxes and wanes according to the availability of personal funds that can be invested in early-stage companies.

Traditional valuation models involving discounted cash flow and discounted residual income analysis, while useful to growing companies with a few years of business operations, are of significantly less value to early-stage start-up companies. These forms of company valuation are used to forecast the present value of a company's expected cash flows (dividends) or future residual earnings. The DCF method generally uses future free cash flow projections and discounts them using a required annual rate. The residual income (RI) method calculates the income that will be generated by the firm after accounting for the true cost of its capital. Considered in these valuation models are the earnings of the company over the period of the investment; changes in the working capital of the company; and various noncash expenses (including depreciation). The calculated free cash flow projections are converted to a current valuation of the company based upon discounting the value of the company and adjusting the costs of financing.

This model for valuing a company may be broken down into two basic components. The first reflects the value of the company over the forecast period, which is typically three to five years. This calculation is accomplished using detailed projections of revenue, expenses, and balance sheet items. The second component is calculated by assuming a fixed or variable growth rate for items included in the last detailed forecast year. This item is then capitalized. Adjustments are generally applied using multiples derived from the financial records of similar companies. In most cases, these multiples may be calculated by comparing enterprise value and earnings before interest, taxes, depreciation, and amortization; this is called the enterprise value multiple.

While analytically valid, these approaches do not often accurately reflect the discounted future value of start-up or pre-revenue companies that have few or no historical sales. In the earliest phases of a company's existence, the accuracy of the company's financial or performance projections is generally only as good as the professional experience of the entrepreneur who creates them. This high degree of uncertainty plays a significant role in investors' assessments of early-stage companies and generally requires the entrepreneur of such a company to accept a significantly reduced valuation of her or his start-up because of investors' perceptions of risk.

The most important lesson for young (non-serial) entrepreneurs to understand about structuring the deal is that valuing the venture in the early phases of its existence is not a science but an art, especially when one considers the high degree of risk for both the entrepreneur and investor. The art of negotiation becomes the critical determining factor in both the structure of the deal, the terms and conditions of the deal, and whether the deal will actually close. This negotiation is strongly influenced by the excellence of the management team and its professional advisors and by the confidence they produce in the prospective investor through frank and open communications during and after the due diligence process. Whether a specific deal appeals to an investor will be crafted around the characteristics of the individuals involved, the nature and attractiveness of the business to the investor, and the deal's setting in time and in terms of the business or investment climate.

Dropbox

College classmates Drew Houston and Arash Ferdowsi identified an unmet customer need for a corporate space that would enable the secure sharing and transfer of files and documents among individuals, and so Dropbox was born in 2007. The company has grown; in 2017, it had brick-and-mortar offices in 13 cities and users in over 180 countries around the world. That year Dropbox reported that it had reached over 500 million users and over 200,000 business customers, including Under Armour, News Corp, and National Geographic. These business customers pay an annual fee of $150 per employee for Dropbox's standard data package. As a result of developing and delivering a product valued in the marketplace by repeat users, Dropbox attained annual revenues of over $1 billion in 2017. Through the thoughtful and diligent leadership of Houston and and Ferdowsi, the company's market valuation had grown to over $10 billion by May of that year.

Sources:

1.　"Dropbox: The File-Sharing Economy," *CNN*, May 16, 2017, https://www.cnbc.com/2017/05/16/dropbox-2017-disruptor-50.html.

2.　See the pages "About" and "Investor Relations" on the Dropbox website, accessed July 2018, https://www.dropbox.com/business/.

For most deals, those involving sensible parties on both sides of the transaction, the following are generally agreed upon frameworks for producing investment in early-stage companies:

- A trust reflected among the parties
- A distributed and shared risk among participants
- Simple, straightforward form of agreement
- Terms that are equitable and fair for all parties

- An agreement between parties that is flexible
- A strong willingness to communicate at all times

To structure the deal, the entrepreneur must be able to communicate the opportunity to potential investors in easy to understand language that is accurate, truthful, and convincing and that conveys the trustworthiness of the company's management. The importance of developing effective oral communication skills cannot be underestimated for the entrepreneur and young business owner. Many entrepreneurs view themselves as knowledge experts regarding their businesses but fail to comprehend the importance of being able to articulate clearly and concisely the value of a business or investment opportunity to investors. These skills in professional salesmanship are absolutely essential when structuring a deal acceptable to both parties and to closing the deal. Every successful serial entrepreneur has learned these skills, but for many first-time entrepreneurs, these skills may not come naturally. Business owners can and should constantly improve and sharpen their communication and sales skills, focusing especially on effective public speaking and one-on-one interactions. Successful entrepreneurs position and sell themselves, their company, and their company's products and services every day. The most successful are those who become more effective communicators and listeners capable of understanding the needs of others, a most critical skill necessary when structuring and negotiating investment deals for your company.

The high degree of uncertainty surrounding the success or failure of entrepreneurial companies can often be mitigated by an entrepreneur's confidence and effective communications with prospective investors. For early-stage ventures, contrary to the belief of many, the structure of the deal and the entrepreneur's ability to close the deal rely primarily on the investor's confidence in the management team of the company, in the lead entrepreneur, and in the ability of both to lead the company and execute and modify the business model to achieve success.

Structuring, negotiating, and closing the deal comprise a process similar to dating and courtship; it may lead to nothing, to an initial agreement, or to success or separation. Entrepreneurs and potential investors must engage in "getting to know each other" through a process referred to as due diligence in which each party will conduct a close examination and evaluation of the other. This process generally includes extensive personal and professional background checks, social and professional interactions among the parties, and a detailed analysis of the strengths and weaknesses of all concerned. Young entrepreneurs are often taken off guard by the level and depth of the examination undertaken by prospective investors. To close the deal, entrepreneurs need to establish a strong level confidence and trust. Doing so will enable them to negotiate a balanced and fair financing arrangement. Further, the trust engendered through the due diligence process should carry forward to establish stronger working relationships among the company's management and its investors.

As an entrepreneur, you should be focused on securing the resources and capital necessary to grow your company. However, you need to examine carefully each source of funding and the structure of every deal with the clear understanding that, when a deal closes, the company and you will have taken on a new investor as an integral part of the company for some time to come.

The most common form of financing for entrepreneurial companies in their early stages of development is the private placement memorandum, or PPM. (An example follows this chapter's discussion.) This document outlines in clear terms the conditions under which investments may be placed into the company and the rights and responsibilities of both parties after the investment has been made.

The PPM specifically sets forth the terms of the financing and includes the following information:

- Type of security
- Minimum amount of the company's offering
- Number of securities (shares) to be offered
- Purchase price of the security
- Capitalization of the company following the close of the round of financing

In addition, the offering memorandum may specify a variety of rights, preferences, and privileges granted to purchasers, as well as give information about the terms of investors' rights agreements and other issues.

Here are some of the issues considered in the section detailing the rights, preferences, and privileges provided to the purchasers of the company's securities:

- Dividends to be paid by the company (rates and terms)
- Liquidation preferences (the order and conditions of disposal of company assets upon the cessation of business operations)
- Conversion (rights related to converting securities from one class to another)
- Automatic conversion (triggering events for securities class conversion)
- Anti-dilution provisions (clauses that protect against the dilution of ownership)
- Voting rights (the terms of shareholders' voting rights)
- Election of company directors (the constitution of the company's board of directors and provisions regarding the board's election)
- Protective provisions (security holders' class protection provisions)

Some of the terms of investors' rights agreements could address the following:

- Information rights (access to the company's financial records)
- Rights of participation (ability of the purchaser to participate in future rounds of financing)

- Registration rights (terms related to the registration of purchasers' securities for sale)

- Expenses (the terms and conditions under which the company will pay to register the securities)

Here are some other issues that might be addressed in the PPM:

- Rights of first refusal (repurchase agreements for securities)

- Co-sale rights (rights of the purchaser to obtain securities offered by other security holders)

- Small business stock (the registration of securities to qualify as a small business)

- Purchase agreement (conditions for the purchase of the security)

- The closing (the conditions necessary to close the round of financing)

- Expenses (who pays legal expenses on behalf of the investor)

See the sample PPM at the end of this chapter for insight into how to structure an effective private placement memorandum.

ENTREPRENEURIAL SPOTLIGHT
LISA CURTIS—KULI KULI

Lisa Curtis is a 30-year-old entrepreneur and a former Peace Corps volunteer in Niger who founded Kuli Kuli with Valerie Popelka, Jordan Moncharmont, and Anne Tsuei in 2011. Curtis, the CEO of Kuli Kuli, is an excellent example of a woman who is a serious social entrepreneur. While in Niger, she discovered a plant called moringa, which is considered a potential super food.

Kuli Kuli sells products made from moringa, which is rich in iron, calcium, vitamins, antioxidants, and plant protein. These products are designed to address the current lack of vegetables in the diet of many persons. Kuli Kuli sells energy bars, powders, organic greens and proteins, teas, and energy drinks (called "shots")—all made from moringa leaves. Curtis's goal is to improve the nutritional input of its customers while supporting the economic development of the women-led farming cooperatives that grow moringa trees. The company reports it has planted over 1 million moringa trees resulting in the creation of over 1,000 current farmers, each of whom can earn a sustainable livelihood.

Kuli Kuli has partnered with women farmers in Ghana, Haiti, and Nicaragua. The company has also established marketing relationships with major retail outlets across the United States.

Sources:

1. See the "About" and "Our Impact" sections of the Kuli Kuli website, accessed July 2018, https://www.kulikulifoods.com

2. "Lisa Curtis," *Linkedin*, accessed July 2018, https://www.linkedin.com/in/lisamariecurtis.

EXAMPLE OF A DRAFT PRIVATE PLACEMENT MEMORANDUM

NUCO

MEMORANDUM OF TERMS FOR PRIVATE PLACEMENT OF SERIES A PREFERRED STOCK

January 1, 2013

NUCO, a Delaware corporation (the "Company"), intends to issue shares of its Series A Preferred Stock to certain qualified individuals and entities (each an "Investor" and collectively, the "Investors"). This memorandum summarizes the principal terms proposed by Band of Angels Fund, L.P. (the "Lead Investor") with respect to the purchase of Series A Preferred Stock (the "Financing").

GENERAL TERMS OF THE FINANCING

Security: Series A Preferred Stock ("Series A")
Minimum Amount of Offering: $1,000,000
Number of Shares: 500,000
Purchase Price: $2.00
Capitalization: Immediately following the closing of the Financing, the Company's capitalization will be as follows:

	Shares Outstanding	Percentage
Common Stock (1)	1,000,000	50.0%
Incentive Stock Plan (2)	500,000	25.0%
Series A Preferred Stock	500,000	25.0%
Totals	1,500,000	100.0%

(1) Held by founders on a vesting schedule in accordance with the stock option plan.

(2) The Company's board of directors has adopted a stock option plan to be administered by the board authorizing the Company to grant options and stock purchase rights to employees and consultants. There are 500,000 shares under the Stock Option Plan that are subject to outstanding options and 500,000 shares remaining available for future issuance.

RIGHTS, PREFERENCES, AND PRIVILEGES

Dividends: The holders of Series A Preferred Stock ("Series A") shall be entitled to receive in preference to the Common Stock ("Common"), noncumulative dividends of $0.25 per share per annum, respectively, when and if declared by the board of directors.

Liquidation Preference:	In the event of any liquidation or winding up of the Company, the holders of Series A shall be entitled to receive, in preference to the holders of Common, an amount equal to the price paid per Series A share, plus all declared but unpaid dividends on such shares. Thereafter, the assets available for distribution shall be distributed ratably among the holders of Common and Series A. A merger or sale of all or substantially all of the assets of the Company shall be treated as a liquidation or winding up for purposes of the liquidation preference.
Conversion:	Optional Conversion: The holders of Series A shall have the right to convert their shares of Series A, at the option of the holder, at any time into shares of Common, at the rate of one share of Series A for one share of Common, subject to adjustment as described below.
Automatic Conversion:	Series A shall be automatically converted into Common, at the then applicable conversion rate, (i) in the event of the closing of an underwritten public offering of the Company's securities in which the aggregate gross proceeds to the Company equals or exceeds $5,000,000 or (ii) upon the election of the holders of a majority of the shares of Series A then outstanding.
Anti-Dilution Provisions:	In the event that the Company issues additional securities without consideration or for a consideration per share less than the price paid for Series A, as adjusted for capital reorganization, stock splits, reclassification, etc., (other than (i) the issuance of options or shares of Common to employees, directors, and consultants, (ii) the sale of shares in connection with a firm commitment underwritten public offering, (iii) the issuance of Common upon conversion of the Series A or other already outstanding convertible securities, (iv) dividends or distributions on Series A, (v) the issuance of warrants to banks or equipment lessors, or (vi) the issuance of shares in connection with business combinations or corporate partnering agreements approved by the board of directors), then, and in such event, the conversion price for the Series A Preferred Stock shall be adjusted using a broad-based weighted average anti-dilution formula.
Redemption.	Commencing on the date that is three years after closing and for three years thereafter, the holders of a majority of the Series A (provided that the Lead Investor consents) may require the Company to redeem their respective shares of Series A at a price equal to cost plus dividends declared but not paid. Any redemption payment not made when due shall thereafter bear interest at the prime rate plus 5%.

<u>Voting Rights</u>:	<u>Generally</u>. The holder of each share of Series A shall have the right to that number of votes equal to the number of shares of Common issuable upon conversion of such share of Series A. The Series A votes together with the Common on all matters except as described below.
<u>Election of Directors</u>:	The Company's board of directors will have five (5) directors. The holders of Common, voting as a separate class, shall be entitled to elect two members of the Company's board of directors. The holders of Series A, voting as a separate class, shall be entitled to elect two members of the Company's board of directors. The Lead Investor will be entitled to elect one member of the Company's board of directors.
<u>Board Composition</u>:	Upon the closing of the sale and issuance of the Series A, the Company's board shall be comprised of Thomas A. Jones and Melissa K. Smith, who will be deemed elected by the holders of Common, and Georg W. Williams and Andrew B. Johnson, who will be deemed elected by Series A, and George L. Walker, who will be deemed elected by the Lead Investor.
<u>Protective Provisions</u>:	Consent of both (i) the holders of at least a majority of the outstanding Series A voting together as a single class and (ii) at least a majority of the board of directors that includes the Lead Investor director shall be required for any action that would allow (a) the repurchase or redemption of Common (except from an employee or consultant upon termination), (b) any increase in the number of authorized shares of Series A, (c) any offer, sale, or issuance of any security senior to or ranking equally with Series A, (d) any amendment to the bylaws or articles of incorporation of the Company, (e) the payment by the Company of any dividends to the holders of Common, (f) any merger, reorganization or sale of all or substantially all of the assets of the Company, (g) any liquidation or dissolution of the Company, (h) the issuance of securities of any subsidiary of the Company, (i) increase to the board size, (j) increase in compensation for any executive officer during any one year in excess of 15%, or (k) any change to the Company's stock option plan.

Consent by at least a majority vote of the board of directors that includes the Lead Investor director shall be required for the Company to: (a) mortgage or pledge or create a security interest in, or permit any subsidiary to mortgage, pledge, or create a security interest in, all or substantially all of the property of the Company or such subsidiary of the Company; (b) make any loans or advances to employees, except in the ordinary course of business as part of travel advances or salary (promissory notes for purchase of |

shares permitted); (c) make guarantees except in ordinary course; (d) grant or issue any equity, options, or warrants representing in the aggregate over 0.5% of the fully diluted capitalization of the Company; or (e) allow acceleration of either the vesting of options or expiration of the Company's right of repurchase as to the equity interest of any service provider.

TERMS OF INVESTORS' RIGHTS AGREEMENT

<u>Information Rights</u>:	So long as a holder of Series A continues to hold at least 50,000 shares of Series A or Common issuable upon conversion of Series A (the "Conversion Stock"), the Company shall deliver to such a holder (each a "Major Investor") audited annual and unaudited quarterly financial statements.
	These information rights provisions shall terminate upon the initial public offering of the Common Stock. Information rights may be transferred to a transferee who, after such transfer, will hold at least 50,000 shares of Series A or Conversion Stock, provided that the Company is given prior written notice of such transfer.
<u>Right of Participation</u>:	Each Major Investor shall have a right to purchase its pro rata portion of new securities in the event of any sale of new securities by the Company, excluding shares sold to employees, consultants, officers or directors in connection with services pursuant to arrangements authorized by the board of directors, and other customary exclusions. Each Major Investor shall have the right of re-allotment in the event any Major Investor chooses not to exercise his or her right of participation.
<u>Registration Rights</u>:	<u>Demand Rights</u>: If, at any time after the earlier of three (3) years from the date of closing of the Series A or the date that is six months following the Company's initial public offering, holders of a majority of the Series A or Conversion Stock requests that the Company file a registration statement for an aggregate offering price of at least $5,000,000 the Company will use its best efforts to cause such shares of Conversion Stock to be registered. The Company shall not be obligated to effect more than one registration under these demand rights provisions.
<u>"Piggyback" Registration</u>:	If, at any time, the Company determines to register its securities, the holders of Series A shall be entitled to have their shares of Conversion Stock included in such registration. The Company and its underwriters shall have the right to terminate or withdraw any registration initiated by the Company and, in the case of the Company's initial public offering, to reduce or eliminate the number of

shares proposed to be registered on behalf of the holders in view of market conditions. For registrations following the initial public offering, the holders of registration rights may not be cut back to less than 15% of the offering.

S-3 Demand Rights:

If Conversion Stock is available for use by the Company, its holders will be entitled to unlimited S-3 registrations provided that the anticipated aggregate offering price, net of discounts and commissions, would exceed $1,000,000. The Company shall not be obligated to file more than one S-3 registration statement in any twelve-month period.

Expenses:

All registration expenses (including expenses of one attorney for the holders of registrable securities but excluding underwriting discounts and commissions) shall be borne by the Company, subject to customary exclusions and exceptions.

Other Provisions:

Registration rights terminate five years after consummation of the Company's first underwritten public offering or earlier as to a particular holder if such holder can sell all shares in a 90-day period pursuant to Rule 144. The registration rights may be transferred to a transferee who acquires a minimum number of shares of Series A or Conversion Stock provided the Company is given written notice thereof. The holders of Series A agree not to sell any shares of the Series A or Conversion Stock for 180 days following the closing of the Company's initial public offering. Registration rights provisions may be amended or waived solely with the consent of: (i) the Company (ii) holders of over 50% of the registrable securities, and (iii) the Lead Investor.

OTHER ISSUES

Co-Sale Right and Right of First Refusal:

Right of First Refusal. The Company will have the right to repurchase shares offered for sale by a founder, subject to customary exceptions for transfers in connection with estate planning, bona fide loan transactions, and sales up to 5% of the total number of shares of capital stock held by a founder. To the extent not exercised by the Company, the right of first refusal will be transferred to the holders of Series A on a pro rata basis with a right of re-allotment.

Co-Sale Right. In the event that a founder proposes to sell any shares of the Company's Common Stock (subject to customary exclusions), the holders of Series A shall be given the right to sell on a pro rata basis a portion of their shares to the proposed purchaser in lieu of the purchase being made from the founder. Such right shall include a right of re-allotment to the extent that the right is not exercised by holders of Series A.

Termination. These rights shall terminate upon the closing of the Company's initial public offering or upon the merger of the Company into another entity.

Small Business Stock:

So long as it does not require the Company to operate its business in a manner which would limit its prospects, the Company's shall seek to have Series A Preferred Stock qualify as a small business stock within the meaning of Section 1202(c) of the Internal Revenue Code and the Company shall perform all acts reasonably necessary to so qualify its stock and shall make all filings required under Section 1202(d)(1)(c) of the IRC and related Treasury regulations.

Purchase Agreement:

The investment shall be made subject to the negotiation of a stock purchase agreement for Series A reasonably acceptable to the Company and the Lead Investor, which agreement shall contain, among other things, customary and appropriate representations and warranties of the Company, covenants of the Company reflecting the provisions set forth herein, and appropriate conditions of closing. The stock purchase agreement shall provide that it may only be amended and any waivers thereunder shall only be made with the consent of (i) the Company, (ii) holders of over 50% of the Series A sold thereunder, and (iii) the Lead Investor.

The Closing:

The closing is subject to the Company raising at least the minimum amount of offering in the Financing and completion of legal and financial due diligence by the Lead Investor.

Indemnification Agreements:

The officers and directors will have standard indemnification agreements acceptable to the Investors.

Expenses:

The Company will bear its legal expenses; in addition, the Company will pay the reasonable legal fees and expenses of one counsel to the Investors up to a maximum of $7,500.

No Commitment:

Nothing in this Memorandum of Terms, or any notes, or any actions occurring after there is an agreement on this Memorandum of Terms, will be construed as a commitment by the Lead Investor or any other Investor to proceed with any stage of the Financing contemplated hereby. However, once closing occurs, Investors' obligations as set forth in the closing documents will be binding upon all parties.

ENTREPRENEURIAL EXERCISES

Entrepreneurial Exercise 12.1

With the financials of your business plan complete, please describe in detail the methods you will used to establish a value for your start-up business venture. Please be specific and show all of your calculations.

Entrepreneurial Exercise 12.2

Assume in this exercise that you are the investor in your business. Please write a complete private placement memorandum (PPM) that covers the issues and conditions under which the investment is being made. What are the anticipated rights and responsibilities of both parties after the investment has been made?

HARVESTING THE VENTURE

It ain't over till the fat lady sings.

Anonymous

Every sale has five basic obstacles: no need, no money, no hurry, no desire, no trust.

Zig Ziglar

CHAPTER LEARNING OBJECTIVES

Upon completion of this chapter you will be able to

- Identify reasons for exiting a venture
- Compare family business succession and exiting a private or public company
- Describe the key elements of an ownership succession plan
- List the factors involved in selling or merging a business
- Summarize the results of a public liquidity event
- Explain the differences between restructuring and liquidation in the bankruptcy process

PREPARING FOR YOUR EXIT

Entrepreneurs are always focused on creating and growing new, vibrant, value-added businesses but rarely, unless they are serial entrepreneurs, on creating and crafting viable harvesting opportunities and exit strategies for their cofounders and themselves. Successful serial entrepreneurs, having created and exited several earlier ventures, have learned the skills necessary to create an exit pathway even as they plan for the creation and launch of a new venture. The decision to exit may be personal, professional, or financial, but the entrepreneur needs to be prepared for this likely event. Both internal and external pressures may precipitate exiting a venture. For some, personal issues, such as being unable to commit sufficient time to personal relationships and family, strongly influence the decision. Others decide to leave so they can pursue attractive alternative business opportunities rather than slowly growing an existing one. Perhaps the exhilaration of starting another business influences their decision to exit the old venture. For still others, the decision to harvest a business opportunity is strongly influenced by their desire to gain financial liquidity and value from their sweat equity and the personal and professional sacrifices they have made. There are many other reasons that can precipitate the exit of an entrepreneur from a venture, and many options on how this can be accomplished.

Entrepreneurs may also be forced to exit a business because they lack the financial resources necessary to operate and grow it. They may leave the company at the request of investors or creditors seeking an alternative leadership team with possibly more experience and business maturity. In addition, entrepreneurs may be asked to exit a business because they did not meet the milestones agreed upon in the terms of their financing arrangements.

Being an entrepreneur requires a strong personal commitment of time, talent, and dedication to the venture—and a very strong will to succeed. Many are the weeks, months, and even years of long, hard work.

Yet I know of few more rewarding personal or professional experiences than creating and growing a business, which creates employment opportunities for others and which produces products and services that can make a positive difference in people's lives. I also know of no other more physically or mentally demanding exercise that one can engage in. The entrepreneur chooses the challenge not because it is easy but because it is difficult and life changing. For the entrepreneur, it is potentially the most rewarding exercise— one that embodies the American Dream—that an individual can use mind and body to create lasting value for others and, along the way, enrich people's lives, including the entrepreneur's, while being actively and positively engaged as a role model and mentor for his or her community. This is what entrepreneurship is all about.

In this chapter, we will examine some of the more common harvesting opportunities and possible exits for entrepreneurs. These include family business transitions, selling the business, utilizing a public liquidity event, and bankruptcy. To achieve a successful exit or harvesting event, the entrepreneur must first identify which options are available and choose the one that best suits the entrepreneur's needs and situation. Before doing so, the business owner should engage in contingency planning and explore succession planning as well.

Contingency planning for harvesting in business involves an analysis by the entrepreneur of his professional and personal readiness and the various options that are available to exit the venture. In an ideal setting, the choice will most likely reflect the best outcome for the entrepreneur, personally, professionally, and financially, and provide for the continued growth and success of the company that the entrepreneur created. For these reasons, succession planning should play an important role in the entrepreneur's preparation of an exit strategy. Issues relating to how long the entrepreneur will be affiliated with the company after her or his departure should be considered. For example, under what terms will the company be able to engage and utilize the entrepreneur's professional skills and networks to provide a smooth and successful transition of leadership? Will the entrepreneur still play a supporting role in the company?

Management succession is a very popular option when dealing with what is termed a "family business." The most critical qualities that need to exist for an effective transfer of the business to a new family member include the following:

1. *A strong set of shared values.* Being a family member does not guarantee that an individual wants to commit fully to operating the business. Determine which family members are qualified to work in the business and which actually wish to continue in the business. Success becomes a matter of both heart and mind.

2. *A willingness to learn and grow.* Many family members may have worked in the business but were never decision makers. Successful succession requires that future leaders be brought into the decision-making process so that they can ask questions about how and why decisions are being made.

3. *An agreement as to how power will be shared.* The family members who will remain active in the business need to reach an agreement on the role each will play in the business.

4. *A liquidity plan for exiting family business members.*

Entrepreneurs who wish to keep the business in the family need to develop and implement a succession plan. An effective succession plan shares critical business knowledge, including the following:

1. *Who the new entrepreneur should trust as advisors and why.* Who has demonstrated in past business dealings that they are worthy of trust? This list would also include the business people with whom the exiting entrepreneur would normally work, including the firm's attorney, banker, accountant, insurance agent, and critical suppliers.

2. *Critical documents, including wills, trusts, insurance policies, financial statements, bank accounts, articles of incorporation, and so forth.* These documents need to be understood and openly discussed in order to ensure a smooth transition.

A second step in the management succession plan is to groom one or more successors and clearly define the roles and responsibilities, if any, for family members who will not remain in operational roles within the company. This step is time consuming but essential. Knowledge of the business and how it operates must be transferred from the founding entrepreneur's mind to the minds of those being considered for succession. The succession candidates must learn the keys to managing the business successfully in the industry in which it competes. The candidates must be provided insight into the potential actions and behaviors of competitors. As the entrepreneur attempts to teach the candidates about the business, she or he will come to recognize which one has the greatest potential for assuming the mantle of leadership.

A succession plan needs to promote an environment of mutual trust and respect. The successor needs to be given opportunities to make decisions, and even make mistakes. The exiting entrepreneur needs to display a trusting spirit and to use any error as a valuable teaching opportunity. When the successor is brought more visibly into the business as a key decision maker, the transition of power will be smoother.

The final step in the management succession plan is determining the most financially equitable way of transferring the ownership of the business. In reality, most family businesses will have family members who wish to continue with the business and others who do not wish to be involved or who lack the competency to contribute. The exiting entrepreneur, along with his or her attorney and accountant, must establish a fair and equitable estate plan that includes the transfer of the business.

SurveyMonkey

Finding that no good options were available to those wanting to conduct rapid and efficient online surveys or marketing assessments of new products and services, Ryan Finley, a computer science graduate from the University of Wisconsin Madison, launched SurveyMonkey in 1999. Having grown the company to sales of over $30 million in 2008, he sold it in 2009. Since that time, he has continued as an employee of the company. His innovative online survey platform has been utilized both in internal assessments and in outward facing product or service evaluations across the country and around the world. Recently, in the 2016 national presidential elections in the United States, millions of voters utilized SurveyMonkey to voice their opinions on the candidates and other concerns related to the candidates' positions on issues important to voters. The company has transitioned through senior corporate leadership and now has a bright future with a current market valuation of $2 billion.

Sources:

1. See the pages "About Us" and "Board of Directors" on the SurveyMonkey website, accessed July 2018, https://www.surveymonkey.com/.
2. Mike Rogoway, "SurveyMonkey Sold," *The Oregonian*, April 20, 2009, https://www.oregonlive.com/business/index.ssf/2009/04/surveymonkey_sold.html.
3. Michael Arrington, "Survey Monkey Growing Like a Weed, Fills Out Exec Team," *TechCrunch*, September 8, 2009, https://techcrunch.com/2009/09/08/survey-monkey-growing-like-a-weed-fills-out-exec-team/.
4. "NBC News & SurveyMonkey Launch Weekly Online Polls for 2016 Presidential Election," SurveyMonkey press release, https://www.surveymonkey.com/mp/nbc-news-surveymonkey-launch-weekly-online-polls-2016-presidential-election/.

SELLING THE VENTURE

The most common exit strategy for many entrepreneurs takes the form of selling either a controlling interest in the company or all of the company to an interested third party. Both of these options may provide a financially suitable exit for the business owner, but each has different factors for the entrepreneur to consider. When selling the company outright, the entrepreneur should select the purchase price that provides the best financial benefit with the lowest tax implications possible. When selling a controlling interest in the company (sometimes referred to as capital restructuring), the owner should consider the purchaser or investor and her or his ability to manage and grow the company to provide increasing value for those with a stake in the company. Remember, the seller will have remaining equity in the company after this sale. In addition, if the entrepreneur owns a property asset, a determination needs to be made as to whether the real estate asset will be acquired, leased, or financed by the new owner from the original owner.

The sale of the business should be considered with professional assistance from accountants and financial specialists to determine the terms and conditions that will be most favorable for the entrepreneur. In addition, issues other than the purchase price will need to be negotiated. These may include whether the purchase will be in cash or stock or a combination of both; whether earn-out agreements will be placed on the departing entrepreneur based upon company earnings that are mutually agreed upon; what, if any, seller employment agreements or noncompetition clauses will be placed upon the exiting business owner; and whether the entrepreneur will be involved in or willing to help the buyer in financing the purchase of the business.

Just as entrepreneurs need to prepare a business plan to create, finance, and grow their business, they must develop a selling memorandum to prepare for the sale of their business. Typically, the selling memorandum will include information grouped under these headings:

- Executive Summary of the Business
- Existing Products and Services
- Current Marketing Operations
- Manufacturing Capabilities
- Financial Statements (Historical and Current)
- Financial Projections
- Management and Employee Agreements and Covenants

MERGERS

Entrepreneurs may also consider the merger of their business with another business to provide an exit for the business owner. There are three factors that might precipitate a merger:

- *Survival.* The company may face loss of market share, the aging of its products and technology, or a low cash position, for example.
- *Safety.* A merger could prevent an unwanted takeover or offer increased intellectual property protection.
- *Added value.* The company could benefit from new management skills, increased financial resources, or new product opportunities.

The benefits of a merger are many. A merger can provide economies of scale, the increased management capabilities of the combined businesses, improved technological innovation, improved access to investment capital, product diversification, new product and service offerings, and the vertical integration of business operations.

PUBLIC LIQUIDITY EVENT

"Going public" or the use of an initial public offering (IPO) of the company's securities can provide an exit strategy for the successful entrepreneur, but this option is not without significant potential risks and costs. Taking a company public is both seductive and intoxicating for the first-time entrepreneur. To see the company that he or she created, bootstrapped, and grew become a publically traded company is often the dream of the entrepreneur. The challenges in considering this pathway to liquidity and harvesting for the entrepreneur are many: (1) the risks associated with the underwriting and registering of the company's securities for the IPO; (2) the costs, both direct (for the registration) and indirect (for the possible loss of productivity during the process of going public); (3) the risk of an unsuccessful public sell of the stock due to external economic conditions; and (4) the loss altogether of a window of opportunity in the securities market for an initial public offering.

First, the entrepreneur must understand that this option is no more or less important than any other exit option. The risks of financial market volatility should be considered carefully. Even a well-planned IPO with a favorable market for the company's securities can be placed in jeopardy or delayed due to unforeseen economic events. The IPO process is long and difficult with numerous pitfalls and very high stakes. Going public has traditionally been a rite of passage for companies, one that provides them with significant access to public and institutional investment capital but saddles them with increasingly more complex regulatory oversight.

Economic and market conditions can and do change quickly. The entrepreneur undertaking an IPO registration needs to prepare for the issues, challenges, and responsibilities that go with managing a publically traded company under the current Sarbanes–Oxley legislation. Close scrutiny by investors and analysts of the company's operations and profitability contributes heavily to the demands of managing a public company. Many texts have been written specifically on the topic of "going public" or "staying private," and much discussion continues today.

The entrepreneurs who consider the IPO as their exit and harvest strategy should investigate a number of additional factors. Under normal conditions, the entrepreneur will be treated as an insider and will therefore be limited, for at least a time, regarding the number of shares he or she can offer for sale during the IPO. Further, restrictions may be placed on the public sale of securities owned by the entrepreneur after the IPO during a "lock-up" period negotiated with the IPO's underwriter prior to the initial offering of the company's securities to the public market. This period may last from a few months to several years, during which time the entrepreneur will be unable to access the liquidity of the sale of the securities. In addition, the entrepreneur may have difficulty selling stock due to the registration of securities for the entrepreneur by the company, timing concerns surrounding the sale of the founder's stock, restrictions on the number of shares that can be offered based upon the company's average trading volume, and the perceived adverse effects on analysts and stockholders of the sale of stock by the founding entrepreneur. The sale of such securities can significantly depress the company' stock price and reduce the entrepreneur's value for the shares sold. Many shareholders may think that the founding entrepreneur is selling stock based upon knowledge that something adverse is going to happen. Such views, though generally inaccurate and unfounded, can and do depress the stock price and may lead to an erosion of confidence in the company and in the value of its stock. All of these factors can limit the founding entrepreneur's ability to harvest ownership in a timely manner, making the value of the harvesting depend on the future performance of the company, over which the entrepreneur has limited control after retiring from an operational role.

BANKRUPTCY

Finally, a possible exit for the entrepreneur is one that most individuals do not wish to discuss. This is bankruptcy, which, although a form of protection for the owner, can cause preemptive or forced restructuring or creditor-forced liquidation of corporate assets. Every business has a defined life cycle—some short, some long. A reality for entrepreneurial business start-ups is that most of them will not do as well as the entrepreneur expects, and many will fail. Bankruptcy provides an exit when forces working against the enterprise are so great that the entrepreneur cannot succeed and needs to leave the venture and move on to a new business opportunity. Although inability to pay debts is the main reason for business failure, other precipitating factors can play a role in a company seeking bankruptcy protection. These include the entrepreneur's lack of understanding of business and economic cycles, shifts in market demand for the company's products and services based upon environmental and competitive pressures, unforeseen expenses, and the poor operational and financial management of the company.

Although the bankruptcy code contains several chapters, two are specifically relevant to entrepreneurial ventures. They are Chapter 7 and Chapter 11.

Chapter 7 Bankruptcy

Chapter 7 bankruptcy is an order for relief for the company that does not have sufficient financial resources to fulfill obligations to creditors while continuing business operations. It involves the liquidation of corporate assets to satisfy creditors in part, and it provides a discharge of debt owed by the company. The goal is to reduce the business to cash or cash equivalents and distribute these resources to the creditors, where authorized. According to the legislated order of distribution of cash, repayment first goes to secured creditors and then to priority claimants, such as employees for unpaid wages. Any surplus monies can then go to the business owner. The entrepreneur may have the right to keep certain exempt properties, but these are minimal if the company is a corporation.

Chapter 11 Bankruptcy

Chapter 11 bankruptcy allows for the reorganization of the business while the company continues operations and begins paying its outstanding creditors. Generally, unless a court-appointed trustee is placed in the company, the entrepreneur continues in the management role of the organization. If the company qualifies as a small business (less than $2 million in unsecured debts and noncontingent liquidated secured debts), it may be placed on a fast track not requiring the immediate formation of a creditor's committee. The company under these terms is required to meet its creditors within 30 days to discuss the reorganization and status of the company. The court then appoints a committee of the company's seven largest creditors (if seven exist) to develop a plan for the business, which must be submitted within 120 days and accepted within an additional 60 days. Once the reorganization plan is accepted, the entrepreneur is relieved of any debts except those specified in the plan, and the company and the entrepreneur can continue the operation of the business under the new plan.

In both cases—Chapter 7 or Chapter 11 bankruptcy—if the company is going to fail, end it quickly, before it affects the personal life of the entrepreneur adversely. The business may have failed, but the entrepreneur is not a personal failure. This is a lesson learned by successful serial entrepreneurs, many of whom have one or more business failures in their history. However difficult it may seem, entrepreneurs need to be able to separate their personal value and worth form that of any entrepreneurial venture. It is better to walk away and begin again than to remain consumed by the temporary setback of a failed entrepreneurial venture. Entrepreneurs learn valuable lessons from adversity and business failure, and successful entrepreneurs learn from their mistakes and failures and do not repeat them in future ventures.

ENTREPRENEURIAL EXERCISES

Entrepreneurial Exercise 13.1

Please assume that you are approached to either sell your business 5 years after it has been established or merge it with another firm. Please list the questions that you would ask the possible acquirer or the person proposing the merger.

In order to evaluate the acquirer of my business, I would seek answers to the following questions.

1.

2.

3.

4.

5.

6.

7.

8.

9.

10.

In order to evaluate a merger opportunity, I would need to have answers to the following questions.

1.

2.

3.

4.

5.

6.

7.

8.

9.

10.

Entrepreneurial Exercise 13.2

The greatest reward for many entrepreneurs is taking a business public. Please conduct additional research on both the process and expense of "going public." What has your research taught you about the following?

1. The process of taking a business public.

2. The expenses involved in taking a business public.

CASE 1: NEVER UNDERESTIMATE
THE POWER OF MARKETING

Natura Therapeutics began as an extension of research conducted at the University of South Florida School of Medicine, now called USF Health. Previous stem-cell research had determined that adult stem cells exist within our bodies and that these stem cells are responsible for the repair of our tissues and for maintaining our immune systems. Because adult stem cells within the body are so important in our natural repair system, it was alarming to note that they age with us. As these repair and immune-building cells age, they become less in number and vitality, leaving the body more susceptible to infections and disease and slowing down the natural repair system. Natura sought to develop a formulation of natural ingredients that could boost the vitality of the adult stem cells existing within our own tissues. Natura, in collaboration with the Center of Excellence for Aging and Brain Repair at USF, developed a patented formulation that did just that. The company later took this technology to the public sector by creating an over-the-counter dietary supplement, NutraStem®.

After 2004, when Natura Therapeutics was founded, and throughout most of its early life, the company existed as a vehicle to further scientific research. The primary sources of funding were STTR and SBIR grants from the National Institutes of Health, which provided roughly 90% of the funds needed for product development. Later, the Florida High Tech Corridor Matching Grants program provided capital to support growth opportunities. The company enjoyed a very high success rate in its grant-writing efforts.

Aside from conducting pure research, the company executed a strategy to prove its technology. As it became aware of related research, it offered its expertise and established a sublicense agreement with Simplexity Health, now known as the New Earth Company. The agreement ran from April 9, 2012, through to April 1, 2014. That way, if one technology wasn't commercially viable, others within the Natura portfolio might be.

Once outside investors were brought on board, the push to commercialize the technology, covered by two US patents, heated up. Not wanting to sell just another untested dietary supplement among the myriad that crowd supermarket and drugstore shelves, the team conducted clinical trials, two, in fact, over the life of the company. Armed with positive results from the first clinical trial, the team was sure that Natura technology was commercially viable.

The political climate surrounding adult stem cell research was not favorable in the United States, however, and the value of such research was not well understood in the US market. So it seemed the wrong time to introduce the product domestically. Soon, though, Natura's scientific community connections abroad indicated that the United Kingdom and France would be more receptive.

So how does a US company get its products into international markets? Perhaps the most straightforward method is through a strategic alliance. As luck would have it, Natura had yet other scientific community connections that were interested, and an alliance was formed in the United Kingdom. This distributor had warehouses in Kent and Bath and would import the product from the US manufacturing facility. Once the product was in the United Kingdom, it was considered an EU product eligible for further distribution. France turned out to be a very lucrative market.

France's adoption of the Natura line of products—now three in total (NutraStem Active®, NutraStem Cardio®, and NutraStem Bone & Joint®)—provided the impetus to expand further east. Markets in South Korea and China were pursued next. It is interesting to note that approval for a dietary supplement to enter the US market requires a simple filing with the Food and Drug Administration (FDA). Much more scrutiny is required to enter South Korean and Chinese markets. Not only is the product itself scrutinized but its packaging is as well. For instance, in the United States cardboard containers are considered the norm; however, this packaging is not acceptable in South Korea or China over fears that foreign organisms may be transported within the cardboard. The review and approval process is lengthy, requiring a minimum of 150 pages of forms to be filed with various regulatory agencies, including the Chinese and South Korean versions of the FDA.

As is often the case with highly profitable product launches, competition is swift to follow. Natura Therapeutics was no exception. The strategic alliance formed in the United Kingdom was not as strong as originally thought. Natura's distributor offered better terms to a competitor with a similar formulation, which lacked clinical data to support its product's claims but made up for that with deep pockets and marketing prowess. Fortunately, Natura Therapeutics had sublicensed the competing formulation some years earlier. So, at the end of the day, the competitor was really just another revenue stream providing commission payments to Natura Therapeutics.

As the UK partnership deteriorated so did hopes of distribution in South Korea. It was later learned that a South Korean company used the data supplied in the original filings to create its own product. It should be noted that only US patents were sought and issued. In the Chinese market, Natura's fate was equally spectacular with the result being the same. In China, distribution agreements were put in place, but the Chinese firm failed, although it is believed that the product is still being distributed there to this day.

To protect itself from further brand and product erosion, the company began registering and purchasing trademarks as well as domain names.

Domestically, an Alabama-based company was first to market. Recognizing the negative political sentiment evoked by the words "stem cell," this company opted instead to brand the product "Cell Support." Later, this company's pricing model was used to benchmark prices for the NutraStem® line of products.

Faced with little to no market penetration, the Natura team looked inwardly to find a way forward and developed a US strategy. Students within the Marketing Department at USF were utilized to develop marketing campaigns. Guidance from the GrowFL program based at the University of Central Florida was obtained, as well as from the Small Business Development Center at USF. This activity took about a year to produce and implement a cohesive go-to-market strategy.

One of the most financially rewarding strategic moves was the hiring of a US-based sales broker who was able to place the company's products into both the Publix and Kroger supermarket chains. Beyond landing this product placement, however, not much was done in the way of marketing the product. Subsequently, the contracts were not renewed.

The company developed an identity crisis. Was it primarily a research company, or was it a marketing company with distribution partners? This is often a challenge for scientist-led companies. The prevailing view was that clinical trials proved the compound effective, and the product could stand on its own. The merits of the product were borne out in the data. What else could possibly be needed to be successful in the market?

In retrospect, the members of the founding team felt marketing was important but did not realize how important until a big player with deep pockets entered their space.

In the way of advice to budding entrepreneurs and in her own words, Cyndy Sanberg, president of the company from 2007 to 2014, offers the following:

As a twice-over business owner, I would suggest you take to heart and mind two pieces of advice:

1. Consider your board members carefully. Ensure that you choose to include experienced individuals from all walks of life, such as business background in maybe a few areas, finance or accounting, the field of interest that you and your business have, and then just all-around experience from an individual you trust, respect, and have known for a while.

2. Marketing, marketing, marketing—it makes the world go round and also continues to make your business profitable. Thus, spend your dollars wisely, but don't skimp on marketing, and make *certain* when you do make a profit to put most of that profit back into marketing, and it will continue to grow your profits exponentially, similar to a matching savings program, the more you put in, that amount will be matched with some interest.[1]

CASE 2: A LITTLE BIT OF SCIENCE NEVER HURTS

The founders of UVentures[1] discovered an unmet need at their university and quickly learned that all research universities and research-intensive organizations face the same problem: how do you commercialize your intellectual property?

UVentures' founders Sam Reiber, Anthony Cascio, and Ed Washington view their company, at its core, as a firm that helps others bring new technologies to market. To do that, they provide a service that finds the right partner in the form of a qualified investor for a certain piece of technology or intellectual property, and then they work to make the appropriate introductions and close the deal. Similarly, they help find technologies for companies looking to expand their product offerings through IP acquisition. These are called scouting engagements.

They also provide patent landscape analytics or, as they refer to it, trend spotting. In this scenario, a typical client company has an overarching need for a better understanding of the overall R&D pipeline. UVentures' research helps this client company formulate its own R&D strategy relative to the company's industry. Additionally, through patented technology, UVentures provides marketing assessments of intellectual property.

Beyond providing business intelligence and consulting services, the company provides marketing, deal-making, and licensing support.

UVentures also maintains a pharma-licensing platform (www.pharmalicensing.com), which is focused on commercializing innovations from the life science, pharmaceutical, and medical device industries. Currently, this platform has over 23,500 registered users in 110 countries.[2]

This journey started 18 years ago at the University of South Florida and was born out of the need and desire to commercialize university technology. The company began as an offshoot of IP Technology Exchange, originally a division of UTEK Corporation. UVentures is not without competition. Thomson Reuters and NineSigma are two big players in this space. As a result of the advances made by UVentures and IP Technology Exchange, new online platforms have emerged, and UVentures' founders anticipate even more imitation in the future.

As we see with many start-ups, funding originally came from family and friends, but the firm has stayed true to its bootstrapping roots by remaining self-funded ever since it broke away from Innovaro, formerly UTEK Corporation, in 2012.

UVentures employs a differentiation strategy. Specialists in the company rely on their personal backgrounds and their business, legal, and engineering skills but do not hesitate to bring in additional resources that exceed the needs of their clients. They boast that their various services provide comprehensible reports right out of the box with little need for the client to massage the data before presenting the findings to investors or executives.

When the founders initially looked at the competitive landscape, they found that most of the company's services were well differentiated. They soon learned, however, that due to the relatively static nature of some of their tools, particularly on the pharma side of the business, customer attrition became a problem, and they took a big hit; however, on the consulting side, business was more predictable. They quickly learned to use customer pain-point analysis and to keep an ear to the ground. The focus over the years has been to remain small and nimble and perform custom engagements, which are very profitable. This strategy worked; client count has remained consistent with growth projections.

Engagements are highly confidential and intimate; customers come to them with a specific need that, for competitive reasons, must be kept confidential. For this reason, they see little competitive imitation. Notwithstanding, UVentures has been approached to join forces with other organizations because it is viewed as a vetting service for private equity companies. What does the future hold? Today, the firm's owners are faced with three distinct possibilities: acquisition, rolling into a public entity, or remaining independent.

The pace of the market is swift, and new capabilities are always discovered. Although they are faced with time and financial constraints, Reiber, Cascio, and Washington think that further differentiation would open up new markets. Frankly, they see UVentures being significantly different a year from now.

How has entrepreneurship changed the founders? Cascio says he has made the transition from being an engineer in a traditional and technical role to being an interdisciplinary researcher and dealmaker. He feels he has been forced to become a "Swiss Army knife" of the business world, and to be agile and always evolving.

Reiber, a former real estate attorney, no longer does the same thing every day; work is fun for him. He has learned persistence and realizes he has to climb the mountain every day.

Washington has, perhaps, made the biggest transition. He started at Innovaro as an employee but after joining UVentures is now so tightly involved with this young and growing company that he has become more sensitive to customers' business needs. He has found himself learning new technical skills and growing more as a technician; now he feels he has the ability to affect change directly. Washington concludes that his experience in this venture has enabled him to develop a deeper appreciation of the business world; working at a start-up forces granularity.

Today, the business is poised to go public. Looking back at how accurately they assessed the market, the three founders have come to realize that there is an even bigger opportunity waiting for them, and they feel the company has not reached its potential yet.

The start-up experience as a whole has been quite fulfilling; knowing that they provide a unique portfolio of services designed for today's largest and most sophisticated companies is satisfying. Given this backdrop, they still face a challenge engaging large companies due to scale, but they are very successful at maintaining repeat customers and enjoy steady, predictable growth. In conclusion, the team sees a constant need to always evolve.

As far as advice for budding entrepreneurs goes, the team advises the following:

1. Evaluate your intellectual property (IP),
2. Be realistic,
3. Protect your IP,
4. Plan funding alternatives, and
5. Think about exit strategy options.

CASE 3: WHEN ADVERSITY STRIKES

The NAICS code for Odyssey Marine Exploration[1] is "transportation," but in reality this is an ocean exploration company that locates and recovers historic trade cargo. In terms of shipwreck salvage enterprises, it is the only company able to work in very deep ocean and perform very precise archeology where human divers cannot go. Seafloor minerals exploration represents a new opportunity for the firm. Mosaic, one of the world's largest fertilizer companies with potash and phosphate mining operations, estimates that there is about a 10-year supply of phosphate left in Florida. Many don't realize, however, that the seafloor has many of these same dry-land minerals.

So how did a shipwreck company get into seafloor mineral exploration? What follows is a great example of a pivot.

It all started in 2007 with the discovery of sunken treasure, including about 17 tons' worth of silver, in international waters off the coast of Spain. The company landed the treasure at Gibraltar and flew it straight to the United States. Then, following admiralty protocol, Odyssey filed an admiralty arrest in U.S. Federal Court, effectively bringing the silver into US jurisdiction. Thus began the firm's legal battles.

In May of 2007, after the admiralty arrest became public, the Spanish government filed a claim against the recovered cargo, stating that it came from a Spanish ship, sunk by the British in 1804 and known to have been carrying more than a million silver dollars at the time. The U.S. Federal Court in Tampa ordered Odyssey Marine to disclose details of the wreck site to the Spanish in 2008.

Meanwhile, although it was not known until *WikiLeaks* revealed various cables in 2010, the US ambassador in Madrid, in conversation with the Spanish culture minister, César Antonio Molina, tried to connect exchanging the Odyssey find to the return of a multimillion-dollar painting looted by the Nazi's and then in Spanish custody. The original owner of the painting, Claude Cassirer, was a wealthy California campaign contributor. The painting in question was *Rue Saint-Honoré, après-midi, effet de pluie* (1887), by French impressionist Camille Pissarro. It was purchased by the Cassirers, wealthy German Jews, and later forcibly traded to the Nazi's in exchange for the family receiving an exit visa from Germany. According to the leaked cables, "The minister listened carefully to the ambassador's message, but he put the accent on the separateness of the issues."[2]

Indeed, the Cassirer family did not get the painting, and the United States District Court for the Middle District of Florida determined that it lacked jurisdiction to proceed with the case and ruled in favor of Spain's claim of sovereign immunity. The lower court's ruling was later affirmed by a Supreme Court justice.

The loss of the silver resulted in huge financial losses for Odyssey Marine. On June 4, 2009, the day of the first court's ruling, Odyssey's stock lost two-thirds of its market value. Mark Gordon, the current CEO of Odyssey Marine, says his company was forced to rethink its core competency, seafloor exploration, and find another arena in which to use it.

In December 2015, Odyssey announced the sale of part of its assets to a company called Monaco Financials for $21 million. This capital allowed the company to reimburse an $11.7 million bank debt. Sold assets included the company's headquarters in Florida; 50 percent of its underwater-mining business, Neptune Minerals; and a profit-sharing agreement on future shipwreck salvages.

Today, Odyssey currently owns valuable seafloor properties around the world, many of them rich in the same land-based minerals being mined today. One such property is a billion-dollar asset of which they own 55 percent. Odyssey Marine has a market cap of $25 million.

Gordon built four companies prior to Odyssey Marine. One, a communications company, is currently still part of the Rockefeller Group. He worked his way through undergraduate and graduate school as a professional diver and has always been intrigued that admiralty law encourages risk taking to recover and return historic cargos to commerce.

Realizing that technology existed to recover such cargo and that it was widely acknowledged that billions of dollars of valuables sit on the seafloor, he considered Odyssey Marine a good fit. Part of Odyssey's differentiation strategy is its archeological approach; the company collects historical site data and preserves the integrity of the recovery area. This runs contrary to the perceptions of academia and governments, which generally think that commercially focused or funded business models do not support archeology. Often, governments view Odyssey as a threat.

As the company applies its core competency in new ways, mineral deposit location and recovery provide two additional revenue streams separate from that of shipwreck recovery. Today, these two new streams represent 50 percent of the firm's revenue although six years ago they brought in nothing. Soon, Odyssey expects they will comprise a majority of the company's revenue. Mineral exploration is like gas and oil exploration but at sea.

The company is 22 years old, and Mark Gordon has been there 11 of those years. The mineral business is about five to six years old. Sea exploration is a growing business, as noted in Roger Trigaux's *Tampa Bay Times* article "Rising from the Deep." The article indicates that Tampa has become a magnet for the sea exploration business, and Gordon feels Odyssey has inspired others to move into the field. As far as threats from new competitors go, he notes that entrants operate as low-end competition and says that no one has moved into mineral exploration, yet.

Early on, the founders recognized the need for a significant steady stream of capital, and the quickest way was to be publicly traded. To get there, they executed a reverse merger into a public shell. The founders, Gregory Stemm and John Morris, were skilled at structuring deals.

How did it all start? On a whim, Stemm lowballed a bid for a research vessel from UNC and unexpectedly won. He wrote a check out of an account on which Morris, a real estate investor was named, so Morris became a partner by default. While the two celebrated their new acquisition at a cocktail party on the boat, the two were contacted by the U.S. Navy, which wanted to continue chartering the boat.

They had no idea how the vessel was going to be used, but they soon learned that the navy was interested in working with remotely operated vehicles but, due to DOD funding restrictions, was unable to own the vehicles outright—leasing them was an option. Being skilled entrepreneurs, they quickly negotiated favorable terms with a speedy payback to acquire the vehicles.

As for early success, they credit the luck they had with the navy, their ability to develop a great team, and their implementation of a decentralized management structure. Authority and responsibility were given to the team members on the boat, the ones closest to the action. Through teamwork and technical know-how, they quickly demonstrated how old technology could be deployed in novel ways. For example, the company located a 15,000-foot recovery site and later set a record for the deepest recovery to date. Out of the box, Odyssey turned a 20-million-dollar investment into a 65-million-dollar return.

Looking back, Stemm and Morris realize that their initial assessment of the market was correct, but one area that they grossly underestimated was the disdain this type of company would receive from governments and the difficulties that would present when coupled with the influence academia had.

Gordon adds, however, that the future looks bright because there are an estimated 3 million shipwrecks, Odyssey has 10,000 of them in its database, and many are high-value sites.

He notes that the industry has high barriers to entry—namely time and money. When Odyssey was founded in 1994, the technology was not quite there, and it took until 2004 for its first commercial success. Shortly after that, the Spain incident hit, which made competitors reconsider entering the market. Lately, though, new firms are cropping up in Tampa and even Key West's Mel Fisher is now reconsidering deep-water recovery, having enjoyed many years in shallow water ventures.

Odyssey Marine knew it had the right formula after the 2003 *SS Republic* recovery, which produced a 70-million-dollar cargo. This promoted the founders to national and international figures, and they soon found themselves on numerous news shows, which made raising capital easier. Gordon adds, however, that in a post-SOX regulatory world, compliance is very challenging.[3] Even today, Odyssey Marine generates a lot of press, and its searches are the subject of a show on the Discovery Channel. As a result of always being on the public stage, Odyssey team members must carefully craft every statement.

Odyssey Marine is Mark Gordon's first public company. His prior four companies were all private entities. He feels that, in many respects, he is much less entrepreneurial today than he was as an owner of start-ups, mostly due the press attention and the public scrutiny he currently receives.

In his own words, "Tenacity is what it takes to be an entrepreneur." He recognized early on that most ideas don't work, and "you need to learn to roll the boulder up the hill every day." He credits his success on learning how to articulate the company's business plan simply.

Most recently, Odyssey survived a short attack. A short attack happens when traders bet against you by shorting their position. It has the net effect of driving down the value of the company's stock.

Currently, Odyssey has many shipwreck projects in the pipeline and is active in a mineral project off the coast of Mexico (mining phosphate). Although the company has lost many of its institutional investors, management feels the firm is on the verge of greatness again.

Deals for mining seafloor minerals are usually constructed in a risk-free manner for the government entity purchasing the service. Governments opt to have a private company take the early-stage risk, which a firm does in the hopes of profiting from royalty payments and permit fees from other mining companies. In this scenario, the government entity takes a cut off the top. In Odyssey's latest phosphate explorations, team members view themselves as wildcatters from the days of the Old Wild West. They discover the minerals and make early profits, but, ultimately, a large-scale miner like Mosaic will take over the operations.

CASE 4: KNOWING WHEN TO REGROUP

Kunal Jain, native to India, considers himself a serial entrepreneur.[1] Today, he has both a start-up and an established business, a medical billing company. The keys to success for Jain are networking and marketing—and taking advantage of opportunities: "Once you realize an opportunity exists, when someone has a problem, then you are on the way to being an entrepreneur."

Practice Forces is a revenue-cycle management company, which basically files insurance claims for a physician's practice. He differentiates himself from the competition by seeing each claim through to settlement, which could mean resubmitting a claim using different billing codes when the original codes submitted were denied or finding alternative settlement solutions, for example, by working directly with the patient to establish payments over time. Practice Forces is in the "healthcare financial resources" market segment.

Jain recognized this market niche as an offshoot of one that he had entered by establishing another of his companies, a medical transcription service. This market began to shrink as digital medical records became more prevalent. He observed that a typical small-practice physician's office would bill out roughly $700,000 a year yet collect only $300,000, so he quickly recognized a common problem among doctors. It would be in their best interest to streamline the settlement process. Given there are more patients than doctors available to serve them, a physician's practice always has the opportunity to grow, but, as it grows, the typical practice does not realize a corresponding rise in revenue. Practice Forces was Jain's solution to these problems. Indeed, the firm's website boasts that, on average, clients experience a 20 percent increase in revenue during the first 90 days of partnering with Practice Forces.

Part of Jain's differentiation strategy for the company includes identifying revenue leaks and putting plans in place to plug them. As an example, an uninsured or cash customer that has insufficient funds for medical services will be set up on a payment plan or offered guidance in enrolling in other assistance programs such as Medicaid. Other times, the fix for a revenue leak is as simple as finding the correct billing code for services provided.

The competitive landscape has changed over the last six years. Athenahealth has emerged as the largest medical billing company and is also a software player. Additionally, other emergency medical record (EMR) companies seek to further differentiate their product offerings by including settlement functions in their programs and platforms, plus capabilities for identifying coding errors.

Jain has bootstrapped his company from its inception, having taken only a small $50,000-dollar loan from a doctor, and he has worked hard selling his service by going door to door himself in search of customers.

As is the case for many start-ups, competition was the status quo for Practice Force. Many small medical practices were mom-and-pop shops with billing done at home in the physician's garage, usually by the nonmedical person entering the data. Jain's strategy included offering a more professional service. To help him scale up the business profitably, he outsourced most of the to employees in India. Today, he employs over 300 people in India, having realized early on that, in order to compete, he had to maintain a low cost structure. By contrast, Athenahealth employs close to 5,000 worldwide, many of them in Bangalore and Chennai, India.

Jain says that Practice Force struggled as a start-up. He underestimated competing with the status quo and how important effective marketing was in growing a business. He views Tampa, specifically, and Florida, in general, as unsophisticated markets that do not appreciate the value of good service. He notes that, by contrast, Athena Healthcare took venture capital money upfront, which afforded it access to better marketing plans and a wider reach than selling door to door. In retrospect, Jain recognizes that he should have left the Tampa market long ago.

He now has clients in eight states. To expand beyond his door-to-door market, he had to iterate. He began using Google Adwords and other Internet advertising services. In the beginning, marketing consumed 10% of his revenues, but his Adwords strategy now consumes 30%, and, unfortunately, he is still not achieving his desired results. His new iteration includes buying out his partner and looking for ways to improve operational efficiency in the hopes of reaching $3 million in revenue. At that point, he will be looking to be acquired.

He has observed that competitors did not really react to his entry into the market but rather took a different route and experienced success much more rapidly than he did. Although, Jain doesn't anticipate going the venture-capital route, he does believe his strategy of consolidation and focusing internally will get him to an exit within a year.

Early on, he realized that he had to plan for his own success, so he designed systems that scaled. His goal was to create the underlying technical infrastructure that would take him to $100 million in revenue with no major changes. To keep costs low, he manages many of the internal functions himself, for example, IT, IP, and HR.[2] And, like many Asian entrepreneurs who came to the United States with limited or no resources, as he himself did, he says he feels that, because he came here empty-handed, any success is to be cherished. His breakthrough moment was when he first started using Google Adwords, which provides leads, and people responded.

As his business grew, he began to take a hit on the software services side and knew that, if he continued down that road, the results would have been disastrous. He realized he was not quite ready to become a software provider, but by maintaining a strong focus on service, he has helped keep the vision alive of eventually becoming a technology integrator.

The entrepreneurial process has changed his perspective. Originally, he saw things only through his own eyes, but today he sees things through the eyes of his employees, customers, and vendors.

He advises others that the most important thing a budding entrepreneur can do is create or form a good team; doing so will help you achieve your dream quicker, which is better than struggling and being alone. He encourages others to develop leadership skills and foster a team environment from the start.

Today, his business is on a slow but steady incremental growth trajectory, but it is not at the pace he expected or desires. He knows he needs to develop better leadership skills and spend more time finding better talent. He feels he is spending too much of his time nurturing business relationships that are not profitable.

Next, he plans to merge his two companies, buy out his partner, develop a better team, and seek a buyer.

CASE 5: WHEN TO TRUST YOUR GUT

"Dez" Williams is a man on a mission.[1] He researched entrepreneurial programs and selected the University of South Florida based on its national ranking with one goal in mind, starting a business. A recent USF graduate with a master's in entrepreneurship, he now operates a company that sells fruit juice and donates part of its proceeds to causes that make a measurable impact. To be selected as a recipient of AquaMelon's charitable giving program, the applicant has to answer one simple question: "Do AquaMelon's customers care about the cause?"

AquaMelon is in the "juice" subset of the beverage industry. Its products fit into that industry's market category of "premium refrigerated beverages," the same category as milk. All AquaMelon's drinks contain watermelon juice, which is extracted from the meat of the watermelon using the cold-press method, much like premium olive oil is extracted from olives. They compete with POM Wonderful®, Suja®, and BluPrint®, as well as with the juices and smoothies available from Naked and Bolthouse Farms. AquaMelon's juices target the health conscious consumers, who tend also to be socially conscious or at least aware of social issues. Williams views this subcategory of the beverage industry as growing the fastest.

He points out four interesting and relevant business facts. First, six fruit crops are turned into very popular fruit juices. He adds that for every dollar a fruit makes on its own, six to seven dollars are made on its juice. Second, before AquaMelon, watermelon was the only fruit that did not have a Florida-based all-natural juice product. Third, Florida is the number-one producer of watermelon. And fourth, the Florida juice infrastructure is mature, which means there is a reduced reliance on building out a business from scratch, and up-front costs are minimized.

Williams feels the competition is following him. In 2016, when this interview took place, there were no big players in watermelon juice drink production, but he expected some to enter soon. As he recalls, the Campbell Soup Company recently called to purchase his raw product. In his opinion, the big players are looking for a proof of concept to succeed before they manufacturer to scale. He believes that the market will mature within the next 24 months. Williams's initial go-to-market strategy was simply to make the juice. His firm did not bottle, farm, or distribute its product but only extracted the juice and sold it in 55-gallon drums. He has since evolved the business to provide a line of products (currently four or five).

Initial resources came from personal savings. Family, friends, and winnings from a pitch competition got the start-up through a product beta test (customer validation and prototype), and later an investor came on board.

Before getting the company off the ground, Williams did research into what Aqua-Melon's competitive advantage might be. He learned that, if the firm offered a premium product, the company would function like the milk business. In other words, its juice could not be made shelf stable and needed refrigeration to maintain the stability and integrity of the product in the retail outlets. He also learned that Florida has the largest volume of raw product and that his potential competitors were not located in Florida. For example, WTRMLN WTR®, a New York company, operates in New York and California. This close proximity to the watermelon crop, then, gave AquaMelon an advantage over the competition. To further differentiate his business, Williams added a social mission. Currently, AquaMelon donates to Make a Splash, which targets densely populated areas with large minority populations and offers low-cost or free swimming lessons.

The idea for the company was developed as recently as 2013 during a graduate entrepreneurship New Product Development class team project at the University of South Florida, and a prototype was test-marketed in early 2014. In April of 2014, a partnership was formed after the founding team began winning competitions. First, the team won a business plan competition, then a product development competition, and finally the USF Fintech award.

The nuts and bolts of the product were put together in classes at USF, and the winnings provided validation of product viability. Team members were on to something. Next, they had to figure out the supply chain, which led them to their first investor.

For Williams and the team, the breakthrough moment came during a tasting event at a high-volume account, an independent grocer, after their product had been on the market for about two months. The grocer ordered three cases of each SKU (stock keeping unit) and depleted their entire inventory. "This tasting was a huge success for me," Williams states. It also taught team members that their customers were more interested in the pureness of the product than in its other aspects, which validated their decisions about producing the juice through extraction.

Indeed WTRMLN WTR® out of New York, in an effort to maintain its leadership position, made strategic adjustments to marketing and production. It changed its labeling and its extraction process, moving away from simply mashing up watermelons to extracting the juice from just the meat. Additionally, other competitors have added flavor blends to their product lineup. Williams views the competition as copying AquMelon's innovations.

As a side note, Williams added, as part of a class project, a marketing strategy based on the nutritional benefits of his product, one of which was that watermelon juice helped athletes hydrate and maintain energy and contained citrulline (that alleviated muscle soreness). Still, the "aha!" moment was when the customer made it clear that they liked the taste and purity of the product. This signaled Williams and his team to stop pushing their own agenda; in other words, they realized the customer was not looking for an athlete on the bottle.

Williams says that starting AquaMelon has taught him many lessons. Today, he sees the world for what it is instead of for what he wants it to be. He adds, "Early-stage entrepreneurs have dream goggles on; they romanticize about being an entrepreneur, which isn't real. The process is totally different; you deal with the real." His recent experiences also made him trust his gut more. He says his gut decisions have been right more often than not. As he notes, this is a contradiction of sorts because you have to listen to your customers to make sure you're getting it right, but, after that, you have to trust your gut.

As of 2016, AquaMelon had raised capital, rebranded, hired a CFO, hired a COO, and hired a marketing firm; in other words, the firm has assembled a viable team and supply chain partners to boot.

What's next? In a word, execute. Team members feel they have reached the starting line for the launch of a national chain.

As far as advice to budding entrepreneurs goes, Williams has this to say: "Don't lie to yourself." He notes that there is a fine line between believing in something and lying to yourself. Trust your gut. Believe in *you*, which is tough for individuals that look for validation.

CASE 6: LISTEN TO CUSTOMERS AND ADVANCE INCREMENTALLY

Julia MacGregor is a serial entrepreneur.[1] She started her first business, a hamster-breeding program, at age seven, and she has been an entrepreneur ever since. Her favorite saying is that engineers and entrepreneurs are a lot alike. They both solve problems except the entrepreneur figures out how to make money from the solution. She says that she was born this way and that true entrepreneurs always have several ideas going through their heads at any given time.

Her latest company, Global Safety Management, creates, manages, and maintains the mandatory product safety documents that companies require to keep employees safe and comply with environmental standards; these are called Material Safety Data Sheets (MSDSs). In other words, the company is in the regulatory and compliance industry. The impetus behind the company is the mandate that MSDSs be made available to those individuals handling potentially hazardous materials. The goal is to promote employee safety. In fact, the Occupational Safety and Health Administration under the Department of Labor requires that all chemical manufacturers create a hazard sheet for each of their products.

Similarly, employers are required to make MSDSs available to their employees. As you can imagine, this can be a daunting task. Every time a formulation is changed, a new data sheet must be created. While MacGregor admits that her business is not as sexy or as exciting as say hamster breeding, she adds that MSDSs are a necessary part of life the world over. Her company's focus is business to business; Global Safety Management does not play in the consumer space.

To provide some perspective, MacGregor reports that data sheets cost the supply chain about $36 billion each year. Over the years, MacGregor and her team have developed a patent-pending process and software to manage MSDSs. Manually creating a data sheet typically takes eight days. Software automates the process. The company's nearest competitor's software takes three hours to compile a datasheet while her platform takes only 15 minutes.

The way the system works is that sellers must create a data sheet and distribute it throughout the supply chain, and buyers must maintain a library of those data sheets. Regulations change frequently based on new findings about chemical interactions, which creates the need to update these sheets and maintain their currency by adding the newly discovered information. Depending on how a new product is differentiated, it might require a completely new data sheet. Take for instance, Product X, which we will say is an industrial solvent. You, as the manufacturer, make only a slight change to its composition, so you can sell into different markets. That slight change could require a completely new MSDS. To further complicate matters, the datasheets must be translated into the languages of all the countries purchasing Product X; there are 150 languages. Global Safety Management's subscription-based system simplifies this process.

MacGregor can't remember, but she believes that this is her fifth or sixth business. Her previous company, which provided international translation, was the genesis for this endeavor. As we have learned, a strategy for finding an opportunity is to listen for problems. That was certainly how things worked for MacGregor. It turns out that one of her translation company's biggest clients voiced its concern over how expensive and cumbersome it was to maintain MSDSs. She quickly realized what others were not doing.

Over the years the company has grown organically. Its job became easier when the United Nations announced the Globally Harmonized System initiative.

Global Safety Management is venture backed and, in 2016, was set for a second round of funding, having met key milestones. As an aside, investors and founders work together to set milestones.

The difficulty of maintaining up-to-date and compliant safety data sheets is not a new problem, and there is competition in this space. However, unlike other start-ups that face an uphill battle when fighting the status quo, Global Safety Management benefits. Usually, as companies mature, internal systems become entrenched, and it is difficult to break away from them and adopt an innovative approach. In the case of producing and managing MSDSs, though, the status quo is costly, burdensome, and time consuming. So signing on with Global Safety Management is an easier choice.

Like many start-ups that tackle a pervasive problem, strategic partnerships prove to be a valuable tool in developing the solution and the market. MacGregor has partnered with Cargill, a global agricultural and industrial services corporation, to gain insight into the complexities of the task at hand, and it has forged a relationship with Patterson Companies to resell Global Safety Management software. A major differentiation for Global Safety Management's platform is the ability to maintain an MSDS library.

Getting the ball rolling was easy. MacGregor and her team bootstrapped as much as possible—her brother wrote code for the software platform—but when funding from family and friends ran dry, they were fortunate to have a viable proof of concept and adequate revenues to make venture funding possible.

Their product is superior to competitors' products, but MacGregor and her team realize they are the little guys. As her company grew, she fell into the familiar catch-22 situation most start-ups face. Although Global Safety Management had a viable product, but the company's scale was not attractive enough for most venture capitalists. Typically, venture capitalists will not entertain talks with a company that has less than $1 million in annual revenue. This situation forced MacGregor to maintain a very lean operation and chart a different course to venture funding, her customers. Part of the company's lean approach involved structuring operations to use remote workers, which allowed for outsourcing. This approach helped the firm enter the market at considerable savings. Additionally, the University of South Florida helped MacGregor formulate her go-forward strategy, leverage channel partners, and keep her day job.

Details about the internal operations of a firm are difficult to come by, and start-ups have to be creative to get competitive information. In MacGregor's case, she and her team posed as potential customers to get as much information as they could. Where their information fell short, they made guesses about the industry. She states, "Forget it if you are the type that needs all the information and variables figured out. It is important to talk to customers, test the market, and fund the initial [product] from a very interested customer set." She summarizes her strategy: "Draw a floor plan, but don't build the house."

Were her guesses about the market correct? Very early, she discovered that most of her guesses were dead on, but the length of time it took for her product to be adopted in the market surprised her. Another group of guesses were off—for example, the regulatory shift following the United Nations initiative.

Her company has always been driven by demand, and she has gotten pretty good at forecasting sales, which has built credibility with investors. She admits that she learned that their forecasting document had to be a living, breathing model that is constantly refined as new data become available. "It is the unknown that forces a pivot."

With all of her success, she still classifies her venture as at the early-growth stage, but she feels the company is at the beginning of exponential growth. Currently, she is experiencing growth at 49 percent quarter over quarter and estimates that Global Safety Management will be at $38 million in four years. Although her industry is fragmented, she is witnessing acceleration in consolidation.

MacGregor and her team view themselves as disruptive to the industry, and currently they are experiencing a 100% sales closing rate. The one single thing she will tell people is "Listen to customers." As she explains, "Your approach should be—I want to help the customer solve a problem."

Just two to three years ago, 90 percent of companies managed MSDS documents manually—on paper in binders. Today, 80 percent still manage documents manually, but MacGregor feels that, after the next five years, only 30 percent will do so. There are only a handful of companies that provide digital files, and she believes that there is room for everybody to benefit from this transition. She concedes that her company is too small to be an industry leader but argues that, with a focus on ease of use, she and her team are designing their processes and systems to support a rapid move to digital media.

Her competitors are the in-house shops of large organizations currently responsible for complying with standards regarding the posting and availability of MSDSs, for example, the safety departments within companies that continue to follow the status quo. These organizations are so large and their processes are so entrenched that embracing innovative methods is not possible for them. GSM offers a different solution, as trying to use an in-house solution to the problem of keeping safety data current is not effective. A typical manufacture can spend $300 thousand per year *not* to solve this problem while the Global Safety Management platform could provide the solution for $100 thousand. Eventually, cost constraints and competitive pressures will affect the status quo and force the adoption of cost effective, easier-to-use platforms. Despite venture backing and verifiable proof of concept, however, MacGregor's firm still faces the issue of scale, or prejudice against small companies, yet it has a waiting list of clients.

The breakthrough moment never really happened for MacGregor and her team. Success came over time, in increments, and through evolution. They view themselves as solving a broad universal problem by solving industry-specific needs. They really knew they were on to something when they noticed they kept receiving affirmation and confirmation, particularly when investors began asking questions.

They found new opportunities for growth and expansion by forging strategic relationships with companies in same industry, ones that were not direct competitors for their core customers. These partnerships seek to solve problems no one has addressed. As Global Safety Management grows, its team remains cautious, optimistic, and focused.

MacGregor's most important lesson was not to be afraid to fail. Failure is part of success. She views changes in bankruptcy law as a damper on the entrepreneurial spirit. Laws should be written to encourage risk taking. One must understand, she believes, that taking risk (and sometimes failing) is part of success.

So, where does her company sit now? She feels it is in a growth stage now, not the seed stage, not an early stage, and it has a proven market. How about the potential for her endeavor? Is she there yet? In her own words, "Hasn't reached potential, not anywhere close." She knows her company is maturing because it is moving from being people driven to being process driven. She adds, "Investors have a way of forcing that."

What's on the horizon for MacGregor? "Ideas come from experiences," she explains. "I have a congenital heart condition, and I will work to solve that problem, but aside from that, I have a list of small and big projects I plan to tackle when I exit this venture in the next four to five years."

Her approach to her next endeavor will remain the same—start with market research, figure out who is trying to solve this problem, and be mindful that, if you've thought of a solution, chances are that someone else has too.

Her counsel: "Don't be afraid to fail. Seek advice and mentors who have done it before."

CASE 7: MITIGATE RISK

Put simply, Jonathan Solomon does product development.[1] In the beginning, he brought ideas to market. Some were successful, and some were not. Today, he looks at the marketplace of existing products searching for those in need of new innovative marketing plans or simply an adjustment to current plans. When reviewing a product, he tries to determine if it has an undiscovered market.

He currently has several projects in the pipeline. He has grown from selling starfish on Amazon to marketing skin care products and health supplements. He realized early on that intuition was not enough to uncover unmet markets, so he developed a formula, now patented, to determine if a product has commercial viability.

Some of the factors of the formula are whether a consumer product has a repeat purchase component, how unique the product is, whether it is moderately priced, and whether it is made in America.

He funded his undergraduate education by working as a product distributor. Originally, he had plans to enter law school, that is, until he was exposed to the entrepreneurship program at the University of South Florida. One of his concerns regarding being employed in product distribution was that he was always working for someone else and, because of the nature of the business, was forced to keep track constantly of the supply chain for fear of disintermediation, the loss of a customer by someone coming into the distribution stream. This typically happens when a larger distributor comes into a market and obtains a lower price from the manufacturer. He found himself performing marketing activities for products he distributed, but he would eventually lose customers while the manufacturer still benefited from his marketing activity.

In a nutshell, he morphed from being a product or manufacturer's representative to taking an ownership interest in the companies he markets. He concludes, "In order to represent a product or to distribute it, you need to maintain control."

He is proud to say his company has matured from developing products made in Tampa to those made in sunny Florida to those made in the United States. He was pushed in this direction because he found that no one knew where Tampa was.

He is not a huge fan of partnerships and advises budding entrepreneurs against them. He finds partnering with a product manufacturer reveals the unrealistic expectations of that firm's founder—often, he has had to convince manufacturers that their products or product lines are worth much less than they think.

His competition is everybody—anybody with a product can get funded with Kickstarter or Idiegogo or other crowdfunding platforms. Recognizing that finding a new customer is more expensive than keeping an existing one, he categorically dismisses products that do not have a recurring purchase component to them. Another competitive threat is often realized once he introduces a product on Amazon, his preferred e-commerce platform. These products are quickly knocked off by another manufacturer, typically in China. In one instance, he pulled a product from his store, branded it, and then restocked his store and filed a conflict claim with Amazon to have the competitor removed. He states that being an online entrepreneur requires diligence.

In the online space, marketing is very important. He learned over the years the power of professional listings that had certain attributes, such as "quick order" and "reorder" features, in securing or increasing the likelihood of success for his campaigns.

Given how easy it is for products to be copied, he now seeks to brand new products before posting them, and, as his company has matured, he is now looking at products that are difficult to copy. Clearly, competition forced many branding, packaging, and listing changes.

Today, he has codeveloped a computer algorithm for which a United States patent has been applied. It is an online tool used to determine whether something has commercial viability. The University of South Florida offers a graduate level course on how to apply this tool in real life.

The initial resources for his business venture came from the little money he saved, and his ventures have remained mostly self-funded. He has progressed from an undergraduate with a distributorship to a company that establishes a clear plan—A through Z, concept through execution—including establishing the right connections up front.

One of his first considerations in choosing a product line is determining what can be sold immediately? What can you manufacture as orders come in? What products have minimal waste, and how many universal parts does it have to complement other items within a product line up? His lean mentality includes maintaining low or no inventory levels.

Solomon never rests on his laurels. He always feels there is a better way. His focus and determination have moved him to a better position than the one he faced while operating under his old distribution model. He now skips trade shows in order to prevent others from gaining insight into his products. He found these shows were enabling knockoffs. He has been at it for over nine years now, and, as a thirtysomething businessman, he says, "Being young and an entrepreneur is tough." It has forced him to transition to products that do well online and require little overhead to manufacture.

An example of a failed project involved the purchase of a patented product, a material that was water, shrapnel, termite, and wind resistant that could be used in the construction of lightweight shelters and easily deployed in third world countries. The versatility of this product was such that one person could build a 600-square-foot house in four hours. He cites owner envy as the reason the deal did not go through. The owner had unrealistic expectations of what the idea was worth.

Also, the patent owner viewed him as a child, did not respect his professional ability, and was constantly saying things like, "You will need my help to market this." Often, because he was young, he was not taken seriously. Also, *everybody* thinks his or her idea is the best.

His online tool has no real competition. The few competitors he has are changing their practices to offer a more comprehensive solution, one that better matches his offerings. He has also noticed that his friends who have companies have changed their strategies to align with his. For example, an afterschool day-care proprietor observed that he had risk in managing a building, employees, children, and other aspects of his business, so he changed his business model to include coaching others wishing to enter this market space.

The "aha!" moment for Solomon was when he experienced a little success. It was a joyous event. He used to spend time getting to know customers, and he admits he actually likes talking to them. Today, however, he takes a more mature approach and strives to get feedback to figure out how long a product can run.

He has come a long way from just figuring out a way to pay the bills. He manages a million-dollar company. He's not finished yet. He still works to increase revenue and strives to lower his personal workload in the hopes of exiting eventually.

Regarding new competitive opportunities, he makes a simple observation: in order to be successful, one must grow and adapt one's model. He now has a select network of entrepreneurs who each have revenue of over $1 million. This interaction helps keep ideas flowing.

Here is what Solomon says about his own personal development through the process of starting and growing a business:

> Entrepreneurship has changed me as a person. I'm not as naïve, I learn quicker from my mistakes, and if a program fails, its business. I take failure much less personally. I have been hardened to the fact that this is just business. I am quicker to act, and I have developed a good sense of what I'm looking for. I am always learning.

He also has some important guidance for new entrepreneurs:

> My advice for entrepreneurs is that the most important thing is to learn to trust your gut. Nine times out of ten you are right. Also, paper remembers what the mind forgets, which is very useful in court. Always get it in writing! And avoid debt and partners because you might be forced to give up creative control. Don't give up control unless it is absolutely necessary.

Jonathon avoids phrases such as "we have matured or plateaued" when asked where his business stands now? He objects to the mind-set. His personality is such that he always has to strive to make something better, whether it be lowering overhead or realizing other improvements. His business model is shifting to more of an online e-commerce model.

Where does he want to go next? He admits he needs a major shift in thinking. Pride of ownership has made it difficult for him to let go of the reigns and gets in the way of his goal of lowering his personal workload. He is working on asking for help more quickly and becoming smarter in the field—and especially on finding assurance in the knowledge that, when he does his part, others will do theirs. He plans to expand his team to more people that are driven.

CASE 8: VENTURE CAPITALIST TURNED ENTREPRENEUR

Gordon Ryerson is a venture capitalist turned entrepreneur.[1] As he reports, he owns an engineering design and development firm that operates primarily in the medical device field. He is quick to point out that intellectual property represents the genesis of ideas but they need design and development to be commercialized. He considers his company a research and development shop, all in one, for individuals or companies looking to bring their IP to market. He is very comfortable staying in that box and is not looking to step into manufacturing, sales, or marketing. His company is part of the Center for Advanced Medical Learning and Simulation located in downtown Tampa.

He admits to not being an engineer by trade although he did engineering work while enlisted in the navy. Still, he is more comfortable as a business manager. His background as a venture capitalist provided exposure to the transactional aspects of the life science industry, particularly to mergers and acquisitions. A small part of his engineering services offerings include developing a product internally and then getting the concept patented for licensing to someone else. He has one such idea in the pipeline currently, but this type of activity is greatly influenced by resource availability. Custom engagements come first.

He and his team are not new to this marketplace, but they are unique in their ability to take an idea to a manufacturing-ready state. This is a byproduct of the industry-specific development work his senior staff members have done for the past 20 years. Their focus is on the life sciences and health care. The skill his team brings to the market is somewhat analogous to cooking from scratch without a cookbook. Typically, every design and development firm has an appreciation for system-level design, but Ryerson's company takes it to another level. This philosophy is embodied in his company's name, currently, the Occam Technology Group. Occam's razor is a problem-solving philosophy attributed to an English Franciscan monk, William Ockham (or Occam), who was born in the late 1200s. Its general principle is that, among competing hypotheses, the simplest one with the fewest assumptions should be selected.

The company has been around since the late 1990s and has over 1,000 patents under its belt. Its primary customers are University of South Florida medical doctors. Ryerson joined the team in 2016. He notes that, locally, Occam has been disruptive. He credits his superior staff for that. To his company's benefit, the local Tampa Bay engineering and design market is a collaborative one. This makes design work efficient because it is easy to subcontract unique elements of the design work to firms with that specialty without fear of one firm trying to capture another's customer. Locally, there is a benign ecosystem with little competition; however, outside of Tampa, Occam and similar firms face competition.

Initial funding came from the company's chief technology officer, who spent several years in the industry working for two very large medical device companies. Basically, in 1997, he retired and needed something to occupy his free time. He quickly found himself being contracted by his former employers to do the same work he had done while their employee. Then, in 2014, he partnered with the current CEO, who is really the company's main investor, which helped transform Occam from a "garage" business into a mainstream one. As of 2016, the company's staff engineers are 1,099 contract employees.

Ryerson's analysis is that the company was focused on being a little bit of everything to each of its customers, with the result of not achieving real mastery in any one specific area. His current efforts are on establishing a niche and developing a plan to execute within that defined space.

Cited as Occam's main competitive advantage is the local engineering ecosystem, in which all companies stick to their own specialties. As a result of this ecosystem, the company has a deep resource pool. A trend that became obvious to Ryerson was that the industry was searching for ways to make its devices smart or smarter. There is a big push to have devices talk to one another, for example. Armed with a patent in this area, he went out to determine what market existed in the medical device field given the company's background.

He looked to MacDill Air Force Base and found that the defense industry had significant reservations about medical devices talking to one another. After executing several tactics to develop a medical niche, he came to realize that the medical space was too conservative for the commercialization of this patented technology. Additionally, regulated industries present unique challenges that are often difficult to overcome. Before enabling medical devices to talk to one another, consideration had to be given to agencies outside the FDA, namely, the Federal Communications Commission (FCC). Also, to add another layer of complexity, HIPPA compliance had to be ensured as well. This set of facts led to a rebranding campaign; the company dropped the MD from its name.

Ryerson considers the company a 15-year-old start-up, as it continues to grow and mature, but he admits that the firm is beginning to move from being people driven to being process driven, a key signal that a company is leaving the start-up phase. To his credit, he has found many applications of Occam's patented technology. The best opportunities, he thinks, are in industries that value devices talking to one another; these devices might include, for example, commercial cooking equipment or bicycles in Europe. This rebirth or pivot, if you will, demonstrates the company still has that entrepreneurial spirit to survive and prosper.

So what strategies and tactics will pave the way to continued success for Occam? The company will continue to build out systems to support its strategy: devices talking to one another, often referred to as the "Internet of Things" or IoT for short. In the United States, the engineers at Occam consider themselves at the forefront of this technology, and globally, they are at the top of the list. They strongly anticipate a huge wave of new customers in the IoT space.

The breakthrough event for Ryerson was when word leaked out about the firm's technology and the phones started ringing. He feels maintaining his competitive advantage is doable because Occam is uniquely positioned to assess the IoT landscape accurately. The current state of things is that the firm is still reviewing internal systems to ensure everything is correct and precise, bracing itself for increased activity. It is also partnering with the University of South Florida to showcase its technology, the LORA network, a platform through which a range of sensors can communicate. The network is a communications medium with long-range capabilities and substantially lower power requirements.

Occam anticipates heavy usage in agriculture because some sensors have an eight- to ten-year battery life. IBM and Amazon are both interested in these sensors and protocols. Holding the IP for this communications medium puts the firm in a unique position to understand and spot trends.

Ryerson's background is in mergers and acquisitions. He has always worked with start-ups and licensing, and he sees the move to this side of the table, actually running a start-up, as fun. "It provides the opportunity for me to put my money where my mouth is," he reports. He has also come to the realization that things aren't as easy as he thought they would be. He finds himself faced with performing opportunity cost analyses, managing change control protocols, and dealing with people issues, as well as with other operational issues. In terms of finance, he now has a deeper appreciation of all the moving parts it takes to run a business.

Among the most important lessons he has learned from his experience at Occam is to be open-minded and to remain flexible, knowing that your first assumption may not have been correct. From a big picture perspective, he has a newfound respect for cash management, particularly receivables, and after 20 years of working with companies, he has learned to take a third-party perspective.

"Right now, I feel we are on the verge of a breakout, and I predicts big differences between what we look like now and what we will look like a year from now," postulates Gordon.

Next on his plate is some internal management, with the focus on getting the right people on board and keeping them looking ahead and out in front. To "future-proof" the firm, he is searching for additional software capabilities, more intellectual property, and trademarks. He is trying to position the company to be in the best position when the "onslaught of competition comes beating at his door."

His advice for budding entrepreneurs is to have an open mind, particularly when settling on something to pursue. Be innovative but avoid just being an "idea guy"—be willing to mature with the business and execute on ideas. And *never* take your eye off cash flow.

CASE 9: LIVING AN ENTREPRENEUR'S LIFE

Greg Ross-Munro operates in the software studio development space and focuses on building applications for the web, smartphones, kiosks, smart TVs, and wearables. More specifically, his company Sourcetoad, LLC, is a cross-platform application development company. Primarily, it uses platform technologies to backward code and emulate front-end systems on multiple platforms. At the enterprise level, its expertise is in the health care and hospitality sectors, primarily in the cruise ship industry. Ross-Munro considers himself to be a technology investment bank with the long-term goal of having an equity stake in his client's IP. His whole team is composed of engineers.

"Quite frankly, I stumbled into this market niche," says Ross-Munro when discussing how he discovered his venture. "Some people fool themselves into thinking they have a method for finding opportunity," he continues, indicating that he considers being in the right place at the right time more important than other factors.

Programming is nothing new to Ross-Munro—he's been at it since he was eight years old. In 2008, his employer, an investment bank focused on health care, offered him his choice of two jobs in a new department. However, his principle contact at the bank convinced him to go it alone and, feeling strongly about his abilities, invested in Ross-Munro's start-up. Ross-Munro began in web development but ended up in application development.

"As young entrepreneurs, we tend to say 'yes' to everything," he explains. Today, though, he says no more often and stays narrowly focused, which has proven to be a more successful approach. His narrow approach led him to a hybrid, cross-platform, code-based structure, which afforded him the opportunity to provide applications when speed to market and low maintenance were required. He admits this didn't happen overnight; there were many incremental steps requiring the careful management of resources to navigate this market landscape.

By 2008, he had left web development and was doing source-code development. In 2013, he started getting much larger customers and is now working on source code version 2.0. He attributes getting there to luck—and hard work. As he states, "I am totally an entrepreneur. I fit the classical definition. I am willing to work 80 hours a week just so I don't have to work 40 hours a week for someone else."

Ross-Munro observes that his market is underserved because demand is so high. "I was forced to grow and be more strategic, and in retrospect, I made smart choices" he adds.

"Primarily, we are an on-demand service company that has grown organically through various stages of evolution," he says. "Think of us as a start-up service that appears to be a service, but we are really a product much like Uber," he continues.

"Today, we are more process driven; we take time to document our mistakes whereas in the past we fought fires without paperwork." He adds, "If you ever take time to read a legal document, you become aware that a clause is in the document because someone else screwed up."

Ross-Munro feels that his company is too small for the national competition to notice it, but locally, he has observed many shops tighten up their business operations and become more sophisticated in response to his entry into the market. He notes that, locally, the Tampa Bay scene is a small group of diverse guys and gals who are all part of the same network. Everybody sends work to everybody else.

He sold his previous venture, a small company, at a young age. Then he bought a car and lived in Japan for a year. His initial funding for this venture came from his former boss after he turned down jobs from the "big four" accounting firms. He had an interesting financing arrangement. His investor would give him $5,000 per month and each month Ross-Munro needed the money, his investor would take 1% of his company. This incentive pushed him to be cash-flow positive in his first month.

His strategy is to stay small and nimble given how large and underserved the market is. He acknowledges he is always under threat because of the brain drain—recruiters call his office each day looking for talent. But he is proud to say that he has had zero turnovers in that last three years. He attributes this to making a really intense effort to give his people freedom. He empowers coders to make decisions, the company has no standardized vacation policy, and he offers four weeks' paternity leave and 12 weeks' maternity leave. Topping off these employee-focused initiatives, no birthday goes unrecognized or uncelebrated. He provides the example of an individual leaving his company to work for a larger team at Tech Data at two times the salary Ross-Munro could offer. That ex-employee was later welcomed back into the organization.

Ross-Munro definitely feels that his corporate culture is his competitive advantage. He looks at it two different ways. From a positive-spin perspective, he has great people doing great work, and everybody in his shop speaks programming, which leads to more work getting done. His cynical take on things is that most people outside the source-coding world understand very little of what his company does. However, even though coding is a complex and generally poorly understood technical skill, he has been able to leverage his knowledge and assemble a team around the world that can compete with larger organizations, such as McKinsey, both on pricing for projects and on the performance of the product delivered. As an aside, he adds that he's noticed that large companies often write sloppy code.

Over the last two or three years, competitive forces have driven his firm to focus on being the best it can be on each engagement. In the process, he has noticed that competitors have become less relevant. In fact, he adds that some of his team's innovations have shown up in competitor's products, which adds credence to his conviction that he has great innovative talent.

When asked about the breakthrough moment, he glibly replies, "I'm still waiting for that." When pressed for an answer, however, he states that he is creating a company like the one he had imagined and has recently met a venture capitalist in Boca Raton who serves as a role model and mentor. Perhaps a more tangible "aha!" moment was being approached to negotiate a partnership deal with a hardware manufacturer, a deal centered on his shop's technology. This made him realize that he has something useful to offer, that someone could use and benefit from his technology. The technology in question is a management platform for the IoT, which allows 900,000 set-top boxes to connect to it. This technology is very useful on cruise ships and in hotels.

New competitive opportunities emerge when companies need something to talk to something else. Lately, he has observed that large systems are great at handling large complex tasks but not very good at talking to one another. So he finds himself writing middleware applications at times. "Competition forces entrepreneurs to consider what else can be done with their products since they have so much invested in them," he muses. As his company grows, he finds it easier to find other uses for the technology he develops. He considers himself lucky that he has a house full of entrepreneurs. It affords him the luxury of sitting back and picking the best entrepreneurial venture to develop.

He admits that being an entrepreneur has made him a nicer person. "In the old days, I was quite blunt. I didn't' care much about the feelings of others," he reflects. "Today, I have higher levels of empathy, and I have become more cynical about people."

Ross-Munro muses that the most important thing he has learned is how to be better at the hiring process. Now, he only hires someone if, after the interview, that person asks for the job. He has become more knowledgeable about how to spot talent, and how to build an effective team.

Today, his company has outgrown its space, but he is not expecting exponential growth. On a personal level, he is still getting better at his job. He realizes that he needs to focus on strategy more because the company can grow only if he can handle the additional workload.

Over the last three years, his business has quadrupled in size, but he doesn't expect that trend to continue, so his main focus now is to raise the level of revenue per employee and map out a strategy to get him to moderate, predictable growth.

Here are his four suggestions for new entrepreneurs:

1. Don't be a single founder;

2. Don't form a 50/50 or a 100% relationship (someone has got to be in charge, and the other person has to have skin in the game);

3. Get the legal work out of the way first; and

4. Never hire out of desperation.

CASE 10: TO SELL OR NOT TO SELL

Dr. Patrick Michael Plummer, Pennsylvania State University

Although this study is based on a real company owner and the actual dilemma he faced, the name of the company and the names of those involved have been changed to maintain privacy and confidentiality.

Patrick Klempner stood at what amounted to the top of an emotional mountain and looked out into the abyss. "Do I sell my company, or do I keep leading my team into a tough market?" he asked himself. He was faced with one of the most difficult decisions he had had to make up to that point in his young life. Klempner knew that his team would follow him anywhere, and he felt as though these people were part of his extended family. So, at least in his mind, he had to take care of them and look after their well-being and that of their families. "I don't know what the correct answer is to this problem," Klempner thought. "How did we get to this point when everything was going so well for us?"

THE PROTAGONIST

Patrick Klempner was the founder and CEO of HealthcareData, LLC (HDL). HDL was the second health-care data and software-as-a-service (SaaS) company that he had started. Klempner had earned his baccalaureate degree in biomedical engineering by attending school part time at night and on weekends while working at his full-time job at a local hospital. His father was a schoolteacher, and his mother was a full-time, stay-at-home mom. No one in his family had any experience in the corporate world. He continued his part-time education by earning his master's in business administration because he realized he needed more knowledge about how businesses operate if he ever wanted to pursue his lifelong dream of having his own company. Within two years of graduation, he realized that dream and started his first company.

His first firm, Medical Publishers, Inc. (MPI), was founded in 1993 before the Internet was a common word, much less a daily destination. MPI began as a market intelligence firm that originally published industry newsletters for the health-care sector. Heavily influenced by his strong technical background in working with computers, Klempner organized all of the content that MPI published into a database and began to assemble a very accurate and up-to-date list of all the hospitals and health systems that his firm was writing about. At the time, most publishers simply wrote their articles using word-processing software and then created the layout using desktop-publishing software. Publishers didn't worry about indexing the articles or content, except for doing so in order to generate a display showing the content of individual issues, for example, via a paper-based table of contents. Although this fact was unknown to Klempner at the time, his decision to track article content within his database was what made it so valuable and unique.

THE "LIGHT BULB" MOMENT

It was during a conversation with one of his readers that Klempner had an "aha!" moment. The client had asked for additional information, and Klempner, using the firm's internal databases, was able to provide the requested information quickly. It was at that moment that he realized that many of his other readers might also appreciate having access to the database in real time. He was right, and the world's first Internet-based, online database on the business of health care was born. His clients found it extremely useful and were willing to pay 50 to 100 times more for online access than they were for a single newsletter subscription. Profits soared because costs remained largely the same as they had been for the paper newsletter.

Within a few years, the dot-com boom of the late 1990s was in full swing. MPI had taken over several more-established competitors in the medical newsletter field that had yet to embrace the Internet; these companies had fallen behind MPI's technology. Klempner received three competing offers to acquire MPI and closed on the sale of his business in March 2000, ten days before NASDAQ hit 5,048.62, the high-water mark of the dot-com boom. His joy in selling his business was short lived. Due to the required one-year waiting period (a common restriction called the "blackout period"), Klempner could not sell the stock he received during the transaction. By the time the blackout period was over, the stock was worth only a fraction of its original value because of the dot-com crash.

But Klempner, the eternal optimist, surveyed the market and saw that opportunity still existed for the same type of business, so he decided to start up his second firm, HDL. In doing so, he hoped that by going directly to online database products and bypassing newsletters altogether, he could quickly build another company and sell it again. This time, when he sold his business, the transaction would be a cash offer only with no stock options; he believed in learning from his experiences.

Klempner started HDL to compete in the same market as his former company had. In the time since he had begun his original firm, however, the market had become a lot savvier about using data and was looking for more advanced analysis and greater data-mining capabilities than those his original business had offered. So he decided to position his new firm by emphasizing strong data-analysis capabilities as its primary competitive advantage. Because his new company was a self-funded venture, Klempner's first task was to build the product as quickly as possible. He hired a top programmer named Steve Stevenson to work full time on the development. Top programming talent was expensive, but Klempner knew it was the core of the business. To him, it was money well spent because he needed Stevenson for both software development and to lead the technical team. The development process took much longer than anyone had anticipated. Because HDL now faced direct competitors—including MPI, Klempner's former firm—the starting product had to be at least as good as what was already on the market. Klempner knew that, in order to be able to leverage the superior capabilities of his new product, it could not be "as good as" but had to be discernibly "better than" the competition's offerings.

After 18 months of development, which was twice as long as he originally planned for, Klempner launched his new product, and it was just what he expected it would be, another winner. The product was indeed superior to anything else on the market. The only downside he could see was that, because he had not anticipated the higher costs associated with the increased barriers to entry, he was forced to price his product slightly higher than the competition's. In the end, he believed that customers would see the product as the winner it was and would agree that the improved value more than justified the higher price point. But Klempner would have yet another obstacle placed in front of him. As he was taking the product to market, he learned that his sales cycle would be longer because his potential clients were locked into one- or two-year subscriptions with his competitors. He would have to wait until their existing subscriptions expired before they would even consider moving to a superior platform like HDL's. Additionally, HDL experienced the negative aspects of switching costs; potential customers were dissuaded from moving to the HDL platform because it was easier to maintain the "status quo" and stick with their existing product choices. Despite these obstacles, Klempner believed in the product and in the HDL team, so he persevered.

Five years from its rocky beginning, HDL was on firmer ground—its products were finally receiving the industry recognition and sales that they deserved. HDL products were acknowledged as being not only the most sophisticated but also of the highest quality. Clients and users of the products embraced them and began making requests for new features that would enhance them, but also add to their complexity. Klempner was apprehensive about adding these advanced features. His fear was that the enhancements would increase the sales cycle of the product even more, as well as require his sales team to acquire greater sophistication and knowledge. Moreover, HDL had reached the breakeven point and was now showing a slight profit; he did not want to interrupt that growth trend. He also knew, however, that he must remain competitive and satisfy his customers' needs. Throwing caution to the wind, he and Stevenson—now HDL's chief technology officer—laid out an ambitious roadmap to accommodate his customers' requests. Klempner was about to find out just how strong, resilient, and committed to one another he and his employees were. He knew his "work family" would buy in to the plan. He no longer considered them employees; he had become very fond of these people over the years, and they had worked very hard to keep the HDL "family" business afloat. They had become an extension of his family.

THE PERFECT STORM

Six months into the implementation of the software development, Klempner received a voicemail on a Saturday evening from Steve Stevenson's wife, who was sobbing: "Patrick, this is Marsha. I have horrible news. Steve was exercising this morning and suffered a massive heart attack. Patrick, Steve is dead!"

Klempner was taken aback. He didn't know what to say or what to do. He sank into his chair and began to cry. He had just lost his long-time friend. He worried about what was going to happen to Marsha and their two small children. And he thought, "How do I tell our coworkers?" Their loss obviously didn't compare to the loss Stevenson's family felt, but Klempner knew his friend's passing would also hurt the HDL family. As reality began to set in, he realized that this death would not only cause emotional pain at work but also place the company at risk. Stevenson was the creative mind behind the firm's success, and with his passing, most of the intellectual ideas for the firm's future died as well. Klempner sat there for what seemed like hours reflecting on the past and thinking about the future. Slowly, he sat up straight and composed himself. He was not sure what to do, but he knew something had to be done. He immediately called an emergency meeting. He gathered all the employees together and broke the sad news. After emotions had settled down, the team began to talk about the future of HDL. Everyone acknowledged Stevenson's untimely passing was a massive setback for the firm, but team members decided they should move forward with the software initiatives. They knew this would place a great strain on everyone at HDL, but they felt they could pick up the torch and accomplish Stevenson's work.

Health care had long been considered recession proof, but the great recession of 2008 (the global economic downturn that began in 2008 and lasted for approximately three years) proved that incorrect. People still got sick and sought relief from health-care providers, but because of the effects of the recession, including drastically reduced profit margins for providers, the health-care industry began to reduce its staff. For the most part, HDL's customers were able to retain most of their staff; however, their workload and responsibilities increased significantly. The additional workload left very little time for HDL's clients to spend working with the type of data that HDL sold. Sales began to fall, and revenues declined. The advanced features that Stevenson had visualized and that HDL had brought to fruition were never utilized by the requesting clients; it seemed as if all was for not. Compounding the problem was the shift in customer needs. Clients still wanted data, but instead of advanced analytics, which was HDL's core competency, customers now wanted bite-sized, simple charts for quick, at-a-glance insights—and all had to display easily on a smartphone.

Last, but not least, Barack Obama was elected president of the United States and promised to reform health care. Klempner was concerned about how these reforms would affect the health care industry in general and, more important, about how they would affect his business and his "work family."

THE SITUATION

As was expected, health care reform had a negative impact on Klempner's business. The computer operating system industry began to decline even more, and the market shrank. The large customer base that HDL once served was quickly dwindling.

Klempner was now faced with the dilemma of whether he should try to weather the current storm of uncertainty in the health care industry or sell his business. He did have a few interested parties that wanted to buy his business, but he did not know what the future would hold for his employees if he sold the company. This uncertainty weighed heavily on him. On one hand, if he sold the business, would the acquiring firm retain current employees, or would they be shown the door in a massive layoff? Additionally, if he sold the company, he would absolutely be removing himself and the company from possible future profits when the recession ended. The prospect of financial rewards had been a significant factor motivating him to continue with the business during the most challenging times. He wondered whether selling now would actually be selling out.

On the other hand, if Klempner did not sell the company, would he be placing his employees in an equally uncertain position? He knew the company was at risk if things continued as they were because management may not have enough capital to keep the business afloat. If he tried to keep the business alive, he knew he would have to get away from his core competencies. And he was concerned because he was not sure if HDL had the ability to do so without Stevenson.

Patrick Klempner was exhausted from the stress and sleep deprivation. He held his head in his hands and thought, "What should I do?"

REFERENCES

CHAPTER 1

1. Jeffry A. Timmons and Stephen Spinelli Jr., *New Venture Creation: Entrepreneurship for the 21st Century*, 8th ed. (Boston, MA: McGraw-Hill Publishing Co., 2009), 41.

2. Howard H. Stevenson and J. Carlos Jarillo, "A Paradigm of Entrepreneurial Management," *Strategic Management Journal* 11 (1990): 17–27, see page 23.

3. David McClelland, *The Achieving Society* (Princeton, NJ: Van Nostrand, 1961).

4. Joseph A. Schumpeter, *Capitalism, Socialism, and Democracy* (New York: Harper & Brothers, 1942), see Chapter 7 "The Process of Creative Destruction." See also Joseph A. Schumpeter, *The Theory of Economic Development: An Inquiry into Profits, Capital, Credit, Interest, and the Business Cycle* (Cambridge, MA: Harvard University Press, 1934).

5. "Infographic: Boomer Entrepreneurs and the State of Entrepreneurship," Kauffman Foundation, February 17, 2015, https://www.kauffman.org/multimedia/infographics/2015/infographic-boomer-entrepreneurs-and-the-state-of-entrepreneurship.

6. "Infographic: Millennial Entrepreneurs and the State of Entrepreneurship," Kauffman Foundation, February 11, 2015, https://www.kauffman.org/multimedia/infographics/2015/infographic-millennial-entrepreneurs-and-the-state-of-entrepreneurship.

7. Thomas D. Snyder and Sally A. Dillow, *Digest of Education Statistics 2013*, NCES 2015-011 (Washington, DC: National Center for Education Statistics, Institute of Education Sciences, U.S. Department of Education, May 2015), see Table 323.20 and 324.20.

8. National Center for Education Statistics, *Digest of Education Statistics 2017*, accessed June 13, 2018, https://nces.ed.gov/programs/digest/current_tables.asp.

9. Robert W. Fairlie and Alicia M. Robb, *Race and Entrepreneurial Success* (Cambridge, MA: MIT Press, 2008), 1. See also U.S. Census Bureau, Table SB1200CSA01: Statistics for all U.S. Firms by Industry, Gender, Ethnicity, and Race for the United States, *2012 Survey of Business Owners*.

10. Robert W. Fairlie, *Open For Business: How Immigrants Are Driving Small Business Creation in the United States* (New York: Partnership for a New American Economy, August 2012), http://research.newamericaneconomy.org/wp-content/uploads/2013/07/openforbusiness.pdf.

11. David Dyssegaard Kallick, *Immigrant Small Business Owners—A Significant and Growing Part of the Economy: A Report from the Fiscal Policy Institute's Immigration Research Initiative* (New York: Fiscal Policy Institute, June 2012), 13. See also Mark Koba, "How Immigrants Are Changing US Businesses," *CNBC*, August 14, 2012, https://www.cnbc.com/id/48646997.

12. Arthur C. Brooks, *Social Entrepreneurship: A Modern Approach to Social Value Creation* (Upper Saddle River, NJ: Pearson Education, 2009), 4–5.

13. Mark J. Perry, "Fortune 500 Firms 1955 v. 2016: Only 12% Remain," *AEIdeas: A Public Policy Blog*, December 13, 2016, http://www.aei.org/publication/fortune-500-firms-1955-v-2016-only-12-remain-thanks-to-the-creative-destruction-that-fuels-economic-prosperity/.

14. Brooks, *Social Entrepreneurship*, 5.
15. From the Global Partnership for Afghanistan website, which is no longer online.
16. Global Partnership for Afghanistan, *Partners at Work: Annual Report 2010*, https://arch net.org/system/publications/contents/9326/original/DTP101809.pdf?1395767580. See also Priscilla Bayley, "Global Partnership for Afghanistan: Building Sustainable Rural Livelihoods to Alleviate Poverty in a Country in Conflict," *Changemakers*, accessed June 5, 2018, https://www.changemakers.com/economicopportunity/entries/global-partner ship-afghanistan-building-sustainable-rur.
17. See "Dana Freyer," *Encore.org: Second Acts for the Greater Good*, https://encore.org/ purpose-prize/dana-freyer/ and Bayley, "Global Partnership for Afghanistan: Building Sustainable Rural Livelihoods."

CHAPTER 3

1. Nicole Dunn, "What Businesses Can Learn from the Health and Wellness Boom," *Forbes*, April 27, 2018, https://www.forbes.com/sites/forbeslacouncil/2018/04/27/what-businesses-can-learn-from-the-health-and-wellness-boom/#2380710a341e. See also "Fitness," *The Statistics Portal*, accessed June 16, 2018, https://www.statista.com/outlook/313/109/ fitness/united-states.
2. Michael E. Porter, "The Five Competitive Forces That Shape Strategy," *Harvard Business Review* 86, no. 1 (January 2008): 86–104.

CHAPTER 5

1. The Risk Management Association was originally called the Robert Morris Associates when it was founded in 1914.

CHAPTER 7

1. Hermann Brandstätter, "Becoming an Entrepreneur—A Question of Personality Structure?" *Journals of Economic Psychology* 18, no. 2–3, 157–77.
2. S. Sanches-Roige, J. C. Gray, J. MacKillop, C. H. Chen, and A. A. Palmer, "The Genetics of Human Personality," *Genes, Brain and Behavior* 17, no. 3 (March 2018), https:// onlinelibrary.wiley.com/doi/epdf/10.1111/gbb.12439.
3. Alan Lickerman, "Personality vs. Character: The Key to Discerning Personality from Character Is Time," *Psychology Today: Happiness in the World* [blog], April 3, 2011, https://www .psychologytoday.com/ca/blog/happiness-in-world/201104/personality-vs-character.

CHAPTER 8

1. The Uniform Partnership Act (1914), II 6 (I).
2. Chief Justice John Marshall, *Trustees of Dartmouth College v. Woodward*, 17 U.S. (4 Wheat.) 518, 636 (1819).

CHAPTER 10

1. Laura Huang and Andy Wu, *The American Angel* (Philadelphia: Wharton Entrepreneurship and Angel Capital Association, 2017), http://docs.wixstatic.com/ugd/ecd9be_5855a9b21a8c4f-c1abc89a3293abff96.pdf.

2. Report quoted in Salman SH, "The Global Crowdfunding Industry Raised $34.4 Billion in 2015," *DazeInfo*, January 12, 2016, https://dazeinfo.com/2016/01/12/crowdfunding-industry-34-4-billion-surpass-vc-2016/

CHAPTER 11

1. The term "balloon" payment refers to the fact that all or part of the interest accrues to the time of repayment of the debt. As it accrues, the total payment "swells" like a balloon and is due at the conclusion of the loan period.

2. "About STTR," *SBIR–STTR: America's Seed Fund* [website], accessed July 2018, https://www.sbir.gov/about/about-sttr.

CASE 1

1. Interview with Cyndy Sanberg, president of Natura Therapeutics from 2007 to 2014, conducted August 10, 2016.

CASE 2

1. Sam Reiber, Anthony Cascio, and Ed Washington were interviewed on August 18, 2016.

2. The website pharmalicensing.com was consulted in July 2018.

CASE 3

1. This case is based on an August 31, 2016, interview with Mark Gordon.

2. Giles Tremlett, "WikiLeaks Cables: Art Looted by Nazis, Spanish Gold and an Embassy Offer," *The Guardian*, December 8, 2010, https://www.theguardian.com/world/2010/dec/08/wikileaks-us-spain-treasure-art.

3. SOX refers to the Sarbanes–Oxley Act of 2002.

CASE 4

1. This case is based on an interview with Kunal Jain, owner of Practice Force. The interview took place August 16, 2016.

2. In other words, he handles information technology, intellectual property, and human resources functions.

CASE 5

1. This case is based on an interview with "Dez" Williams, the founder of AquaMelon, on September 6, 2016.

CASE 6

1. This case study is based on an interview with Julia MacGregor, CEO of Global Safety Management, conducted on September 12, 2017.

CASE 7

1. This case is based on a September 13, 2016, interview with Jonathan Solomon, who is currently the president of both Sollyco and Proleve.

CASE 8

1. Gordon Ryerson was interviewed on September 15, 2016.

INDEX